SENSE AND NONSENSE IN RELIGION

SENSE
AND
NONSENSE
IN
RELIGION

An Essay on the Language
and Phenomenology of Religion

STEN H. STENSON

NASHVILLE ABINGDON PRESS NEW YORK

SENSE AND NONSENSE IN RELIGION

Copyright © 1969 by Abingdon Press

Standard Book Number: 687-37457-X

Library of Congress Catalog Card Number: 69-19737

Scripture quotations unless otherwise noted are from the Revised
Standard Version of the Bible, copyrighted 1946 and 1952 by
the Division of Christian Education, National Council of
Churches, and are used by permission.

The quotation from "Evil and Omnipotence" by J. L. Mackie, in *Mind*, LXIV (1955),
is used by permission of Basil Blackwell & Mott, Ltd., Oxford, England.

Material from *Being and Nothingness* by Jean-Paul Sartre, translated by Hazel E. Barnes,
and published by Philosophical Library in 1956, is used by permission of the publishers.

Quotations from *Humanistic Existentialism: The Literature of Possibility* by Hazel E.
Barnes, published by the University of Nebraska Press in 1959, is used by permission
of the publishers.

The quotation from *The Idea of the Holy* by Rudolf Otto, translated by J. W. Harvey,
and published by Oxford University Press in 1958, is used by the publishers' permission.

The selection from "The Enigma of Job: Maimonides and the Moderns" by H. Joel
Laks, in the *Journal of Biblical Literature* (Dec., 1964), is used by permission of the
Society of Biblical Literature.

The quotation from "Anselm's Ontological Arguments" by Norman Malcolm, in *The
Philosophical Review*, LXIX (1960), is used by permission of the editors and the author.

The lines from "Little Gidding" by T. S. Eliot, in *Complete Poems and Plays*, published
by Harcourt, Brace & World, Inc. in 1952, are used by permission of Harcourt,
Brace & World, Inc. and Faber & Faber, Ltd.

The quotation on pp. 95-96 is reprinted by permission of Schocken Books, Inc. from
Franz Rosenzweig: His Life and Thought, edited by Nahum N. Glatzer. Copyright ©
1953, 1961 by Schocken Books, Inc.

The quotations from *Time and Eternity* by W. T. Stace (Princeton University Press,
1952) are used by permission of Princeton University Press.

The selections from pp. 69, 72-73 of *Metaphysics and Religious Language* by Frank B.
Dilley, 1964, are used by permission of the publishers, Columbia University Press,
New York, N.Y.

Parts of Chap. II appeared previously in the author's article "Evil and Absurdity"
in *The Christian Scholar,* and are used by permission of *The Christian Scholar.*

Parts of Chap. VI were published earlier in the author's article "Prophecy, Theology,
and Philosophy" in *The Journal of Religion* and are used by permission of *The
Journal of Religion.*

SET UP, PRINTED, AND BOUND BY THE
PARTHENON PRESS, AT NASHVILLE,
TENNESSEE, UNITED STATES OF AMERICA

For
Jan and Eric

PREFACE

Because I was once sharply critical of all traditional and contemporary manifestations of religion, but have now written a book in defense of religious belief, for which the Abingdon Press has graciously honored me with the Abingdon Award for 1968, it is perhaps advisable to tell my readers something about the events that led me to write this particular essay. In a preface—even if it prefaces a philosophical and scholarly treatise—a somewhat personal and confessional note may be permissible and even helpful.

This book was initially projected more than ten years ago as a much different sort of work. At that time I intended to write a devastating criticism of all forms of religion. But in particular—since some Eastern religions do not necessarily involve "believing in God"—I especially planned, at that time, to compose the ultimate, irrefutable philosophical destruction of all forms of Western theistic belief. Should any Jew or Christian persist in his religious indulgences after reading the book I projected, it seemed to me that he would do so in face of the clear fact that I had shown up his moral and intellectual irresponsibility.

7

I finished that manuscript several years ago, but I did not publish it. To my surprise and despair it turned out differently than I expected. What had been initially conceived as a demonstration of the utter impossibility of believing in God, in any reasonable sense, ended as a half-hearted argument in defense of certain traditional forms of religious belief in both the East and the West. I had promised myself and my readers a final philosophical destruction of Synagogue, Temple, and Church, but I concluded by going back surreptitiously to look at the foundations that I had begun to suspect I had not in the slightest disturbed. I had, perhaps, done a bit of housecleaning, but a great deal of the dust I had raised was my own. The manuscript I had in my hands was neither a tearing-down nor a building-up. Instead, it was an unwelcome invitation to start again.

I began by reading Jewish and Christian religious testimony—particularly the Bible—with what was for me a new kind of alertness and growing sophistication. I also set out to observe (comically, as an outsider) the religious communities around me with more care and sympathy than I had done before. This, of course, exposed me to the danger of "catching religion," but there was no way to avoid this if I really wanted to observe the religious phenomenon at first hand.

In the meantime, I had a living to make as a teacher of philosophy; there were other things I had to write; and this book was pushed into the background of my academic activities. Indeed, it became the horizon of my personal and professional life: all my philosophical problems related to it. I had to clarify my philosophical method, my theory of knowledge, my ethical theory, and so on before I could make progress in my philosophical understanding of religion.

In 1960-61, while still a member of the Department of Philosophy at Smith College, I received a fellowship from

8

the Church Society for College Work (a division of the Epis-
copal Church) to spend a year doing postgraduate study in
religion and theology at Harvard University. I am indebted
to the former director of the Church Society, the Reverend
Jones B. Shannon, for helping me obtain this generous aid at
such a crucial time in my private life and professional career.
The year after I returned to Smith, I was invited to teach
philosophy of religion and related subjects in the Department
of Religion, and I accepted. As a member of this Department
since 1963, I have been much helped in my writing and research, not only by the subjects that I teach, but by my daily
conversations with colleagues who are also involved in the
scholarly examination of the many-sided phenomenon of religion.

I owe special thanks to the following: to Professors Bruce
T. Dahlberg and Jochanan H. A. Wijnhoven, of the Department of Religion, for reading the first draft of my manuscript
and making careful and extensive comments; to Professor
Kenneth Stern, of the Department of Philosophy, who examined the manuscript and criticized helpfully; to Mrs. Charles
J. Hill, retired from the English Department, who scrutinized
my writing and conferred with me with generous patience
about exacting details of syntax and style; to Mr. John Green-
berg, an undergraduate at Amherst College, who read the entire finished manuscript, at almost one sitting through a day
and a night, and pronounced it fit; and, finally, to Mrs. A. B.
McArthur who has patiently turned my cluttered tracks into
clean typescript.

I take this opportunity to thank the editors of *The Christian Scholar* for giving me permission to use, in Chapter I,
portions of an article of mine that previously appeared in that
publication. To the editors of *The Journal of Religion* I am

indebted for their permission to use, in Chapter VI of this book, portions of an article of mine that previously appeared in that journal.

Students of religion, and scholars who read this book and then wish to re-examine certain of the ideas or arguments it presents, will appreciate the Index. It was meticulously compiled by two Smith College undergraduates, Anne Rognstad and Taj Diffenbaugh, to whom I here express my gratitude.

STEN H. STENSON

Smith College
Northampton, Massachusetts

CONTENTS

When the Economic Problem will take the back seat where
it belongs . . . the area of the heart and head will be occupied, or
reoccupied, by our real problems—the problems of life and of
human relations, of creation and behaviour and religion.

J. M. KEYNES, *Essays in Persuasion*

INTRODUCTION

THE PROBLEM OF BELIEVING IN GOD

If religion is as important as Lord Keynes, an economist, apparently believed—if, in an affluent society, religious problems deserve priority of some sort over economic concerns—then one of the "real problems" of the Western world is religious, and we must allow it to occupy, or reoccupy, our hearts and heads. We must reconsider our usual, perhaps almost automatic, response to the testimony of our religious traditions. How is genuine religion related to real morality—i.e., how have they been, and how ought they to be, conceived? What does it mean to believe, or not to believe, in God?

In an article directed at Harvard alumni and later quoted in the popular press, Professor Morton White observed that many intellectuals were turning "religious" in some broad sense of that word, but that they did not endorse "the simple old-fashioned declarative statement of theology, God exists." [1]

---

[1] Morton White, "Religion, Politics, and the Higher Learning," *Confluence,* III (Dec., 1954), 402. This article is quoted extensively in *Time* (Jan. 24, 1955), p. 44.

13

This comment was made in 1954, but today, more than a decade later—especially since the publication and enormous sale of the Anglican Bishop of Woolwich's book, *Honest to God*,[2] and the recent notoriety of the "death of God theologians" [3]—White's slightly sensationalistic remark seems to have gained considerable support from what is surely, for many people, an unexpected quarter. Not even the Bishop, nor the theologians he cites most frequently—Paul Tillich, Rudolph Bultmann, and Dietrich Bonhoeffer—can plumply assent to the statement, "God exists." More surprising is the assertion of some of the death of God theologians—take Thomas J. J. Altizer, for example—that the death of God is a historical event that has occurred in our own time.[4] Whatever this statement means, it is obvious that most theologians agree that the concept of existence has never been ascribed to God in a "simple old-fashioned" manner by the classical representatives of Jewish and Christian religious thought.

Professor White was fully aware of the complexities of the problem when he addressed his Harvard audience, but it is quite apparent that most critics of religion hardly suspect the theological subleties of the statement, "God exists," or of the question, "Does God exist?" Scholars who are formally aware of the difficulties involved in such discussions often forget them in fact in the heat of their arguments about religion. And the average member of most religious denominations is even more easily confused.

Devout members of Church, Synagogue, and Temple who are impatient with the corrosive scrupulosity of religiously in-

[2] (Philadelphia: Westminster Press, 1963.)
[3] See, for example, Thomas J. J. Altizer, *The Gospel of Christian Atheism* (Philadelphia: Westminster Press, 1966); Altizer and William Hamilton, *Radical Theology and the Death of God* (Indianapolis: Bobbs-Merrill, 1966); Altizer, ed., *Toward a New Christianity* (New York: Harcourt, Brace & World, 1967).
[4] Altizer, *Radical Theology and the Death of God*, p. 24.

terested but skeptical intellectuals, even some theologians of sorts, are often the unwitting victims of their own lack of philosophical complexity or of their well-intentioned pietistic carelessness. They not only miss the nuances of the question of God's existence, when they discuss it, they also misrepresent it to others. This leads not only the faithful but also the critics of the faithful astray. Thus, the criticism of religion that characterizes much modern culture is frequently irrelevant to the tradition that it thinks it is attacking. By obscuring the real issues in this unintentional fashion, it discredits a phenomenon of the human spirit that many present critics of religion would otherwise wish to protect. For this reason if for no other, whether we think of ourselves as apologists for religion or as critics of it, we must periodically re examine our understanding of this enormously complex phenomenon if we want to hold a responsible position in regard to it. This means that we must keep abreast of contemporary religious thought, as far as our opportunities allow. For, like other areas of culture, religion is a facet of human consciousness that is constantly changing the nature and degree of its own self-understanding.

One of the major concerns of contemporary Jewish and Christian theology and philosophy of religion is with "religious meaning"—with "hermeneutics" and the "philosophical analysis of religious language." In Western society the religious community has during the recent past become painfully aware of the enormous semantic complexity of its traditional symbolic modes: of myth, liturgy, and theological discourse. Thus, hermeneutics, a specialized branch of theology, searches for and tries to apply "scientific" principles of interpretation to biblical exegesis.[5] And the philosophical analysis of reli-

[5] Rudolph Bultmann, "The Problem of Hermeneutics," *Essays: Philosophical and Theological* (London: SCM Press, 1955); also, Bultmann, *Jesus Christ and Mythology* (New York: Scribner's, 1958), pp. 18, 45 ff., 54.

15

gious language (a special bailiwick of linguistic philosophers with a professional interest in religion) attempts to apply certain techniques of logical and linguistic analysis to the clarification and illumination of religious meanings in all their fluid variety.[6] We will illustrate and clarify all these concepts and activities in the discussions that follow.

Both hermeneutics and the philosophical analysis of religious language have been spurred, within the last two decades, by certain corrosive criticisms of religious belief. Contemporary philosophers have not only borrowed and sharpened arguments that like-minded philosophers of the past have thrown at religion, they have also pointed up most of the philosophical reservations concerning religion that are heard in day-to-day discussions of the subject. Sigmund Freud and some of his followers have, in addition, revitalized an old psychological criticism. As a result, in intellectual circles, the most serious objections to believing in God today are these: 1) an allegation that such belief is "sick"; 2) that it is "silly"; 3) that it is "meaningless"; and 4) that it is "self-contradictory."

1. Belief in God is said to be *sick* in the psychological sense that many people understand when they refer to religion contemptuously as a "crutch." Freud has embellished this common suspicion with the terminology of the new science (or art) of psychoanalysis. Accordingly, religion is described as a "universal neurosis" of which mankind must now be cured.[7]

2. Traditional belief in God is said to be *silly* because it

---

[6] For a bibliographical start see Ruel Tyson, "Philosophical Analysis and Religious Language: A Selected Bibliography," *The Christian Scholar*, XLIII (Fall, 1960), 245-50; also, Frederick Ferré, *Language, Logic and God* (New York: Harper, 1961), pp. 167-73.

[7] Sigmund Freud, *The Future of an Illusion* (Garden City, N.Y.: Doubleday, 1957), pp. 79 *et passim*.

apparently involves the acceptance of testimony that patently violates "common sense." The butt of this criticism is the belief in miracles, which has been a traditional ingredient of both Jewish and Christian piety. This criticism does not usually maintain that miraculous events are logically impossible; it customarily holds that there is nothing self-contradictory, for example, in the concept of the Jewish Passover or in the Christian conception of Easter. It merely suggests that nobody can accept such testimony unless he resorts to "double-think," setting aside the basic principles of common sense and adopting different (and murkier) ones when he enters the area of his religious practices. Such turncoat behavior avoids strict logical contradiction, perhaps, but only because it indulges in a kind of philosophical treason, vacillating between two basically different world views—one practical and conformable to modern life, the other superstitious and primitive.[8]

Critics of religious belief in miracles often point out that even if so-called miraculous events occur, men of consistent common sense must assume that however unusual such events might be they are still natural effects of natural causes. Accordingly, no matter how difficult the explanation may be in fact, in principle the event is still explainable in terms of common sense and science.[9] Since traditional religion does not offer "good evidence" to support its claims that such events

[8] In modern times, the most famous statement of this criticism is, perhaps, Section X of David Hume's *Inquiry Concerning Human Understanding*, first entitled *Philosophical Essays Concerning Human Understanding* (London: Millar, 1748). For a more recent example, see Patrick Nowell-Smith, "Miracles," *New Essays in Philosophical Theology*, A. Flew and A. MacIntyre, eds. (New York: Macmillan, 1955), pp. 243-54.

[9] See Nowell-Smith, *ibid.*, p. 253. Note: If, as some scholars maintain, Hume considered belief in miracles self-contradictory and not merely silly, then his objection falls into our fourth category of criticism rather than our second.

17

occurred, and because such events would be explainable experimentally even if they had occurred, philosophers whose methods and criteria are strongly determined by common sense and experimental science accuse religion of being a silly anachronism in a modern age. We do not need one set of principles (those of religion and theology) to interpret one set of facts, and another radically different kind of interpretation to explain the facts of everyday life.

3. Whereas our second criticism was directed against religious testimony that seems to be clearly comprehensible but incredible, the third objection to traditional religion is aimed at certain religious statements that are accused of being downright meaningless—neither true nor false in any sense.[10] Take, for example, such fundamental statements of Christianity and Judaism as those which occur in Christianity's Nicene Creed and in the Jewish *Shema*. The ancient affirmation of the latter states that "the Lord is our God, the Lord is one." [11] And Christians reiterate that testimony: "One God, the Father Almighty [is the] Maker of heaven and earth." [12] Such statements seem sensible at first glance, but many philosophers contend that they are not.

How can one ever determine whether or not such statements are true or false? What imaginable sorts of conditions would the faithful acknowledge as tending to falsify their

[10] See, for example, A. J. Ayer, *Language, Truth and Logic* (2nd ed. rev.; New York: Dover, 1950), pp. 31, 53-54 and 102 ff. This book was first published in London in 1936 and has now become a minor classic. Its criticism of religious belief has been given a fresh twist in Antony Flew's contribution to the discussion on "Theology and Falsification," *New Essays in Philosophical Theology*, pp. 96-99.

[11] Perhaps the single most definitive statement of the Jewish faith, the *Shema*, consists of three sections of the Torah or Pentateuch (Deut. 6:4-8; 11:13-22; Num. 15:37-42). Recitation of the *Shema* is a high point of most Jewish worship services.

[12] The Niceno-Constantinopolitan and Chalcedonian formulae, generally and collectively known as the Nicene Creed, is one historic definition of Christian faith and an essential part of the regular worship of many churches.

faith? If, as many philosophical critics of religion believe, no theist can give satisfactory criteria for establishing the truth or falsity of such statements even in principle (let alone practice), then these expressions must be like Lewis Carroll's nonsense verses, statements which seem to be genuine assertions, but which, like the Jabberwock poem, have no cognitive significance at all.[13]

From this it would follow that religion must not even be taken as seriously as traditional atheism took it. If religious language is cognitively empty, devoid of all content except emotional impact, it does not merit an elaborate rebuttal. That is why the standard tactic of contemporary philosophical critics of religion is to ask those who profess to believe in God what they mean by such testimony, and then to let them demonstrate to themselves, through their inability to provide clear and sufficient criteria of the truth or falsity of their expressions, that they literally have no idea what they are talking about.

4. Should the faithful foolishly persist in their "illusions," they are confronted with another perhaps even more unnerving objection to traditional religious belief. Both Judaism and Christianity are condemned as self-contradictory. Thus, whether or not the definitive statements of traditional religious faith have any cognitive content, the fairly obvious fact that such belief is ultimately self-contradictory (or "logically false," as philosophers say) would seem to put it unquestionably beyond the pall of intellectual respectability. Although one might wish to argue, in defense of some traditional religion, that its basic statements have cognitive meanings of some sort, it may well seem impossible to defend a religion whose fundamental creed denies what it also affirms —or entails such a denial. A statement "S" may have mean-

[13] See Flew, *New Essays* . . . , pp. 96-99; 106-108.

19

ing of some strange sort, but the statement "S and non-S" is apparently—like the statement "2 + 2 =7"—a logical falsehood. Yet, traditional religious language is full of such absurd locutions.

The Judeo-Christian religious tradition is not only involved in the sort of meaninglessness that I discussed in my third criticism, it is also characterized by the ultimate self-contradictions that are the concern of this fourth and final point against religion. Witness, as a concrete example, the theological problem of evil, which I will discuss in Chapter I. Judaism is in the same boat, in this regard, as Christianity, despite the latter's more obvious creedal paradoxicality. Logical falsity and factual meaninglessness—paradox and mystery —are the Scylla and Charybdis between which every belief in a transcendent yet immanent God must come to philosophical disaster.

It may seem odd for an author to express this opinion as his own, in a book which is intended to show the intellectual respectability of traditional religious belief and practice; nevertheless I believe that religion has always been renewed by such hazard and that it can continue to survive only if it remains true to its origins in the midst of such Scylla and Charybdis situations. Although this book is not intended as an addition to the current death of God theology (the principles of which are too vague and diffuse for this author to endorse deliberately), yet I share with Altizer, for example, the conviction that experience of the sacred is essentially mystical, that it can be expressed most adequately in various sorts of paradoxes, and that this always involves "the death of God" in the sense that I shall try to illuminate in the following pages.

Returning now to the four intellectual objections to traditional religion which I have been describing, we see that they can be summarized in a single sentence: Belief in God is accused of being (1) a *pathological* manifestation of man's refusal to grow up, involving (2) *overcredulous* endorsement of miraculous testimony and promises, emotionally attached to (3) certain *senseless* pronouncements—creeds, dogmas, and shibboleths—all of which entail a philosophy of life that is (4) *logically false.* Some intellectuals would also emphasize the alleged *irrelevance,* in modern times, of such an apparently ridiculous philosophy of life, but my response to the four criticisms described above will also constitute an incidental refutation of this additional charge.

Obviously, the Judeo-Christian tradition cannot be honestly or effectively defended against these earnest and intelligent criticisms unless it can provide some sort of reasonable rejoinder to them. The strident anti-intellectualism and obdurate theological obscurantism of some religionists—an untypical minority in the contemporary theological community —are no real help in this respect. Accordingly, the title of this book has already introduced our central and pervasive problem: What can we say about the nature of religious meaning which both accounts for the element of truth in the criticisms which I have described, and yet provides a reasonable defense of traditional belief in God? It is in the light of this question that the title of this book receives its pluralistic significance:[14]

A. In the title, the word "sense" is itself intended in two senses: (1) as a synonym of the word "valid"—as when we speak of the sense (i.e., the logical consistency) of an argu-

---

[14] The deliberate ambiguous use of the word "nonsense" in the title suggests a somewhat similar approach to the problem of religious meaning as that which was taken by Charles J. Ping, *Meaningful Nonsense* (Philadelphia: Westminster Press, 1966). The idea that some forms of "nonsense" make an important kind of "sense" is not new. As the following chapters will show, it is an important element in the thinking of several philosophers of religion today. What is distinctive about the present work is not its subject matter but its method and point of view.

ment or demonstration—and (2) as a synonym of the word "meaning"—as when we speak of the sense (i.e., the cognitive content) of an argument or explanation. In short, the word "sense," in the title, refers both to the odd logic and to the odd content of religious language.

B. The word "nonsense" is meant to direct our attention to at least three things: (1) to the patent self-contradictions, the logical paradoxicality, of religious language; (2) to its factual meaninglessness; and (3) to the overcredulous character of "literal" belief in miracles.

C. In my title and throughout this book, unless it is otherwise stipulated or is obviously narrowly confined to some specific context, the word "religion" will be used in a broad sense, as it is ordinarily, to mean not only revelation but theology, and religion not only as an experience but also as an institution. Although my discussion will often apply to many, if not to all major religions, for convenience my concern will be limited to the Judeo-Christian tradition. When it is impossible to generalize responsibly even in this narrower area, I will make further qualifications.

Since I am interested in both the form and the content of religion, the pages that follow must deal with the problems of religious meaning and the nature of religious truth from two different but intimately related perspectives: (1) from an *existential* point of view (as in existential philosophy), and (2) from an *analytical* point of view (as in linguistic analysis). While I am explaining and illustrating these methods, I will, therefore, occasionally alternate between them, passing back and forth between the phenomenological method of contemporary Continental existentialism and the methods of syntactical and semantical analysis that vaguely characterize British and American philosophizing at the present time.

Inasmuch as the four criticisms I have mentioned seem to

convict traditional religion of violating all the criteria of sound thought and responsible scholarship that Western society is laboriously trying to teach in schools and colleges— since religious belief seems to be foolishly contrary to the canons of good evidence, clarity, and cogency on which Western technocracy is founded—we must either show that religion is not foolish in that pernicious sense, or acknowledge that it is a troublesome anomaly in our present age. We must either rid campus and community of churches and syna- gogues—at least we must allow religion to collapse from neglect—or we must find that belief in God is still profound- ly relevant to, strangely consistent with, and important for, our present culture.

Members of our various religious communities must not take the sort of criticisms I have mentioned as being simply wrong or merely malicious. Indeed, careful consideration of them conduces toward a more humane and profound spirituality than is usual in conventionally religious circles. Nor should those who are interested, but who are unable to abide religion as they understand it, hastily take stock of these criticisms and then despair of seeing through them to something better than they had previously dared to look for. In the twentieth century, the words that I quoted from Keynes echo a perennial conviction of a noteworthy and per- sistent remnant of mankind. In the eighteenth century, the philosopher-bishop George Berkeley struck the same note, and in the following pages I intend to show why we should listen: "Whatever the world thinks, he who hath not much meditated upon God, the human mind and the Summum Bonum, may possibly make a thriving earth-worm, but will indubitably make a sorry patriot and a sorry statesman." [15]

[15] George Berkeley, *Sirius* (London and Dublin: C. Hitch; C. Davis, 1744), par. 350.

Why are not times of judgment kept by the Almighty
and why do those who know him never see his days? . . .
From out of the city the dying groan,
and the soul of the wounded cries for help;
yet God pays no attention to their prayer.

JOB 24:1, 12

CHAPTER I

EVIL AND ABSURDITY IN RELIGION

The sense in which the traditional Judeo-Christian belief in God is logically false (self-contradictory) is nowhere more succinctly demonstrated than in the theological problem of evil. Every reasonable and moral person who is caught up in that tradition must sometime echo the question of the Lord's good servant Job: "Why are not times of judgment kept by the Almighty, and why do those who know him never see his days?" What person pondering the question with Job is not also thunderstruck by God's dreadful response: "Shall a fault-finder contend with the Almighty?" (Job 40:2.) Indeed, can any decent and intelligent person avoid it? Certainly the literature of Western civilization is freighted with such highly moral and closely reasoned contention. Job's question has always been, for many intellectuals especially, both a moral and a logical deterrent to conventional theistic belief.[1]

[1] See, for example, the following: Bertrand Russell, *The Scientific Outlook* (New York: W. W. Norton, 1951), pp. 130-31; Albert Einstein, *Science, Philosophy and Religion* (New York: Conference on Science, Philosophy and Religion in their Relation to the Democratic Way of Life,

24

In 1955, in an article entitled, "Evil and Omnipotence," which is now frequently referred to, Professor J. L. Mackie described the *logical* aspect of the problem as follows:

God is omnipotent; God is wholly good; and yet evil exists. There seems to be some contradiction between these three propositions, so that if any two of them were true the third would be false. But at the same time all three are essential parts of most theological positions: the theologian, it seems at once *must* adhere and cannot consistently adhere to all three.[2]

And Mackie concludes:

Of the proposed solutions of the problem of evil . . . none has stood up to criticism. . . . This . . . strongly suggests that there is no valid solution of the problem which does not modify at least one of the constituent propositions in a way which would seriously affect the essential core of the theistic position.[3]

Professor Henry D. Aiken has more recently discussed the *moral* dimensions of this dilemma. In an essay called, "God and Evil: A Study of Some Relations between Faith and Morals," he formulates the problem very much as Mackie does, but then goes on to describe its practical effect on an intellectually fastidious but would-be theist. Declaring that faith in God consists in believing that "(a) there is an almighty and omniscient being who is a perfectly good person and who alone is God," Aiken adds that, in apparent contradiction of this "theological thesis," a religious person must also acknowledge an "ethical thesis," that "(b) there is some-

1941), pp. 209-14; Nelson Pike, ed., *God and Evil* (Englewood Cliffs, N.J.: Prentice-Hall, 1964), selections from Feodor Dostoevski, David Hume, John Stewart Mill, and others, plus a bibliography.

[2] J. L. Mackie, "Evil and Omnipotence," *Mind*, LXIV, No. 254 (1955), 200; see also Flew, "Divine Omnipotence and Human Freedom," *New Essays in Philosophical Theology*, pp. 144-70.

[3] Mackie, "Evil and Omnipotence," p. 212.

thing in the finite universe created by that being which is evil." [4] Aiken then proceeds to describe the "religio-moral crisis" which must inevitably result from an attempt to hold both of these conflicting theses simultaneously and in full awareness. We are told that in such a crisis a person is driven to "renounce his profoundest loyalties, to cease, that is, to be the very person he is." [5]

The following observation of Aiken's is particularly germane. In it, and in other similar remarks, he emphasizes the despair and passion of a person caught in such a dilemma. "Whatever he does," says Aiken, "his way of life will never be quite the same again, for something that has hitherto been a cornerstone of that way of life has now been shaken to its foundation." [6]

Between them, Mackie and Aiken summarize the logical and moral contradictions involved in the theological problem of evil and express the psychological anguish that often accompanies an awareness of those contradictions. This is a noteworthy contribution to the philosophy of religion. For if interested individuals are to experience a *religious* solution to the theological problem of evil, reason and passion must strike against each other at some point to ignite religious consciousness.

Although Mackie's argument has been criticized by several authors writing in *Mind* and elsewhere,[7] and in spite of the fact that Aiken is taken to task by Nelson Pike in the same

[4] Henry D. Aiken, "God and Evil: A Study of Some Relations Between Faith and Morals," *Ethics*, LXVIII, No. 2 (1957-58), 79.

[5] *Ibid.*, p. 96.

[6] *Ibid.*, p. 80.

[7] For example: S. A. Grave, "On Evil and Omnipotence," *Mind*, LXV (1954-55), 259-62; I. T. Ramsey, "The Paradox of Omnipotence," *Mind*, LXV, 263-66; P. M. Farrell, O.P., "Evil and Omnipotence," *Mind*, LXIX (1958-59), 74-76; Ninian Smart, "Omnipotence, Evil, and Superman," *Philosophy*, XXXVI, No. 137 (1961), 188-96.

issue of *Ethics* in which Aiken's article appears, the paradoxical peculiarities that constitute the theological problem of evil demand more amplification than is provided in those discussions of it. Of course, as one of the discussants, I. T. Ramsey, in effect suggests, no strictly philosophical explanation of the theological problem of evil can completely alleviate the sort of distress that Aiken expresses. Religiously speaking, the price of "common sense" in this context is spiritual bankruptcy. It may, thus, appear to philosophers—especially to professed defenders of "common sense"—that the value of religion is counterfeit if the theological problem of evil cannot be solved by strictly consistent reasoning from accepted moral principles to obviously moral conclusions.

However, whenever we try to stipulate quite clearly what our religious terms mean, Judeo-Christian theism is revealed as a self-contradictory system of concepts. A clearly defined religious faith seems to involve a foolish abrogation of reason; and if we try to flee from that absurdity toward a less scandalous object of worship—if we try to make our conception of an omnipotent God logically and morally respectable—the object of our theologizing becomes increasingly vague.[8] As the scandal is washed away our object of worship fades with it. If we are reasonable, moral, *and* religious, we are caught in a vicious dilemma from which there is no exit short of a miracle. But how can we appeal to a miraculous solution of this problem without appearing, to common sense, to be both silly and sophistical?

There is a way. Yet, we can never totally eradicate the theological problem of evil from the creative passion of religious life. We cannot dismiss it as Pike attempts to do when

[8] Flew has demonstrated this point in several places. See, for example, *New Essays* . . . , pp. 144-69. Bernard Williams demonstrates the same point from a different angle, *ibid.*, pp. 187-211. Perhaps the clearest is C. B. Martin, *ibid.*, pp. 212-26, particularly the last page.

he says, "I suppose for some, Aiken's question: 'What am I to do?' is . . . a cry of utter bewilderment. . . . For most, however, the commitment to the 'rational' way of life is, I think, adjustable without radical change of attitude." [9] Pike concludes that, if one believes in God, "the traditional problem of evil reduces to a noncrucial perplexity of relatively minor importance." [10]

Pike's response to the theological problem of evil is a misleading description of intellectually responsible religious life. To say of Job, for example, that his faith "is tested, but not threatened," [11] is to forget that the test God inflicts on Job is not merely academic, as though Job were a spiritual athlete who is only required to do a short sprint. God's testing of Job is obviously a threat to Job's initial religiosity. It brings about a radical change of attitude and understanding in Job. Because he is passionately involved in his perplexities, Job finally experiences a deep spiritual upset and illumination, but not before his original moral and religious resources are completely exhausted. Indeed, in contradiction to his thesis, Pike himself suggests that Job eventually experienced a crisis: "When the theological thesis is affirmed," says Pike, "Job teaches, the crisis is past." [12] My criticism of Pike is mainly concerned with the importance of that sort of crisis, and of the need, when discussing the theological problem of evil, to illuminate its logical, psychological, and religious function.

Pike's failure to dispel the sort of ethico-religious perplexity that Aiken describes and expresses contains an important lesson for all who seek wisdom in addition to knowl-

[9] Nelson Pike, "God and Evil: A Reconsideration," *Ethics*, LXVIII, No. 2 (1957-58), 124.
[10] Nelson Pike (ed.), *God and Evil*, p. 102.
[11] Pike, "God and Evil: A Reconsideration," p. 121.
[12] *Ibid.*

edge, and who thus come to wrestle with the sort of questions that are poetically dramatized in the Book of Job. Like many others who wish to affirm the ultimate conceptual intelligibility of basic religious assumptions, Pike does not replace, or show how we could replace, our relatively clear conception of a paradoxical Deity with an equally clear conception of God that is not paradoxical. Pike denies the existence of logical contradiction in the "theological thesis," but when he admits that his "world theory invited a charge of incompleteness," [13] his argument fails to come to a satisfactory conclusion. It ends like a frayed rope, apparently attached to nothing. It is possible to avoid self-contradiction by emptying conflicting terms of their usual meanings, but if one cannot then point to some new or still remaining significance, one has hardly effected a real escape. In a philosophical sense, Pike avoids execution by committing suicide, a procedure which, if not formally self-contradictory, is at least materially self-defeating. But Pike did not intend to trap himself in such an embarrassing philosophical cul-de-sac.

The trouble with the familiar argument that Pike, in effect, employs—a variation of "seeing through a glass darkly" —is that it leaves us with a verbally non-paradoxical definition of God that is, however, substantively vacuous. His rejection of Aiken's anguish only replaces the latter's relatively clear paradox with an equally painful vagueness. Pike avoids the Scylla of logical falsity (the paradox of self-contradiction) only to encounter the Charybdis of semantical emptiness (words without sense). We are given no hint of how we might escape such unattractive alternatives except that we must " 'feel' our way on these basic issues anyway." [14] Thus, Pike does not advance us much, methodologically, beyond the haphazard procedure of the philosophically unsophisti-

[13] *Ibid.*
[14] *Ibid.*, p. 124.

29

cated person who occasionally tries, in vain, to unravel the conundrums inherent in his worship.

To defend traditional religious practices more effectively, some apologetical procedure must be found to avoid *mere* paradoxicality on the one hand, and *mere* emptiness on the other. Religious illumination must be described in a way that is fresh and arresting, a way that will show us that the ancient promise of an adequate answer to the theological problem of evil is a real and, in some sense, human possibility.

Notice that the word "paradox" has several overlapping meanings. We, however, are primarily concerned with only three of them. Thus, the word "paradox" may characterize statements that are (1) contrary to the tacit assumptions of common sense (like the religious injunction that it is better to give than to receive), or (2) practically self-defeating (like a reminder to forget your troubles), or (3) logically self-contradictory (like the idea of a married bachelor). Theology and religion are fraught with such paradoxical statements and demands, and we shall have to consider their different contexts and functions. For example, with regard to the theological problem of evil, all three senses of "paradox" are simultaneously involved.

One need only read the Book of Job, or Ecclesiastes, or the 89th psalm (verses 46-52) or listen to the religious discussion that is part of our general culture to be convinced that the Judeo-Christian belief in God is ordinarily understood in a way that is explicitly or implicitly self-contradictory. It is indeed possible to assert that the Judeo-Christian conception of God is *not* self-contradictory, though God alone knows how, but that does not help most sedulously reasonable and religious people to avoid paying a high price for their faithfulness. They cannot forget the logical absurdities and moral dilemmas that disturb their religious reflections. It is the perennial conclusion of countless numbers of concerned and responsible people that the theological problem of evil marks a strict logical self-contradiction in their religious understanding that cannot and ought not to be reduced to a "noncrucial perplexity of relatively minor importance." Quite the opposite! Yet, as the story of Job or the life of Dostoevsky illustrates, not everyone who comes to such a conclusion then rejects the traditional Judeo-Christian belief in Providence.

Such people are reasonable enough to see the absurdity of conventional belief in God, moral enough to be deeply disturbed by it, but religious enough to believe in (to act on) promises that are logically false, practically self-defeating, and contrary to common sense. Must we then assume that these people are all merely neurotic? Or is it, in a larger sense of the word, reasonable to suppose that some religious people actually find, again and again, a valuable illumination in the very midst of their ethico-religious dilemmas? If so, they must repeatedly experience a passage from mere self-contradiction (our third sense of "paradox") and mere self-defeat (our second sense of paradox) into meanings (akin to our third sense of paradox) that are beyond the logic of ordinary discourse. This is not to say that in theology we can reduce one sense of paradox to another until we arrive at a single meaning that is basic. For example, all three senses of paradox that I have mentioned are dynamically related to one another in the reports and confessions of the prophets and saints, yet each of these types of paradox is logically distinct from the others. Consequently, if we are to develop an adequate philosophy of religion, we must show, even to common sense, that it is reasonable to believe in the occurrence and human value of such extraordinary passages of mind, from one experience of paradox to another, each with its own logical character and religious function. To address our philosophy effectively to common sense, we must show, moreover,

31

that such religious occurrences are not *utterly* different from certain sorts of experience in ordinary life, and that we can all understand what it would be like to experience the multiple facets of religious truth. Generally, in what follows, I will not limit my use of the word "paradox" to any one of the senses I have discussed. All three sorts of paradox will usually be involved. In different contexts, however, it will often be obvious that it is some one or another of those senses of paradox that is especially connoted by the discussion.

Assuming that it is futile to deny the self-contradictory character of religious belief to which Aiken and Mackie have once again drawn our attention, we must nevertheless avoid the foolish reveling in paradox and unreason that sometimes characterizes "crisis theology." We must not, for example, echo great Luther's occasional rashness and cry, "Reason is a whore!" [15] If there is an inherently nonrational dimension or depth to human life that is reflected in religious consciousness—if, for example, intellectual agony is one cost that resolutely reasonable men must pay for religious enlightenment—it is not something to welcome without trembling. There is good reason to eschew "religious enthusiasm" in the present investigation, and yet we must exercise ingenuity and imagination if we are to bring out and exonerate the logical, psychological, and religious function of paradox in religious life and language.

Once we become aware, as Mackie and Aiken have, of the ineradicability of self-contradiction in traditional religion— once we are aware that the only theological alternative to this kind of paradox is to move into the sort of vagueness that

[15] See W. Kaufmann's comments and his quotations from Luther, *Existentialism from Dostoevsky to Sartre*, ed. Kaufmann (Meridian Books; Cleveland: World, 1957), p. 18. Those who think Luther is being unjustly characterized here may substitute occasionally rash castigations of reason from the writings of Tertullian, Kierkegaard, and Barth instead.

characterizes so-called "rational theology" (the conceptual vagueness that results from having to qualify endlessly what theologians have said about God)—then, although we may *wish* to avoid logical falsity of the kind of which the theological problem of evil is but one example in religion, we will only be able to do so by inviting the disturbing charge that our theological discourse has now become senselessly vacuous, or by abandoning traditional religion altogether.

Many intellectuals reject traditional belief in God at this point. They value clarity and consistency too much ever to put them knowingly in jeopardy. They shun vagueness—especially concepts that trail off, as they see it, into no sense at all—and they eschew self-contradiction. Yet, surely, it is possible, perhaps even likely, that every tidy and self-contained rationalism is bought at a high price. If we are unknowingly shut up within our conventional systems of discourse, we may forfeit spiritual values that could profoundly enrich our days if only we would permit those values to break into the insulated dominion we occupy within our systems of conventional explanation and evaluation.

In the nineteen thirties and forties, even the self-assurance of certain positivistic philosophers was shaken when they discovered that they could not expunge every degree of vagueness and ambiguity from their own philosophical principles. Their theory of meaning was designed primarily to explain the semantic character of scientific statements on the one hand and that of pure mathematics on the other, and deliberately to reject both metaphysics and theology as meaningless and misleading forms of discourse, for the sorts of reasons I have already discussed briefly in the Introduction. But, unexpectedly encountering complicated technical difficulties that I need not trace out here, they found that they

could not define and defend their own criteria of meaning

33

without employing self-defeating arguments.[16] They were, so to say, "hoist on their own petard." They found that they could not entirely rid their own house of the plague—the twin bacilli of endemic vagueness and paradoxicality in human discourse—for which they had planned to blow up the houses of others. The attempted purge of metaphysics, theology, and the language of worship threatened to spread to the very disciplines that the purge was intended to establish as inviolate.

Eventually, the late Ludwig Wittgenstein began to point out that there are "family resemblances" among the most dissimilar linguistic types. Thus, we may reasonably suppose that merely because the traditional language of worship leads philosophers into the sort of quandry that is exemplified by the theological problem of evil this does not *entirely* isolate the logic of religious language from the forms of discourse that are more generally and unquestioningly accepted by a technocratic society. Philosophers of science and mathematics also encounter various kinds of paradoxicality and various kinds of vagueness when they attempt to push the concepts and principles that define a science or a mathematical system to the absolute extremes of theoretical clarity and philosophical justification. Wittgenstein's description of ordinary language as a profusion of "language games"—each ineradicably vague to some extent, all overlapping in various (and contrary) ways—suggests that common sense itself is not as free of paradox and indefinability as many commonsense critics of religion had once taken for granted.[17] Apparently, as Ralph Waldo Emerson once remarked, there *is* such a thing as a foolish consistency which is the hobgoblin of little minds.

[16] See J. O. Urmson, *Philosophical Analysis* (London: Oxford University Press, 1956), pp. 114 ff.
[17] Ludwig Wittgenstein, *Philosophical Investigations* (New York: Macmillan, 1953), pp. 5-15, 31-45.

"God offers to every mind its choice between truth and repose," he said:

Take which you please—you can never have both. Between these, as a pendulum, man oscillates. He in whom the love of repose predominates will accept the first creed, the first philosophy, the first political party he meets—most likely his father's. He gets rest, commodity and reputation; but he shuts the door of truth. He in whom the love of truth predominates will keep himself aloof from all moorings, and afloat. He will abstain from dogmatism, and recognize all the opposite negations between which, as walls, his being is swung. He submits to the inconvenience of suspense and imperfect opinion, but he is a candidate for truth, as the other is not, and respects the highest law of his being.[18]

In less poetic fashion, this theme was also stressed by the great philosopher-logician, Charles S. Peirce, in explanation of his own religious belief. "God is a vernacular word," he points out, "and, like all such words, but more than almost any, is vague." And then he continues on the same tack as that along which we ourselves have been advancing in this chapter. "Every concept that is vague is liable to be self-contradictory in those respects in which it is vague."

No concept, not even those of mathematics, is absolutely precise; and some of the most important for everyday use are extremely vague. Nevertheless, our instinctive beliefs involving such concepts are far more trustworthy than the best established results of science, if these be precisely understood. . . . Men who are given to defining too much inevitably run themselves into confusion in dealing with the vague concepts of common sense.[19]

[18] Ralph Waldo Emerson, quoted in the frontispiece of *Knowledge and Value*, eds. E. Sprague and P. W. Taylor (New York: Harcourt Brace & World, 1967).
[19] Charles S. Peirce, "The Concept of God," *Philosophical Writings of Peirce*, ed. Justus Buchler (New York: Dover, 1955), pp. 375-76.

Peirce reminds us that, whenever we attempt to clarify the persistently vague concepts and ambiguous language of common sense, we take the chance of running into the confusions and self-contradictions that stick up directly beneath the surface flow and froth of daily discourse. To the extent that religious faith is expressed in ordinary language, it is an invitation to theological and psychological disaster for all who accept a challenge to deepen their religious understanding by philosophical means. Yet, no thinking person can approach the conventional language of religion without trying to understand it as clearly and consistently as possible. It is quite natural for a "rational animal" to attempt to clarify what is unclear in his comprehension of the religious myths he inherits; and, as Peirce points out, it is quite inevitable that in doing so he will experience paradoxes, like the theological problem of evil, that appear only when one tries to think clearly and consistently about the original mythopoeic revelation. The Bible may make some loose but precious sense to us, for example, but cease to do so when we read Calvin's predestinarian and double predestinarian interpretation of it.

However concrete the imagery of revelation may be (subsequent chapters will offer examples), its full religious significance is always ambiguous and almost surely to become self-contradictory when we attempt to make its meaning more precise. We should keep in mind, however, that religion is not entirely different, in this respect, from some of our relatively clear and self-consistent modes of discourse. Nor should we forget that religious myths are spontaneous and recurrent expressions of certain profound levels of human experience: of guilt and remorse and forgiveness, of death and anxiety in the face of it, of disappointment and loss, of love and the lack of it, of value and its absence, of ecstasy and boredom. Like primitive drawings in a cave or cries in the

36

night, the full significance of religious myth and liturgy cannot be expressed in any leaner or more prosaic form.[20] Ambiguous and self-contradictory signs are often the most adequate kinds of symbols of such experiences; the best way of bringing one person to share the precious insight of another. The repeated eruptions of what we roughly classify as religious expression is a profound and ambiguous sign: it points to something mysterious and wonderful (but not unknowable) in the creative relationship between every human individual and his world order. And, if this is what Nelson Pike meant by saying that his "world theory invites a charge of incompleteness," we have no quarrel to pick with him on that score.

It follows that the theological problem of evil is not merely a problem of the kind that Mackie has suggested. Its significance is far deeper and different than he suspected when he wrote the article that I have quoted. The theological problem of evil is what Aiken recognizes it to be, a crisis in the life of a person whose allegiance is split between obedience to the Word of God as that person presently understands it, and obedience to the everyday logic of his moral life. God, it seems, is both loving and malicious, omnipotent and impotent, all-knowing and unknowing—a worthy object of both worship and scorn.[21] The problem is not merely a theoretical difficulty. It is, in its full and proper sense, an existential crisis in individual after individual, in one age after another. The theological problem of evil functions in religion as an end to the intellectual's conceptualistic and relatively abstract approach to God, and as the beginning (perhaps) of another approach. And if it does not initiate this latter ap-

[20] John Wisdom makes the same point. See John Wisdom, "The Logic of 'God,'" in *The Existence of God*, ed. John Hick (New York: Macmillan, 1964), pp. 275-98.
[21] A point emphasized by C. G. Jung. See C. G. Jung, *Answer to Job* (Meridian Books; Cleveland: World, 1960), pp. 32 ff.

proach, one will never fully understand the problem, for the religious answer is in part a reflexive illumination of that initial difficulty.

When we reflect on the fact that one purpose of theology is to clarify and explain revelation—when we appreciate what it means to try to rationalize religious myth—then we will not be surprised that philosophical theology leads to such inconsistencies as the one we are discussing, nor will we be so quick to condemn religion out of hand when we are told that the problem is not one to be answered in the intellectualistic fashion of that initial theological project. In its full religious significance, the theological problem of evil is a marker: it establishes the point at which philosophers must learn something radically new, or, like tourists who wander unaware past the gate to the Old City, they will not know that they have missed the turning that would have made the whole trip worthwhile. What appears to philosophy, narrowly conceived, as nothing but a logical absurdity or a senselessly ambiguous equivocation can be seen in the light of a wider philosophical perspective as an odd sign of our own mental and moral limitations, and as an encouraging promise of repeated spiritual fulfillment. Religious knowledge is a matter of repeated emptiness, repeated fulfillment, cherished memory, and faithful anticipation.

Because of the extraordinary passion that must accompany religious insight if it is first to be acquired and then sustained, the kind of dilemma to which Mackie and Aiken draw our attention serves an essential purpose in the attainment of full religious life. It functions *logically* as a transcendental sign of the odd "object" which we will consider in Chapter III, and *psychologically* as the occasion for that sign's *religious* functioning. Although rationalistic theologies of "finite divinity" succeed in circumventing the theological problem of evil, the result, for both philosophy and religion, is less than a triumph. Such religious philosophies attempt to demonstrate the present existence or evolving emergence of cosmological and human factors that they label "divine." But the relatively clear and paradox-free notion of such a finite god is not the conceptual equivalent of the God of our Fathers. Nor does it have the psychological power to enflame the passions of men that previous generations have spoken of in their religious testimony. For most religious people, the conception of a finite god is a religiously stunted notion, and in the opinion of most philosophers of science it is a useless speculative addendum to scientific procedure. To the extent that they really succeed in talking sense to the scientific and philosophical communities (which largely ignore what they have to say) theological cosmologists like Samuel Alexander, Alfred North Whitehead, Teilhard de Chardin, Charles Hartshorne, Daniel Day Williams, and others sacrifice the sort of passion-in-the-face-of-paradox that is one essential characteristic of biblical religion. They give up the characteristic intensity of religious passion, the fire of the prophets and the saints, without gaining any real philosophical or scientific advantage. Admittedly, the God of the Judeo-Christian tradition is finite in one sense, in the sense that every historical appearance is finite—and God, we are assuming, has indeed revealed himself to Jews and Christians—nevertheless (and paradoxically) he is also said to be wholly transcendent.

Paradox characterizes the language of religion at its highest point. Yet, because of the paradoxical promises of traditional religion, and because of the paradoxical spiritual needs of every human individual, the theological problem of evil does not merely repel—it both repels and attracts. And when it becomes psychologically provocative, it may come to have religious reference. In such a moment the heat of passion may indeed help generate and repeatedly regenerate the

39

hoped for illumination—the extraordinary change of general perspective or "insight" that is characteristic of what we call "religious intuition"—which is much more than merely an emotional experience. In such a crisis an individual's knowledge of God and of himself may fuse and interpenetrate, and the languages of both psychology and religion become equally proper but differently revealing descriptions of the individual's condition. Onlookers may describe what is happening to such a person, either in the language of some psychological system of explanation—in terms of Freud or Jung or Skinner, for example—or in terms of some religious myth. We may talk in different logics and thus enter different areas of discourse, enter different realms of being through what is in a sense—but in only a limited sense—the same datum.

Religious paradoxes like the problem of evil are, in part, expressions of the limited character of the myriad modes of discourse in which men encounter their worlds and their own phenomenal selves. Religious consciousness is thus, among other things, an apprehension (however unsophisticated) of the pinchbeck nature of all interpretations of reality—even of the inadequacy of every religious myth—and that is why its own expression must be ultimately self-destructive.[22] Philosophers who are more than superficially interested in religion must ponder the testimonies and confessions of religious literature, not only because that is the source of the paradoxes with which philosophical theology and philosophy of religion must wrestle, but also because it is the environment, the Word, in which the answer lives in the midst of the community. Whoever is sincerely interested in that answer must enter its environment, the religious myth, with his whole heart and mind, for no armchair philosophy of religion can be more than superficially relevant to its

[22] See Paul Tillich, *The Courage to Be* (New Haven: Yale University Press, 1952), pp. 182 ff.

subject matter. Just as traditional empirical philosophy has insisted that ordinary and scientific meanings must be based on sense perception, so every philosophy of religion must be rooted in its appropriate religio-mythic intuition and communion.

The religious answer to the philosophical difficulty which Mackie, Aiken, and others have delineated so carefully is to be given only by "the spirit of God," as religious people say. This is, of course, an abandonment of philosophy—but not without the promise of a more perceptive return to it. In religious life, as contrasted to mere philosophical speculation about religion, one experiences solutions to such questions as that posed by the theological problem of evil, not by avoiding but by suffering those paradoxes in a way that fuses those violations of conventional logic with the existential enigmas of human existence. In religious life one cannot always avoid logical absurdity. Professor Henry Sidgwick used to say, jokingly, that he never knew when a contradiction was simply a contradiction and when it was a sign of a profound truth,[23] and this remark is worth remembering when we consider the theological problem of evil. In religious life one cannot always avoid believing what is logically and morally inconsistent in some conventional sense, not because one is so foolish, but because human life is so ambiguously significant and morally complex, a crosshatch of sense and nonsense which is our spiritual environment. Thus, one must find the answers within, not without, the dilemmas to which religious language brings us. "Through the dark gate," writes Martin Buber, "the believing man steps forth into the everyday which is henceforth hallowed." [24]

We can now see that a subtle but important change has

[23] See H. R. Mackintosh, *Types of Modern Theology* (London: Nisbet, 1952), p. 234.
[24] Martin Buber, *The Eclipse of God* (New York: Harper, 1952), p. 36.

41

taken place in our discussion—one that must always occur when the odd logical and psychological function of the theological problem of evil is allowed to operate. Whenever we become existentially involved in that question, it aims our relatively abstract theological reasoning directly into the heart of human existence as we find it in ourselves. If our hunger for wisdom prompts us to continue in that direction—from a relatively dispassionate to a relatively passionate consideration of the promises of our traditional religious myths—we must move from the conceptual neatness of philosophical speculation into the concrete disorder, into the "absurdity," of human existence. We will then become aware of ourselves existing in dialectical tension between a projected ideal (our idea of God and the sort of world we think he should have created) and the radically different reality in which we find ourselves (confronted by a "meaningless" universe and the logical impossibility of the existence of the God we had projected). This may be the beginning of our religious awakening. If it occurs in us, the answer we are looking for will happen as an existential solution to our deepening speculative disturbance. The answer to the expanding ramifications of our initial speculative problem must occur as a revolutionary "encounter" or *noesis* which wrings the paradoxical name of God from us. To have faith in God, in contrast to immediate knowledge of him, is to have an impassioned belief that although it is logically impossible—although no self-consistent system could adequately account for it—nevertheless such an encounter may actually happen. In essence, the answer to the question that Mackie and Aiken raise is not a proposition or set of propositions but an unexpected change in the quality of our own individual existence. Our ethico-religious crisis must cause us to exclaim with Job, "I had heard of thee by the hearing of the ear, but now my eye sees thee;

42

therefore I despise myself, and repent in dust and ashes."
(Job 42:5-6.)

Some remarks and illustrations from John Wisdom's article, "The Logic of 'God,' " will help clarify the direction our
discussion is taking. "Imagine someone is trying on a hat,"
says Wisdom:

She is studying the reflection in a mirror like a judge considering
a case. There's a pause and then a friend says in tones too clear,
"My dear, it's the Taj Mahal." Instantly the look of indecision
leaves the face in the mirror. All along she had felt there was about
the hat something that wouldn't quite do. Now she sees what it
is. . . . It isn't true that the words about the hat only influence
the hearer's feelings to the hat. They alter her apprehension of the
hat. . . . It isn't true that the words "It's the Taj Mahal" meant
"It's like the Taj Mahal." This more sober phrase is an inadequate
substitute . . The still more sober substitute "It is in some respects like the Taj Mahal" is still more inadequate. It's *much*
too feeble. . . . What she said wasn't the literal truth like "It's a
cobra" said of what is, unfortunately, a cobra. But what she said
revealed the truth. Speaking soberly what she said was false but
then thank heaven we don't always speak soberly.[25]

Religious testimony is notoriously intoxicated talk, and
even the relatively sober apologetics of traditional theology
are still reeling from the night before. The prophetic testimony of religion is often inelegant and disruptive, and its
theological amplification cannot help violating our intellectual and sensible conventions. This is what we experience in
the theological problem of evil. But there is a point to all this.
To experience the theological problem of evil as you are trying on religion is like hearing someone behind you murmur
about your conception of religion, "My dear, it's the Taj
Mahal."

[25] Wisdom, "The Logic of 'God,' " pp. 277-79 *passim*.

We must enlarge our present consideration of the theological problem of evil and absurdity beyond the confines of a theological crotchet to a consideration of the universal condition of man. The question that has occupied us in the preceding pages—How can an omniscient, omnipotent, and good God be the creator of a world containing evil?—aims beyond the area of discourse in which it is raised. It is the sort of question that Stephen Toulmin calls a "limiting question," and Karl Jaspers a "boundary problem" (*grenzproblem*).[26] We are, thus, forced out of the topic of this chapter and into the subject matter of the next one.

[26] Stephen Toulmin, *The Place of Reason in Ethics* (London: Cambridge University Press, 1953), pp. 202-25; Karl Jaspers, *Way to Wisdom*, trans. Ralph Manheim (New Haven: Yale University Press, 1954), p. 204. Cf., Jaspers, *Truth and Symbol*, trans. Jean T. Wilde, William Kluback, and William Kimmel (New Haven: College and University Press, 1959), trans. intro. and p. 33.

A man is a god in ruins. . . . Man is the dwarf of himself.
. . . The problem of restoring to the world original and
eternal beauty is solved by the redemption of the soul.
The ruin, or blank, that we see when we look at nature is
in our own eye. . . . The reason why the world lacks unity
and lies broken and in heaps is because man is disunited
with himself. He cannot be a naturalist until
he satisfies all the demands of the spirit.
Love is as much its demand as perception.

RALPH WALDO EMERSON, *Nature*

CHAPTER II

EVIL AND ABSURDITY IN EXISTENTIAL PHILOSOPHY

1. Introduction to Existentialism

One of the most important aspects of the theological problem of evil is also one that is most frequently overlooked. We forget that traditional religion did not start as a theory. Essentially, religion is not a metaphysical system; and when it becomes one, its essential testimony has been suborned. Religious testimony is a mythopoeic, a prophetic expression of certain momentous insights into the conditions of human existence; and the Book of Job is a classic example of such a disclosure. That book is a *poetic* response to an intuition of evil that is indigenous to human existence as such and which far exceeds the competence of any merely prosaic or "literal" description or solution. As far as the origin of this problem is concerned, the lesson of religion is perfectly consonant with

45

the lesson of modern depth psychology, including existential psychoanalysis.[1] Man is his own worst enemy!

In religious myth, the classic adversary, Satan, is man against himself in some profounder sense than is usually suspected. And in the terminology of the myth, only God can save that self-alienated victim from his foe. Thus, every man cries out with Job for help: "Oh, that I had one to hear me! . . . Oh, that I had the indictment written by my adversary!" (Job 31:35.) Yet, in the mystery of human existence, that indictment is ghost-written by man himself, and the acquittal, when it comes, must come from man in a sense that is wrapped in the ambiguous and paradoxical swaddling of the prophetic promise.

The ancient teachings of religion and the modern researches of depth psychology agree that the well-being of every human individual depends in part on his becoming aware of his own surreptitious involvement in moral evil and self-destruction. Job is a prophetic archetype of every individual whose conventional virtue and superficial rectitude alienate him from the spirit of the moral law and a gracious acceptance of the conditions of self-fulfillment. Thus Job experiences the fundamental problem of human existence as that problem is expressed in traditional religious language. He knows the absence of God which is the very presence of his Adversary. Job's basic affliction is a subsurface rejection of self-knowledge, a rejection of a moral and psychological con-

[1] See, for example, Karl Menninger, *Man Against Himself* (New York: Harcourt, Brace & Co., 1938), *passim;* C. G. Jung, *Psychology and Religion* (New Haven: Yale University Press, 1938), Chap. 1; Erich Fromm, *Psychoanalysis and Religion* (Yale University Press, 1950), Chap. 5; Paul Tillich, *The Courage to Be,* Chap. 3; Gregory Zilboorg, *Psychoanalysis and Religion* (New York: Farrar, Strauss and Cudahy, 1962), pp. 54-62; David Roberts, *Psychotherapy and a Christian View of Man* (New York: Scribner's, 1950), Chap. 1; Victor White, O.P., *God and the Unconscious* (Meridian Books; Cleveland: World 1952), pp. 47-100, 188-202. The last two books contain bibliographical addenda of further readings in this area.

frontation of self that is essential to religious wisdom. It is his initial lack of reflective self-awareness, his inadequate moral and emotional maturity, that is expressed in mytho-poeic terms throughout most of the Book of Job. This freely chosen estrangement from his own "larger self," as the Upani-shads might say, increasingly withers Job's life, and the flower and fruit of his labor, as his story unfolds.

So it is with all of us. The theological problem of evil has the form of an academic conundrum, but it expresses a universal problem of human existence. When it appears on the surface of theology or philosophy of religion, it is a seis-mographic response to a deep fault in human nature, like a crack in the earth's crust that plunges out of sight and deeper than we can plumb. This is the "abyss" which fasci-nates all existentialists, and which draws us now to consider their descriptions of it.

Existentialism is a many-sided and complex phenomenon in the history of Western thought, but as a method of phi-losophy and as an intellectual attitude it is uniquely relevant to the moral and psychological concerns that we have so far only touched upon. The profundity of some of the existen-tialists' insights partly accounts for the notorious obscurity that characterizes the most original and influential examples of their writings. At other times a less laudable obscurity muddies relatively commonplace observations that reek of overdramatic and sentimental jargon. Every thoroughly re-sponsible discussion of existentialism must avoid obscurity when it occurs at the needless expense of clarity, but it must also dare to be obscure when a simplified clarity would itself conceal the chiaroscuro mysteries of human existence which existentialists seek to bring to our attention. Anglo-Saxon commentators on existentialism often violate this latter prin-ciple; Continental commentators just as often disregard the former; but I, in this chapter, shall try to avoid both of these extremes. By describing and then criticizing the thought of only one existentialist philosopher, I shall try to show what the existentialist descriptions of human existence are like in general—taking care to note when our model is a misleading example of the group—and in particular how certain existentialistic conceptions are related to such traditional religious ideas as "original sin" and "salvation."

Inasmuch as I am writing with both the Jewish and Christian traditions in mind, we must remind ourselves that although the notion of original sin has been notoriously over-emphasized in some Christian quarters and foolishly under-emphasized in some Jewish contexts, nevertheless the idea of original sin is not as foreign to historic Judaism as strenuously non-Christian Jewish polemicists would sometimes lead us to believe.[2] This is worth noting if Jews and Christians are both to appreciate the religious significance of the concept of man's "fallenness" as it occurs in atheistic existentialism. If we focus our attention on the philosophy of Jean-Paul Sartre, it will, for example, eventually confront us with existentialist parallels to the problem of religious meaning that started our investigations, and this in itself may help us view the often obfuscating peculiarities of religious language in a new light. It may also improve our understanding of the existentialists.

There is, however, a dual note of caution and encouragement that must be sounded before we begin. This chapter attempts to be comprehensive enough to touch all the points of existential philosophy that are importantly related to the broad question of the meaning of religious discourse and religious behavior. Moreover, the exposition is intended to

[2] For the concept of "the evil inclination" (the evil *yetzer*) in Judaism, see C. G. Montefiore and H. Loewe (eds.), A *Rabbinic Anthology* (London: Macmillan, 1935), Chap. XI.

achieve such comprehensiveness without slighting the technical complexity and philosophical profundity of this popularly trivialized philosophical movement. My discussion is bound to fall short of both of these ideals, but it will be guided, nevertheless, by a sincere attempt to attain them. As a result, readers who are already thoroughly familiar with existential phenomenology may be bored if they feel they are being asked, here, to study what they already know; and readers who are relatively unfamiliar with the technical intricacies of existentialism may be discouraged if they feel that they must understand everything in this chapter before they proceed to the chapters that follow. But neither the well-informed nor the relatively uninformed should be put off by such erroneous suspicions. For each may read this chapter profitably according to his own ability and interest.

Readers who find that they do not need the instruction in existentialism that follows are encouraged to skim it and to skip, if they wish, to the conclusions in section four of this chapter. On the other hand, readers who are relatively unfamiliar with the material being described are encouraged to expose themselves to its modest technicalities. These slightly academical considerations are really intimately related to the vital matters of heart and mind that have brought us to this point, and even if a person is not satisfied with his understanding of this somewhat scholarly digression, he will subsequently discover that the chapters that follow are not only a vacation after his work but are also enormously germane to the existential insights and oversights that we are now about to consider. Thus, although we may sometimes feel in this chapter, as Spinoza did in the last sentence of his *Ethics*, that "all things noble are as difficult as they are rare," perhaps we may also come to feel, as he did, that we have moved a bit toward that high standard and that our travail has been worthwhile.

We will concentrate on Sartre, rather than on some other author, because he is more than the best known existentialist and the most provocative. He is also one of the most systematic and perhaps the most readily explained. The limitations of our endeavor in this chapter will therefore make it possible for us to travel more deeply and more systematically into the tangled undergrowth of existentialist philosophy than would be possible, in the length of one chapter, if we advanced on a broader and more scattered front. Moreover, since the works that made Sartre famous express some of the most tragic insights of all existentialist literature, our consideration of his earliest and most unalleviated pessimism will bring us unambiguously into the presence of moral evil and suffering that so much concerns traditional religious writers.

Although Sartre's general position now includes some important qualifications of his earlier views, and despite the fact that it is difficult to develop an entirely clear picture of his present position regarding all the matters on which he has written,[3] nevertheless his philosophy of freedom is a thoughtful and brilliantly articulate response to questions that men are said to ask themselves in every climate of opinion, under every sky. His description of freedom is a bridge over which we can pass from questions with which we are all intimately familiar—the basic and inescapable questions of

[3] See his most recent major work: *La Critique de la Raison Dialectique* (*Précédé de Question de Méthode*) (Paris: Gallimard, 1960). The first portion of this has been translated into English by Hazel Barnes under the title *Search for a Method* (New York: Knopf, 1963). For comments on the inconsistencies and ambiguities of Sartre's overall position, see Barnes's comments, pp .xv, xvii, xx-xxi. Also, Norman N. Greene, *Jean-Paul Sartre: The Existentialist Ethic* (Ann Arbor: University of Michigan Press, 1963), p. 206; Wilfred Desan, *The Marxism of Jean-Paul Sartre* (New York: Doubleday, 1965), *passim*; Raymond Aron, "Sartre's Marxism," *Encounter* (June, 1965), pp. 34-39; Mary Warnock, *The Philosophy of Sartre* (London: Hutchinson, 1965).

all mankind—into the mood and method of existential analysis as it describes the prevailing situation and deepest personal concerns of modern man.

As it occurs in this chapter, the word "philosophy" will usually have a meaning that is roughly the same as that suggested by the Greek word *"theoria,"* the German word *"weltanschauung"* and the English phrase "world view." The Greek term suggests a "mental vision," the connotation from which we derive our modern conception of theory. To compare philosophy with *theoria* thus implies that just as our scientific theories determine our hypotheses, condition our expectations, and affect what we notice in our laboratories, so a person's *theoria* is a constituent part of his experiencing; and to the extent that his philosophy is common to his culture it enables him to live in the "same world" as his contemporaries.

In classical German philosophy, for example, the word *"weltanschauung"* literally means "world view" or "world perspective" in a sense that strictly entails the notion that "our world" exists only in the light of our common philosophical orientation. This thesis is broadly characteristic of contemporary existentialist philosophers.[4] Sartre, for instance, maintains that a person "realizes" his world only in his philosophy.[5] In the following discussion of existentialism, the term "philosophy" will therefore refer to whatever conceptual system, however naïve or sophisticated, a man or culture uses to make sense of the raw material of experience. We

[4] See Wilfred Desan, *The Tragic Finale: An Essay on the Philosophy of Jean-Paul Sartre* (Cambridge: Harvard University Press, 1954), pp. 55-57; John Wild, *Existence and the World of Freedom* (Englewood Cliffs, N.J.: Prentice-Hall, 1963), Part II.

[5] Jean-Paul Sartre, *Being and Nothingness: An Essay on Phenomenological Ontology,* trans. Hazel E. Barnes (New York: Philosophical Library, 1956), pp. 179-80.

must notice two important facts connnected with this view of philosophy.

The first is that it integrates philosophy and existence! At least it links the concept of philosophy essentially with the concept of existence. It requires us to think of every fact as itself a part of the logical system that is used to interpret that fact. Both Martin Heidegger and Sartre insist, for instance, that an "uninterpreted world" is a contradiction in terms, like a "square circle." [6]

Second, this view of philosophy involves both philosophy and the world it interprets in the very being of the person whose world and philosophy they are! Each person is regarded as himself a part of every fact he calls "a fact." He realizes his world in his philosophy, but in so doing he also realizes—creates—himself. This idea is basic in Sartre's conception of existential psychoanalysis, and for all other existential psychoanalysts. "The only theory of knowledge which can be valid today," says Sartre, "is one which is founded on the truth of microphysics: the experimenter is part of the experimental system." [7] Study the world that confronts any individual, and you have a depth-psychological symbol of that person's basic choice of self. Consider the world that is structured by some culture, and you have a psychoanalytical basis for understanding the individual human projects that support and conflict with each other in that society. "Since," according to Sartre, "each example of human conduct symbolizes in its own manner the fundamental choice which must be brought to light, and since at the same time each one disguises this choice under its occasional character and its historical opportunity, only the comparison of these acts of conduct can effect the emergence of the unique revelation

[6] *Ibid.*, p. 181; Martin Heidegger, *Being and Time,* trans. John Macquarrie and Edward Robinson (New York: Harper, 1962), pp. 93 ff.

[7] Sartre, *Search for a Method,* p. 32 n.

which they all express in a different way." [8] Although we may try to separate one from the other in our thinking, neverthe-less, a person, his philosophy, and his world are integral aspects of one another and should not be isolated from one another in our descriptions of them.

"One could consider Sartre both as a realist and as an idealist," says Wilfred Desan. "As a realist because he accepts the 'brute existent' as being independent of human inter-vention, and as an idealist because he charges human con-sciousness . . . with the task of giving meaning . . . to this 'brute existent.' " [9] Desan points out, quite rightly, that "what is at stake" is an attempt on the part of existentialists like Heidegger and Sartre to affirm the "paradoxical neces-sity" of the "contradictory and simultaneous existence of subjects and objects." Thus, Sartre's ontological position (his conception of the basic and universal characteristics of existence) may be summarized as follows: mind is in no sense prior to its objects, as the philosophical idealists have held; neither are objects prior in some sense to mind, as philosoph-ical realists have argued. There is no transcendent reality that is more fundamental than the dual appearance of mind and matter; both consciousness and its objects are held to be mutually dependent on each other, and are so defined by Sartre. The world of man is a *meaning* given to an otherwise inexplicable and meaningless "brute existence" in the mys-terious light of human consciousness. This, basically, is why Sartre describes existence as meaningless. When he asks him-self, "What is the original relation of human reality to the 'being of phenomena,' " he answers as follows: "We are obliged to reject both the realist solution and the idealist

---

[8] Sartre, *Existential Psychoanalysis*, trans. Hazel E. Barnes (a Gateway Edition; Chicago: Regnery, 1962), p. 46. This book consists of excerpted portions from *Being and Nothingness*.

[9] Desan, *The Tragic Finale*, p. 56.

solution. . . . 'The relation of the regions of being is a primitive upsurge,' we said, 'and it forms a part of the very structure of these beings.' The concrete is revealed to us as the synthetic totality of which consciousness, like phenomena, constitutes only the articulations." [10]

Sartre seeks to evoke in his readers what is for him a fundamental mood: awe before the absurd coming-to-be of things. Along with Heidegger, Sartre attempts to renew a primitive amazement in modern man: that there *is* something rather than nothing at all. Many philosophers and theologians have expressed a similar sense of the world's contingency, of course—take Thomas Aquinas as a famous example—but their development of this "metaphysical intuition" (as Jacques Maritain calls it) has usually been dramatically different from Sartre's.[11] Thomas is led to posit the peculiar existence of God (*Ipsum esse subsistens*) as the necessary cause of the nonnecessary things that constitute the natural order. In contrast, Sartre seeks to increase our sense of the world's inexplicable existence by stressing its apparent lack of cause or purpose, and (as we shall see) by describing human life as inescapably self-defeating, tragic, and absurd.

Using methods that are fairly typical of contemporary existentialism, Sartre tries strenuously to avoid all questions that cannot be answered merely by describing appearances carefully, and yet he answers all the "big" questions of traditional philosophy. For existentialism is nothing if it is not an attempt to make us aware of certain perennial "deep" problems of mankind, and to suggest the road one must take if he is not to fall, or remain fallen, in the half-hidden fissures

[10] Sartre. *Being and Nothingness*, p. 171.
[11] See Thomas Aquinas, *Summa Theologica*, Question II, Arts. 1-3; *Summa Contra Gentiles*, Bk. I, Chap. 13; Jacques Maritain. *Approaches to God*. trans. Peter O'Reilly (New York: Macmillan. 1954). Chap. 1; *Existence and the Existent*. trans. L. Galatiere and G. B. Phelan (New York: Image Books, 1956), pp. 11-19.

—the potential hell—of human existence. It is a response to the problems that the analytical psychologist Carl Jung calls "the serious problems of life." Jung says that these problems "are never fully solved. If it should for once appear that they are, this is the sign that something has been lost. The meaning and design of a problem seem not to lie in its solution, but in our working at it incessantly. This alone preserves us from stultification and petrifaction." [12]

Students of contemporary philosophy will recall a well-known remark of Ludwig Wittgenstein's that seems to contradict Jung. In his *Tractatus Logico-Philosophicus* (para. 6.521), Wittgenstein observes that "the solution of the problem of life is seen in the vanishing of this problem." This is true of course of pseudo-problems. But we need not assume that the major concerns of existential philosophy are all that mistaken, nor should we presuppose that the theological and religious problems with which we are concerned in this book are all pseudo-problems either. We must wait and see what we can decipher. Perhaps there are indeed "serious problems of life" that are not solely logical or merely psychological. If there are, they will probably have logical and psychological aspects, but they will not be only the result of "linguistic cramps" or of neurotic compulsions. Sartre and other existentialists contend that there are such problems as Jung describes, and that they have an existential (an ontological) basis which men universally conceal from themselves, but which is symbolically revealed in the ambiguous and agonizing possibilities and frustrations of all human life. If so, then as Jung suggests, each of us is a constant problem to himself, a living complex of questions of a kind that Wittgenstein might not have been considering when he made the statement quoted above.

[12] C. G. Jung, *Modern Man in Search of a Soul* (New York: Harcourt Brace & Co., 1933), p. 103.

2. The Basic Questions and the Existential Method

What are these alleged questions? And how does the existentialist suggest we should respond to them? What are the questions (assuming there are some) that every human individual, lying awake and alone in the dark while the rest of the world sleeps, must put to himself merely by virtue of his existence as human? And how can he answer them?

I have occasionally asked this question of an audience: "Imagine that each one of you has inherited a large fortune. All of your obvious cultural and material wants can be satisfied. Suppose that you are in good health both mentally and physically, married or unmarried, childless or with children, with few or many friends—whatever you please. In such enviable circumstances, would there still be problems that would plague you, not (so far as you can tell) as idiosyncracies, but just because you are human, and for which, apparently, no amount of material advantage and technical training could provide the usual sorts of solution? Do you think you are confronted with such problems even now?"

After the initial surprise, the invariable response to this question has been a whisper of sibilant yeses. And the questions that people have confessed—often eagerly, in order to hear them discussed—have always been of profound philosophical interest. Apparently, most people in this century are deeply bothered by the same questions that were described by Immanuel Kant, in the eighteenth century, as the four basic questions of "universal philosophy."

In the *Handbook* to his lectures on logic, Kant describes philosophy in terms that put it at the very center of every examined life. According to him, philosophy is a search for "knowledge of the ultimate aims of reason"—a quest for "knowledge of the highest maxims of the use of our reason." [13]

[13] Quoted by Martin Buber, *Between Man and Man* (Boston: Beacon Press, 1955), p. 119.

Kant means by this that the fundamental questions of philosophy cut across all other disciplines, intersecting every human activity, penetrating every human life. His four basic questions seek *ultimate* rules of rational life—maxims that will provide the *final* justification of all existence! What is the meaning of human life, Kant wondered—what is the value of the world itself—if we cannot find a rational justification for rational life? Both science and morality must drive men, he thought, to seek "knowledge of the ultimate aims of reason." [14] One might summarize the intentions of all existentialists by saying that they are trying to provide a freshly candid and deliberately unconventional discussion of the four questions that Kant declared to be the necessary foundation of authentic human existence. [15]

  a. What can I know?
  b. What ought I do?
  c. What may I hope?
  d. What am I?

The first question motivates traditional theories of knowledge. The second asks for a foundation on which we can reasonably base our moral judgments and serious practical decisions. It is the foundation of moral philosophy. The third expresses the religious, though often skeptical, longing of mankind that our ideals of love and personal worth be somehow realized. The fourth voices the private shy puzzlement of each one of us as we realize, in ourselves, that we are somehow different from every other being.

In *The Critique of Pure Reason,* in the section called "Of the ideal of the supreme good," Kant says that the first three questions sum up every interest of speculative and moral

[14] *Ibid.*
[15] Cf. Karl Jaspers' use of these questions in "On My Philosophy," *Existentialism from Dostoevsky to Sartre,* ed. Walter Kaufmann (Meridian Books; Cleveland: World, 1957), p. 139.

reason, but then he proceeds in his *Handbook* to subsume even these three "big" questions under the fourth as the one that is absolutely paramount in any rational and responsible human life. Accordingly, in Kant's opinion, before we can proceed to answer and *justify* our answers to all the other problems of our unique existence as human individuals, the rock-bottom foundation that must be uncovered by each one of us for himself is a proper response to the question "What am I?" This question in its general form—the question, "What is man?"—is the basis of "philosophical anthropology" (or "philosophical psychology"), and it is hardly an exaggeration to say that existentialism is largely an anguished and often brilliant example of that inquiry.

Whether or not we have reservations about Kant's formulation and treatment of these "ultimate" problems, most people will agree that these questions are more than academic logomachies, and more than expressions of sheer confusion. For most individuals, no matter how sophisticated they have become, these questions smolder throughout life as honest, proper, and often insistent concerns. Like Jung, most people find that they *do* ask these questions over and over again—that they must. And although some philosophers and psychologists have proposed ways of getting rid of these questions—by dissolving them rather than by stirring them up—nevertheless, neither psychoanalysis nor philosophical analysis has succeeded in making them disappear. Whether or not we think they should, these questions continue to plague the private lives of men and women in even the most intellectual and sophisticated circles. Sartre thinks that everyone asks these questions and that, although we try to conceal the despair of our asking and the vanity of our self-deceiving answers from ourselves, we each experience the tragic implications of these questions in our lives. We are all victims, according to him, of a rebellion that we have each freely de-

58

clared against the inexpugnable conditions of human existence, and it is to this poorly concealed rebellion and its
failure that he wants to draw our attention.

Notice that no matter how one proceeds to deal with these
questions, one can reasonably be challenged to justify the
way in which one proceeds. To meet the problem, one needs
both a *place* to start and a *method* to proceed—and both
must be above all reasonable reproach! But who is so free of
tribal or personal prejudice, so unaffected by "idols of mar-
ket place and theater," as to be above such criticism? Any
method one chooses to answer or ignore these questions is
also a sign that he has already chosen the only kinds of answers he will accept. This means that his basic criteriological
principles have already been selected. Sartre characterizes
this spontaneous selection as the "primitive upsurge" which
constitutes one's fundamental choice of being—the choosing
of one's character and the character of one's world. Later we
shall criticize Sartre's own conclusions in the light of this
dilemma, but for the present it is sufficient to observe that,
according to Sartre, a poet's world reflects a poet's chosen
response to brute existence; a common world reflects one's
choice of "common sense."

Why then is the world we all inhabit so full of tragedy
and pain? From the possibilities presented to us, why do
we choose the unwholesome moral and cultural environment
that we have chosen? Since it is the actual but unnecessary
bane of our existence, why do we continue to support it?
This is a question that Sartre answers in a way that is, paradoxically, both conventional and surprising. By asking this
question—in itself a kind of summary of Kant's four questions—we discover (if Sartre is right) that any world we
choose will be rationally unjustified in a strict sense. Whatever we call "reasonable" is an expression of our free choice

of criteria and cannot be justified in terms more basic. Although, as Desan puts it, we must accept "the 'brute existent' as being independent of human intervention," human consciousness must give existence its value and ultimate purpose. The tragedy is that, although we are each free to choose a better world (a world we would rather inhabit), inevitably we choose the worst possible sort and then rationalize our choice in terms of "facts," "common sense," and "logic."

This discovery, or conviction, is central in existentialist thought. It is, for instance, the single most important constituent in Sartre's (and Heidegger's) conception of man's "fallenness." In the face of our ultimate questions—with the unavoidable necessity of answering them somehow in order to exist, however poorly—man becomes aware that he is "condemned to be free," that his *will* alone is the ultimate justifying authority in logic as well as in morals. But that will is itself unjustified. According to Sartre, we can never really be conscious of any moral, logical, or metaphysical support to relieve us of our creative and destructive responsibility. In his opinion, every thoroughly self-critical philosophy must start from a blunt awareness of human freedom and proceed to the rest of its business from there. Existentialists agree, in this regard, with the eighteenth-century British empiricist, David Hume: "Reason is . . . the slave of the passions." [16]

The "rational" is whatever conforms to the styles of life we have selected for ourselves out of innumerable possible ways of interpreting reality. All casuistical systems—as, for example, the moral precepts of our great religious systems—must be recognized as expressions of human freedom, as expressions of the way individuals and societies *choose* to live their lives, and not as precepts that are rooted in some

[16] David Hume, A *Treatise of Human Nature*, Bk. II, Part 3, Section 3; cf. Bk. III, Part 1, Section 1.

nonhuman reality.[17] Thrown up in an otherwise amoral and nonrational universe, man is the creator of the basic precepts of morality as well as of science: all norms are conventions established by men on their own absolute responsibility. Out of his own spontaneous upsurge, each individual must define himself, must stipulate the kind of being he will become, and in that way contribute also to the still unfolding general definition of mankind.

There is at least one being in whom existence precedes essence, a being who exists before he can be defined by a concept, and . . . this being is man, or, as Heidegger says, human reality. What is meant here by saying that existence precedes essence? It means that first of all, man exists, turns up, appears on the scene, and, only afterwards, defines himself. . . .

Man is nothing else but what he makes of himself. Such is the first principle of existentialism. It is also what is called subjectivity. . . . For we mean that man first exists, that is, that man first of all is the being who hurls himself toward a future. . . . Man is at the start a plan which is aware of itself . . . man will be what he will have planned to be. Not what he will want to be. Because by the word "will" we generally mean a conscious decision, which is subsequent to what we have already made of ourselves . . . but all that is only a manifestation of an earlier, more spontaneous choice. . . . Thus, existentialism's first move is to make every man aware of what he is and to make the full responsibility of his existence rest on him.[18]

[17] This way of regarding moral systems and of relating religion to them is interestingly expressed by one of Hume's philosophical descendants: R. B. Braithwaite, "An Empiricist's View of the Nature of Religious Belief" (New York: Cambridge University Press, 1955). Cf. also, R. M. Hare, "Religion and Morals," in *Faith and Logic*, ed. Basil Mitchell (London and Tonbridge: Whitefriars Press; Boston: Beacon Press, 1957); a similar moral theory and a relation of morals to religion is elaborated by Paul M. van Buren, *The Secular Meaning of the Gospel, Based on an Analysis of Language* (New York: Macmillan, 1963).

[18] Jean-Paul Sartre, *Existentialism*, trans. Bernard Fechtman (New York: Philosophical Library, 1947), pp. 18-19.

According to the existentialists, at least according to Heidegger and Sartre, every human individual is a plan that is at first spontaneously projected, and, if that individual subsequently attains "authentic existence," only later projected in full self-conscious awareness. Were it not for the objections to Freud's psychology that spring out of Sartre's "phenomenological method" [19]—if Sartre did not argue so strenuously that Freud is too uncritically wedded to mechanical preconceptions and that this results in a deterministic account of sex and morals, and an ultimate denial of individual responsibility—one might attempt to translate Sartre's language of "freedom" and "spontaneous upsurge" into Freud's now familiar language of the "libido" and "id." It is the uncaused, free activity of human willing that Sartre and other existentialists want to bring to our attention. This unfounded, unjustified upsurge *is* the human individual, according to them. This conviction is the basis of the existentialists' insistence that every individual is responsible for his own character, and that the historical circumstances into which he is born, or in which he now finds himself, are only a stage on which the individual enacts a role he freely chooses—at first, spontaneously, and then ultimately (perhaps) deliberately— for himself. Once we become aware of this, once we become thoroughly self-conscious, we may enter a deeper (and more anguished) level of human responsibility and "authentic" individuality.

Although some existentialists do not agree with Sartre that we will all individually continue to reject authentic existence, although Sartre thinks, as some do not, that Job's cry for a "redeemer" (as the myth expresses it) is necessarily in vain, nevertheless, all existentialists are in sympathy with Sartre's insistence on the ineradicable character of human freedom,

[19] See Sartre, *Existential Psychoanalysis*, pp. 43-59, 167-71, *et passim.* Cf. Greene, *The Existentialist Ethic*, p. 66.

and with Sartre's unwillingness to excuse human individuals from responsibility for being whatever they are. In this connection as in others, the existentialist argument refers us to our subjective experience of ourselves as moral beings—i.e., to the fact that each individual's inadequately concealed bad conscience bespeaks an intuition of his own inescapable freedom and absolute responsibility.

That sociologists and psychologists can regard me as a statistic and correctly predict that the probabilities are ten to one that I shall act tomorrow as I have today does not alter the fact that I *experience* myself, that I *appear* to myself, as a being who may indeed choose an unexpected course. My friends very sensibly expect me to do what I have done before, but this does not alter the fact that I must often wrestle with my conscience to decide what I will do. It may help someone else to have a pollster predict how I am going to vote, but it does not help *me* one bit, for it is I who must decide whether or not to make the prediction correct. Although one may use a deterministic theory to explain my behavior, what appears to me as my own inmost reality is an awful freedom, a necessity, to *make up* my own mind, even (since I can choose to alter my habits) to the choosing of my own character. In this sense, the existentialist contends that his conception of human freedom is no mere theory. Human freedom is, so to speak, a brute appearance, and if it is, existentialism cannot be refuted by phenomena (which support it), nor by philosophical theories that try to reach beyond appearances.

The existentialist description of human freedom does not imply that choices are easily made or easily carried out. Take the usual example of the "hopeless" drunk who reforms. There was a time when it would have been fairly easy for him to stop drinking, and perhaps he would have chosen to stop then if he had realized how difficult it would one **day** become to change his habit. Yet, now he must stop drinking or die of it. These are the painful alternatives between which he must choose. To choose not to choose will be to choose to keep drinking. But even if he elects now to stop, he must do so again five minutes from now when his throat is drier. He will have to choose again and again. And the fact that next minute or next month he may give up his resolution—spontaneously turning into a bar as he was passing—and then feel guilty for it, only shows that as a matter of fact he *does* acknowledge himself to be responsible for, the absolute originator of, his deeds. To encourage him to think that he acts as he does because certain events and conditions *cause* him to do so is to tempt him to abdicate, as Sartre sees it, both his moral responsibility and his very existence as a human subject. But this he cannot wholly succeed in doing. And if he tries, he will only plunge himself deeper into despair.

Observe, further, that although existentialists tell us that each human individual is free, this does not mean that we must necessarily attain the ends we elect. One may choose to be the darling of millions (as does many a stage-struck girl), yet fail to make Broadway. This does not alter the fact that such a person exists—that she is present to herself in the midst of one failure after the other—as a constant necessity to choose to try again, or to choose to quit. We may not be able to attain what we choose—one may collapse or die in the attempt—but we are doomed, as humans, to exist while we are alive as one moment of freedom after another. Whether we succeed or fail in our projects neither robs nor relieves us of this ontological (ubiquitous, inescapable, and irreducible) burden. Indeed, we shall see that, according to Sartre, we all fail ultimately—utterly—but we are nevertheless responsible for choosing our projects.

It is sometimes said that the existentialists' description of human freedom ignores the importance of natural necessity or causation.[20] This is a misinterpretation. However, in view of the obscurity of existentialist writing on this point, it is not an inexcusable or stupid mistake. In *The Critique of Dialectical Reason*[21] and in other publications since *Being and Nothingness*, Sartre attempts to clarify his position on this score. He insists that the particular situation in which we each find ourselves is one that is largely of our own choosing, and that its value and rational structure depend on the interpretation we give it; nevertheless he does not deny that every situation is partly constituted by the uninvited presence and limitations that characterize material existence.[22] Suppose, for example, that one is born in a slum. Here are certain material conditions to be met. The question is: What will one make of them? What statistic will one choose to be? One may elect to become a revolutionist or a reformer, or a "victim of circumstances." But in any case, one will be, in Sartre's sense, a self-made man.

According to Sartre, we have now uncovered one of the two prerequisites needed for answering the basic questions of human existence. We have a *starting point*, human freedom, which is the absolute foundation of every philosophical system and way of life, whether or not it is acknowledged. Now, if we are to establish a consistently self-critical philosophy on this foundation, we need a *method* that will systematically prevent us from falling into any form of speculative self-deception.

Most contemporary existentialists think that they have

[20] See, for example, Pierre Naville's questions and comments in the discussion at the end of Sartre's published lecture, *Existentialism*, pp. 65-91; cf. Barnes's introductory comments to her translation of Sartre's *Search for a Method*, p. vii, *passim*.

[21] Sartre, *La Critique de la Raison Dialectique*, as yet, as we have noted, *supra*, only partly translated into English.

[22] *Ibid.*, pp. 246-47, *et passim*; cf. Greene, *The Existentialist Ethic*, Chap. 8; also Desan, *The Marxism of Jean-Paul Sartre*, Chap. 1; and Aron, "Sartre's Marxism."

found this method in the "phenomenology" of the German philosopher, Edmund Husserl (1859-1938), who was not himself an existentialist. Indeed, because Husserl's purpose was limited to a description and classification of the types of "essences" that appear to consciousness, inasmuch as Husserl was not concerned with the investigator's awareness of his own individual existence, some students of existentialism have argued that Husserl's method is really incompatible with the personal and self-conscious concern of "classical" nineteenth-century existentialism.[23] Nevertheless, the majority of present-day existentialists believe that there is a basic ("existential") structure that is unique to human existence as such, observable by every individual himself, that can be described without speculative embroidery if we follow certain somewhat modified rules of Husserl's phenomenological method. If so, the results of such an analysis will yield a list of "existentialia"—the essential characteristics of human existence as such—as a guide to self-knowledge for every interested person. Thus it is maintained by Sartre and others that the phenomenological method can be joined to the central concern of classical existentialism: to make each one of us aware of his own unique existence as a human being, and to encourage one's own responsible acceptance of a creative role in moral action and speculative reason. To the extent that it can be adapted to this purpose, Husserl's phenomenological procedure has become the standard method of contemporary existential philosophy.

In order to understand this method, we must briefly consider Husserl's own intentions. Husserl started his career as a mathematician interested in the foundations of mathematics and convinced, as so many mathematicians have been, that that discipline is the master key to all the dark closets of

[23] See, for instance, Herbert Spiegelberg, "Husserl's Phenomenology and Existentialism," *The Journal of Philosophy*, LVII (Jan. 21, 1960), 62-74.

reality. To show this, however, he eventually discovered that he needed the help of philosophers to clarify certain basic conceptions of ordinary life. How, for example, are concepts like space and time, number and knowledge, appearance and reality, and so on, to be defined? Here he ran into trouble. Common sense seems to involve unexamined philosophical presuppositions. Suddenly, unsuspecting, he stumbled over the roots of traditional epistemology and landed in a thicket of contradictory theories among which the claims of "scientific philosophers," offering experimental evidence, were just so many more branches of a thorny confusion. On what basis could he pick and choose from this profusion of explanatory systems without being blindly or willfully arbitrary?

Like René Descartes, who had faced a similar problem in the seventeenth century, Husserl decided that he had to rediscover the absolute foundations of all knowledge once again by himself! This means that he proposed to return to a completely naïve standpoint—to an intuition of those (as he alleged) "pure" appearances that men have learned to embroider with words and philosophical systems, with the prejudices of common sense and science. Assuming that it is possible, he decided to go back to the uninterpreted objects of consciousness (essences or *noëmata*) which our competing descriptions of reality—the Babel of traditional philosophies—have long evaluated in contradictory tongues. Husserl's description of appearances, his phenomenology, was to be an acutely ingenuous description and classification of the generic characteristics of whatever raw material consciousness intuits, just as it appears, before we organize those phenomena into our competing world orders. Phenomenology, as he practiced it, was an attempt to recapture philosophical innocence (if man ever had it) in order to look once again, with intuition uncorrupted by philosophical bias, at the source of all knowledge about "the world." He proposed to start out "from that which *antedates* all standpoints: from the totality of the intuitively self-given which is prior to any theorizing reflection, from all that one *can* immediately see and lay hold of, provided one does not allow oneself to be blinded by prejudice, and so led to ignore whole classes of genuine data." [24] He even refused to become involved in "the question of existence," the problem of judging whether or not certain appearances are of the "real" world, choosing instead to "bracket" or put aside the question of existence in order to study whatever appears without prejudice. This "bracketing of existence" is what first distinguishes Husserl's phenomenology from that of the existentialists.

Although existentialists endorse Husserl's proposal to conduct a "reflective analysis" (a carefully controlled kind of recollection) using a method that merely points to the contents of consciousness without becoming involved in explanations that go beyond the bare classification of those appearances (Sartre's *Being and Nothingness* is even subtitled "An Essay on Phenomenological Ontology"), nevertheless, all existentialists hold that an awareness of existence-as-such accompanies every object of intuition. They do not find that the investigating self is able to detach itself from its concrete involvement in existence to the extent that Husserl envisaged. It seems to them that they are unable to intuit appearances of any kind except as objects *that exist* in some sort of relation to the self to whom they appear. *Existents* of one sort or another are exactly what always appear. No matter how an object of intuition happens to exist—whether it *is* as an aspect of a material thing, a feeling, mood, concept, or imaginary entity—existence-as-such ("being-in-itself") is one of the constituent elements in every object of intuition. A human in-

[24] Edmund Husserl, *Ideas*, trans. W. R. Boyce-Gibson (New York: Macmillan, 1952), p. 86. Cf. *ibid.*, pp. 110-11.

dividual is steeped in existence, and there in his peculiar fashion he remains as long as he lives. The result of this discovery or conviction is *existential* phenomenology.

Our procedure is now phenomenological, a modification of Husserl's method; and our procedure is existential, continuing the moralistic interests of such nineteenth-century philosophers as Søren Kierkegaard and Friedrich Nietzsche. A contemporary existentialist can now proceed to describe existentialia like "freedom," "bad faith," "despair," and so on—peculiarities of subjectivity that color all objectivity— and try to make each one of us aware of the extent and manner of his own responsibility for the values inherent in his world order. In plays, novels, and treatises, existentialists use the world as a mirror of man in order to bring him "from concealment into unconcealment," as Heidegger says. Existentialists agree with Emerson: "Nature always wears the colors of the spirit." Some of the world's most objective characteristics are, according to Sartre, the reflections in it of the human reality that confronts it.

To borrow Heidegger's definition, the world is "that in terms of which human reality makes known to itself what it is." . . . Without the world there is no selfness, no person; without selfness, without the person, there is no world. . . . Yet this quality of "myness" in the world is a fugitive structure, always present, a structure which I *live*. The world (*is*) mine because it is haunted by possibles, and the consciousness of each of these is a possible self-consciousness which I *am*; it is these possibles as such which give the world its unity and its meaning as the world.[25]

Think of pain and death. Their values, good and bad, are shown to be the reflection of man's own spontaneous valorizing activity. Paralleling the problem of evil and absurdity in

[25] Sartre, *Being and Nothingness*, p. 104. Cf. *ibid.*, pp. 107-218.

theology is a problem of evil and absurdity in existential philosophy. And in the context of existential analysis the responsible source is no less surprising to common sense than it is in the context of traditional theology. As the theological problem of evil indicts the God of our philosophizing, the existential problem of evil indicts what man has made of himself. There is a lesson to be learned in this about the relationship between theology and existential psychoanalysis, and further consideration of Sartre's analysis of human existence will help to explain it. For now that we have followed Sartre in establishing both a method (phenomenology) and a starting point (human freedom), we may resume our asking of basic questions: What is man? What can he know? What ought he do? What can he hope for?

3. *The Method Applied, and the Answers*

Our primary question is still the same: What is man? But now let us proceed phenomenologically to answer it. What does one intuit when one reflects on oneself? What confronts one's consciousness when one seeks to surprise that elusive waif called "I" with one's own presence?

Although he came at it somewhat differently, "the father of modern philosophy," René Descartes, made this question famous in the seventeenth century; and today the existentialists follow his lead. It was Descartes' so-called method of doubt that led him to this starting point, and his methodical search for an indubitable basis for philosophy is closely associated in the minds of contemporary existentialists with their own phenomenological procedures. To establish a foundation for philosophy and science, Descartes also found himself confronted, in effect, with Kant's questions, the most basic of which proved to be the one I have indicated. Thus, Descartes was led to his famous *cogito ergo sum* (I think, therefore I am) and then on to ponder the essential nature of this thinking self. Out of his somewhat lugubrious lucubrations came what is now a fairly commonplace world view; human experiencing is held to be the result of an interaction between two kinds of metaphysical substances, mind and matter—the philosophical realities *behind* appearances—which are brought together according to mathematically describable "natural laws" established (Descartes argued further) by the creative will of God. Today Sartre explains what he believes to be the phenomenological mistakes of the earlier man.

What is the basic reality of this self that thinks? Sartre's answer is remarkably different from Descartes', and it is bound to seem strange at first to the "common sense" that is so deeply colored by recent centuries of Cartesian thought. Where Cartesians look for and profess to discover knowledge and eternal truths, existentialists can find only pragmatic beliefs and passionate commitment. Whereas Cartesians describe the inferred existence of entities (minds and bodies) beyond the everyday phenomena that are said to be only their appearances, Sartre argues that our consciousness of phenomena (including, as we have noticed, the phenomenal appearance of *existence* itself) is the whole of reality. Although Cartesians offer rational proofs that God exists—the logical justification and sufficient reason of all that appears —existentialists find that the notion of God is a self-contradictory concept that atheistic existentialists reject as a hopeless ideal, in spite of the fact that theistic existentialists deliberately commit themselves to a paradoxical trust in it. Where Cartesians claim to intuit values—truth, goodness, and beauty—which exist independent of man, most existentialists argue that all values are created by human freedom in the presence of an otherwise brute and valueless universe.

In *Being and Nothingness*, Sartre starts his criticism of

71

Descartes with the very first step that Descartes takes. Descartes' method, his so-called method of doubt, is intended to be critical of all alleged knowledge, excepting only such propositions as are proved by the method to be indubitable. Thus, Descartes' first step toward certainty is his putative discovery that every attempt to doubt his own existence is self-defeating. *He* doubts, *he* thinks, *he* is conscious in some fashion, therefore he must exist. This is a simplified version of how Descartes arrives at his famous *cogito*—"*cogito ergo sum*," "I think, therefore I am"—to which Sartre repeatedly refers. Descartes thought that he had proved the existence of a self. He supposed that he had proven that a mental substance (or being) exists whose essential attribute is to be conscious in some way. And this is the contention that Sartre denies.

It is true that every time we make a judgment, that judgment can be construed according to our subject-object form of grammar. We can always say, "I doubt that so and so is the case," or "I think (feel, believe, experience) that so and so is the case." But does this subject-object form of discourse indicate that we have intuited a self as the subject of our sentence in the same way that we have intuited the objects of which we are conscious? Is the subject-object form of our discourse (1) a mere peculiarity of grammar, or is it (2) an indication that we are conscious of a continuously existing entity, called the self, which is completely self-conscious, at least every time we say, "I think," "I doubt," "I feel" and so on? Descartes came out for the second alternative. But Sartre, in effect, maintains the first, and in this he is supported by most contemporary psychologists and secular philosophers. According to Sartre, we can always express our judgments in the form "I think (doubt, feel, am conscious) that so and so is the case," but we can never intuit the presence of a self

72

(a knower, like a homunculus within the works) whose name is "I," the "I" of the "I think." According to Sartre and many other contemporary philosophers and psychologists, we do not intuit a self that thinks its thoughts and wills its wants and feels its feelings. We just think, will, feel, and so on. And, since we are forbidden to make doubtful assumptions, by both Descartes' and Sartre's method of doubt, we cannot assume the existence of a self such as Descartes (and many traditional theologians) have postulated. We cannot—except wishfully and fallaciously—assert that we *know* that we have souls or minds, like metaphysical ghosts within us, that do the thinking, willing, feeling, and so on that our judgments express. We must not think that a grammatical propriety—"I think that so and so"—is an ontological revelation.

Sartre concludes his own futile search for self with what may seem to be a paradoxical conviction not dissimilar from that which is expressed by William James in his essay, "Does 'Consciousness' Exist?" Sartre contends, like James, that knowledge does not entail the existence of a knower, in the Cartesian sense; nor does phenomenological investigation discover one behind an arras of introspective appearances. What *does* appear is all there is for us to talk about, and although that includes my ego—me—an object of which I, and others, are more or less conscious, *that* self is just another object that I and others can describe. It is not the pure subject, the pure consciousness, that I had set out to find. Our basic consciousness never appears as an object of itself says Sartre. It is not anything in the world; it would not appear in an inventory of all the things that can be counted. In that sense, Sartre, like James, can say that consciousness does not exist. In effect, both James and Sartre agree with the contemporary British philosopher, Gilbert Ryle, that there is no good evidence that there really is a "ghost within the machine." [26]

Suppose, for example, that I am aware of an object. I may next become aware *that* I am aware of it. I was conscious without being self-conscious—i.e., without being conscious of being conscious—but now my attention is drawn to myself. Suppose I could go on to extend this introspective series, becoming aware of being aware of being aware—and so on. In this way I might also become aware of a persistent absence that would begin to "haunt" me, as Sartre says. But, to use Ryle's figure of speech, it is the absence of a "ghost" and not its presence that is so disturbing. Every time I am aware of being aware of some object, even if that object is my own ego, it seems as though there is still another level of consciousness, a deeper self, that is not coming to light. This deeper consciousness, my "pre-reflective consciousness," constantly eludes objectification by dropping back (so to speak) from the object of which I am conscious in order to be conscious of it. Only my reflected self (my ego) appears in the light of a consciousness that (significantly) I cannot even call "mine," for I cannot capture it in objectivity. Thus, the self I *do* objectify—*my* self, *my* ego—reflects the absence of the primordial self I am seeking. Since, according to the phenomenological method, only appearances of one sort or another can meaningfully be said to exist—since phenomenology is carefully limited to a description of appearances as such—the self for which I am searching, and which does not appear, cannot be said to exist. Instead, to use a figure of

[26] Gilbert Ryle, *The Concept of Mind* (New York: Barnes & Noble, 1949), Chap. I ff.; cf. Sartre, *Being and Nothingness*, pp. 73-84 ff.; also Sartre, *The Transcendence of the Ego*, trans. F. Williams and R. Kirkpatrick (New York: Noonday Press, 1957), pp. 42 ff.; William James, "Does 'Consciousness' Exist?" in *Essays in Radical Empiricism* (New York: Longmans, Green and Co., 1947), p. 9; cf. Martin Heidegger, *Being and Time*, p. 185 *et passim*.

speech, it stands revealed as an insistent "nothingness" in the center of my world—in the center, so to say, of my soul. "Nothingness," says Sartre, "lies coiled in the heart of being—like a worm." [27] That "worm" is the serpent of Eden.

Following certain philosophical conventions long established in Hegelian circles, Sartre's generic term for all actual or possible objects of consciousness is "being-*in*-itself" (*l'être en soi*). His term for consciousness, for subjectivity as such, is "being-*for*-itself" (*l'être pour soi*). But we have just seen that we can never be conscious of *ourselves* except in a reflective manner, in the presence of some object (an instance of being-*in*-itself) that invariably reveals consciousness to itself in a negative way, as *other* than the object that is present to it. Self-consciousness (being-*for*-itself) is, thus, an awareness that, in our deepest subjectivity, we are always *wholly other* than the objects, physical or mental, that appear (so to speak) *before* our consciousness. Self-consciousness is, therefore, an awareness of oneself as a lack, as the "nothingness" that is referred to in the title of Sartre's most influential book, *Being and Nothingness*. The word "being" in that title signifies "being-*in*-itself," the being of objects; the word "nothingness" is a synonym for "being-*for*-itself," the being (more accurately, the *lack* of being) of every subjectivity. To obey the ancient dictum, "Know thyself," is, thus, to become painfully aware of oneself as a question, a void, a "hole" (as Sartre says) in the center of the universe of objects with which (to use Sartre's figure of speech) we each "surround" ourselves. However, strictly speaking, objects *cannot* surround us in our deepest subjectivity, for inasmuch as consciousness persistently refuses to be objectified, being-*for*-itself (one's "primordial self") is utterly transcendent. Paradoxically, one's self is not *in* one's world; it cannot be located

[27] *Being and Nothingness*, p. 21.

in space or in time. The "self" that we find in *space* is merely physical, a material object (an instance of being-*in*-itself); and the "self" we find in *time* is also just an object (being-*in*-itself)—a role remembered or a role projected. "Being-*for*-itself," the "nothingness" that we self-defeatingly seek to objectify—the subject that we want to confront as an object —forever eludes us. It can never appear as an object, except as a question that "haunts" each one of us, and in that sense, Sartre says, *the self does not exist.* Each one of us must finally admit that his pre-reflective consciousness is a sort of awareness *ex nihilo*—unfounded, mysterious, inexplicable—a spontaneous upsurge. It is that condition of my inmost subjectivity which drives me to despair.

According to Sartre, every human being is an "absurd passion" to realize an ideal that can never be obtained. Every human individual wants to possess himself as a consciousness that is free of the hollow core that is the present mode of his deepest subjectivity. We wish to know our primordial selves as *objects* that we can establish and sustain in the world the way we once thought we could establish empires on which the sun would never set. Each of us seeks to make an objective fact out of his own pre-reflective consciousness, without thereby sacrificing any of his subjectivity; in other words, each individual seeks to make himself a "being-in-itself-for-itself," as Sartre calls God, but no one will ever succeed, for God cannot exist. Every individual wants to free himself from the "worm" that gnaws at him night and day, but only death will be surcease, and that is a self-defeating way of escape. Each human being must live out his days anxious about his existence, fearful of his ultimate oblivion: in death oblivion, and in life an "unhappy consciousness," as Hegel called the individual's awareness of his own finitude and separation from God. But where Hegel promised ultimate at-onement, success, Sartre holds out no such hope. Sartre's "theology" of self—his description of the spontaneous upsurge that is every man's self-defeating project to be God—is largely negative and pessimistic:

The fundamental value which presides over this project is exactly the in-itself-for-itself; that is, the ideal of a consciousness which would be the foundation of its own being-in-itself by the pure consciousness which it would have of itself. It is this ideal which can be called God. Thus the best way to conceive of the fundamental project of human reality is to say that man is the being whose project is to be God. Whatever be the myths and rites of the religion considered, God is first "sensible to the heart" of man as the one who identifies and defines him in his ultimate and fundamental project. If man possesses a pre-ontological comprehension of the being of God, it is not the great wonders of nature nor the power of society which have conferred it upon him. God . . . represents the permanent limit in terms of which man makes known to himself what he is. To be man means to reach toward being God. Or if you prefer, man fundamentally is the desire to be God.[28]

According to Sartre, man logically cannot and actually will not fulfill his ideal and paradoxical destiny. He is doomed to live in alienation from nature and neighbor, with no hope of obtaining the object of his ultimate concern. Like Moses, each individual is doomed to die outside the "promised land"—that mirage of self-deception, as Sartre sees it—for the object of every man's ultimate concern transcends the limitations of human existence. Nevertheless, Sartre's description of the human situation often resembles, and, in effect, frequently supports the Judeo-Christian religious tradition.[29] Thus, as I have already indicated, the theological

[28] *Ibid.*, p. 566.
[29] See Barnes's introductory comments, *ibid.*, pp. xxviii-xxxv; also Greene, *The Existentialist Ethic*, pp. 154, 204.

77

problem of evil is paralleled by a similar problem in Sartre's existential philosophy—as though theology and atheistic existentialism were opposite sides of a single path in this respect. For if man (not God) is solely responsible for the creation of his world's values, why does evil exist?

By recognizing the contribution that is made to every world order by the pre-reflective consciousness ("nothingness"), the author of *Being and Nothingness* makes each human individual responsible for the values that appear in his world—including the values of such "natural" evils as earthquakes and storms! Sartre's strange explanation of evil must be considered thoughtfully by anyone who is interested in the existential significance of the mythological accounts of evil that occur in the Bible. His analysis even suggests that there is something existentially proper and phenomenologically defensible in the notorious theological description of evil as "non-being." Indeed, Sartre's atheistic account of evil corroborates, in its way, the mythological and theological contention that all evil is the result of sin, sustained by human perversity alone. Undoubtedly, Sartre's account of evil resonates a deeper and more complex relationship between the conceptions of God and man than most of us are accustomed to think about.

In a sense . . . man is the only being by whom a destruction can be accomplished. A geological plication, a storm do not destroy—or at least they do not destroy *directly;* they merely modify the distribution of masses of beings. There is no *less* after the storm than before. There is *something else.* Even this expression is improper, for to posit otherness there must be a witness. . . . If a cyclone can bring about the death of certain living beings, this death will be destruction only if it is experienced as such. In order for destruction to exist, there must be first a relation of man to being . . . and within the limits of this relation, it is necessary that man apprehend one being as destructible. . . . It is man who renders cities destructible, precisely because he posits them as fragile and as precious and because he adopts a system of protective measures with regard to them. . . . Destruction is an essentially human thing . . . it is man who destroys his cities through the agency of earthquakes or directly. . . . But at the same time it is necessary to acknowledge that destruction supposes a pre-judicative comprehension of nothingness as such and a conduct *in the face of nothingness.*[30]

The destruction of art, in the flooding of Florence by the River Arno, did not occur to the insouciant immortals whose images were ravished by the flood. Disaster and tragedy cannot occur unless some human or nonhuman force frustrates a human plan, or eradicates or prevents the existence of some state of affairs that the creative nothingness of man has chosen to valorize. In this regard, Sartre puts one in mind of Protagoras, the sophist of the fifth century B.C. For Protagoras taught that the good man is one who transforms what *appeared* evil and so *was* evil into what *appears* to be good and so *is* good. Like Protagoras, Sartre asserts that man himself makes things appear evil and be evil, which, given a different will, he could make appear good and be good. Here is where every man's freely elected rebellion against the ontological conditions of human existence acts, in Sartre's view of things, as an existentialist parallel of the theologian's concept of original sin. For the "atheist" as for the "theist," man queers his life at its source in himself.

Sartre's account of the appearance of evil is not offered as a denial of the existence of evil phenomena. Nor is it offered as a solution to the theological problem of evil, although it is relevant. It is an unvarnished description of the absurd state of affairs that Sartre sees everywhere as a characteristic of human existence. Although men may always have to put up

[30] *Being and Nothingness,* pp. 8-9.

with the "geological plication," and with storm and death, the *quality* of human suffering could be transfigured (Sartre seems to be saying) if only men would adopt a radically different attitude toward the inescapable limitations of their human existence. As it is, however—and as it always will be, apparently—men will inevitably elect evil. We will renounce Eden because we will choose, in vain, to be God. The result is that we give up our original freedom (the freedom of authentic human existence) in order to live in bondage: yoked to a world of objects, treating ourselves as objects— earning bread, but not human fulfillment, by the sweat of our brows—harnessed to conventional values of success and failure that invariably turn out to be reins that check and drive us against ourselves.

Sartre is not unaware of the odd manner in which his atheistic description of evil, and human responsibility for it, echoes the traditional religious admonition not to "sin" (not to try to be God) nor fall into "bondage to the world." His writing suggests, in full accord with biblical religion, that evil can be overcome in the life of the individual if only he will commit himself to the original (i.e., the ontological) conditions of human freedom. But he will not. Instead, every man recoils from these conditions. He has no faith in them. He chooses, rather, to escape them—i.e., he aspires to be God—and then, as a shrunken god, he becomes the world's adversary and its victim.

Every man's "bad faith" or "self-deception" (*mauvaise foi*) expresses itself in the myriad sorts of distractions that characterize human life as we choose to make it. We divert our attention from our inauthentic existence and despair by worshiping our false idols even more frenetically than ever —sacrificing our freedom as much as we can to success, power, popularity, wealth, pleasure, excitement, forgetful- ness, and fatigue—all of which only makes it still more necessary for us to forget our treason to ourselves. Thus, the "abyss," the "nothingness" from which each man surveys the world becomes a fissure from which his own satanic self emerges.[31] Like a demon rising from the bottom of a spring, the ego one makes of himself spreads a ring of violence around itself. The rage to be God, which *is* each inauthentic individual, has tragic social consequences. Hell is oneself— and other people! [32]

Think of the times you have been talking to an acquaintance when suddenly, in the full flight of conversation, you have caught the other's eye. According to Sartre, nothing so effectively unmasks the badly disguised violence of man for man as "the Look." [33] Nothing is more inimical to easy chit-chat and conventional good fellowship than to obey the platitude about looking one's neighbor in the eye.

One of us is talking. Suddenly our eyes meet and for a breathless moment the conversation reels, until we look aside, and then our talk regains its easy way again, perhaps. But what has happened? This was not like the times our eyes drifted inattentively over each other's faces as we chattered. This time, says Sartre, the usually lidded violence of the other's inauthentic existence was revealed to each, and each was numbed by the sudden shock of power sweeping over him which is his neighbor's judgmental glance. Each individual designs a world of "facts" by naming them according to a plan: "my hat . . . my wife . . . my view . . . my life. . . ." But when I catch the other's eye, I catch him in the fearful act of naming *me!* The reluctance of primitive man to give another person his name is not a mere superstition. It expresses a profound phenomenological insight into the nature

[31] Cf. Jung, *Answer to Job*, pp. 66-74, 158-69, 178-79.
[32] See Jean-Paul Sartre, *No Exit and Three Other Plays*, trans. S. D. Gilbert (New York: Vintage, 1955), p. 47.
[33] *Being and Nothingness*, pp. 363 ff.

of man's inauthentic relation to man. We treat our neighbors as mere objects in the world orders we construct around ourselves and seek to possess.

"Give a dog a bad name and hang him," says an old adage. But every name is a label with a lethal intent, Sartre thinks, when it is applied to a person. Every label is a nail, like a lepidopterist's pin, which we use to fix our neighbor as a thing in our own world order. That is the tiny sting of death we feel in the Look of the other. And even though the full realization of that murderous project is doomed in advance —since one's pre-reflective consciousness (being-for-itself) cannot be objectified (being-in-itself)—nevertheless the awful intention of each toward the other is revealed. And, indeed, we succeed in encircling our neighbor's inviolable freedom with the alien environment that is our own inauthentic glance and project. The nagging parent, the jealous lover, the tyrannical boss are only some of the most obvious examples of every man's satanic attempt to establish himself as an individual who transcends the conditions of human existence by making the world he inhabits his own possession, and by identifying himself with his possessions, vainly trying to escape the mysterious hollowness that haunts him in himself.

The Lord's Prayer—"and lead us not into temptation, but deliver us from evil"—indeed expresses a miracle to wish for, for we are each tempted to do violence, and, constantly succumbing to that temptation, are each in need of deliverance from the Evil One in our neighbors and ourselves. The central problem, in both the Bible and in Sartre's writing, is alienation. In the Look each individual finds himself in the alien world of the other, and each seeking to turn the tables on his neighbor is in turn responsible for compounding that alienation. In the Look each individual judges, classifies, and dispatches the other as this thing or that, and each experiences a fall into a twice alienated existence: once as the judge who alienates the other with a glance, and once as the victim who is alienated in turn by him.

Sartre believes that no one escapes from the hellish predicament of the Look. In one sense we do not choose to escape, and in another sense we cannot. At the end of Sartre's play, *No Exit*, the door of Hell opens but each of its inhabitants refuses to leave. There is an aspect of Hell that each of us chooses and makes for himself everyday when he chooses the manner of his own individual flight from the inescapable conditions of human existence. Each of us has his own self-defeating way of fleeing from guilt and death, for example. This, to use a technical word of Heidegger's and Sartre's, is what plunges one into the "ontic" Hell, the unique environment in which an individual immures himself on an even deeper level of tragedy within the general tragic condition, the "ontological" condition, of human existence as such. As "inauthentic"—i.e., in his "flight" from the conditions of human existence as such—the "fallen" individual refuses to leave the personalized Hell he has created for himself within the circumambient Hell of human existence. Instead, he blames his ontic condition on the very world order he has built around himself. He takes that world "seriously" (as Sartre says), pretending that *it*, not that he himself, is the origin of his suffering. The drunkard, for example, blames his drunkenness on nature and not on himself. He tries to convince himself that his ontic Hell is not the creation of its sole inmate, and that he could not escape from it even if he sincerely wanted to. But he can, if—by the agony of his thirst—he will pay the price.

Of course, there is an aspect of Hell from which there is absolutely no exit, according to Sartre. This Hell is an element of man's ontological condition, a facet of human existence *as* such. Nevertheless, paradoxically, we are strangely responsible for evil at this level also, and our actions and statements reveal that our consciences are uneasy about it. It is Sartre's belief that no matter what we do, the social involvement of man with man must always be rapine. The class struggle that his later Marxist writings discuss is an extension, in the area of ethics and politics, of the ontology he develops in *Being and Nothingness*. To live oneself, one must violate the freedom of the other, according to Sartre (but not Heidegger), and even suicide cannot absolve one of his guilt. Human freedom occurs in a tragic material and historical context from which there is no ultimate or miraculous deliverance. When we become aware of the nature of our existence, we are already existing as guilty, violent, and ego-centered in a world of hostile egos. Our remorse, if we feel it, cannot erase our past (the series of evil causes we have initiated) nor entirely change the future (the demonic series of effects we have already chosen). Having already chosen a world of violence, that is where we come to full self-awareness. And, given the cause-and-effect character of historical existence, we must all reap the fruit of our planting. Hazel Barnes summarizes this complex and agonizing dialectic of evil and human responsibility.

In our examination of existentialist literature, we have met with the problem of evil in two different contexts. The first of these is the complex structure of good and bad faith. The fundamental principle is one of authenticity. The only way for a person to realize his true being is to recognize that his being is his individual freedom, that he is responsible for all his acts and determined by nothing. Here there is no question of being born in sin. Man renders himself unauthentic by pretending that his environment is a Serious World and by submerging himself within it. . . . There is also a sense in which we are indeed, all of us, born in original sin. . . . By my very existence, in everything I do, I make an assault upon the other's freedom. When I look at him, I bring into being

84

his self-for-me. . . . Moreover, by my acts I help to frame the world within which he will make his choices. . . . In so far as his own absolute freedom is his greatest good, I am the enemy. . . . From this kind of guilt there is, of course, no deliverance.[34]

First, by my own self-deception or "bad faith" (*mauvaise foi*), in my passion "to be God" (though God cannot exist) —i.e., by my repeated refusal to accept the inexpungible conditions of human existence—I have created and now sustain the private Hell I draw around myself. In this sense, I was not born in "sin," but I chose it; and I choose it again every day, in schizoid frenzy, even when I am *also* choosing to live in "good faith." My name is Legion: I am a will divided against itself.

Second, because I have been "thrown" into life and am already existing as a human individual when I become aware of it, I *am* born into "sin." In a sense, I am born into the evil that was my first spontaneous act of selfhood. The ambiguities and paradoxes of Sartre's writing are intended to reflect the ontological peculiarities of human existence as such, and, presumably for that reason, his writing often echoes traditional religious descriptions of "fallen man."

According to Barnes, "the old words keep recurring in the writings of humanistic existentialism. The absurd," she says, quoting Camus, "is among other things 'sin without God.' " Of both Simone de Beauvoir and Sartre, she remarks, significantly, that "the goal of sainthood appears mostly in perverted form as temptation . . . yet these authors too cherish an ideal of moral purity." [35] She concludes (although not unequivocally) that this ideal is never realized in the writings of atheistic existentialism: "Sartre goes so far as to say that all

[34] Hazel E. Barnes, *Humanistic Existentialism: The Literature of Possibility* (Lincoln: University of Nebraska Press, 1959), pp. 371-72.
[35] *Ibid.*

man's conduct—at least all of his most basic desires and the bad faith which is for most men their natural environment—is the manifestation of man's wish to *be* God." [36] Moral purity remains a mere ideal. Man is incurably infected by the inauthentic existence of his original choosing.

Despite his profession of Marxism, Sartre does not look forward to a withering away of strife between groups of men or toward a lessening of conflict within each individual himself. Sartre's pessimism is closer to Reinhold Niebuhr's assertion that "sin is natural for man in the sense that it is universal but not in the sense that it is necessary." [37] For Sartre as for Niebuhr, man does not sin because it is his "nature"; he sins because that is, at first, his spontaneous *choice*, and then his deliberate, desperate pursuit. That Sartre renews, in his way, the Augustinian-Lutheran-Calvinistic emphasis on original sin is well worth pondering. According to him, each one of us is Cain and the other is Abel. And each raises Cain within himself, to his own undoing. There is no real love between persons—that remains an unobtainable ideal—and there is no real self-love. There is only everywhere, in public and in private, the vain and violent objectification and utilization of the human spirit.[38] According to Sartre:

It is from this singular situation that the notion of guilt and of sin seems to be derived. It is before the Other that I am *guilty*. I am guilty first when beneath the Other's look I experience my alienation and my nakedness as a fall from grace which I must assume. This is the meaning of the famous line from Scripture: "They knew that they were naked." Again I am guilty when in

[36] *Ibid.*, p. 106.
[37] Reinhold Niebuhr, *The Nature and Destiny of Man* (New York: Scribner's, 1941), I, 242. Compare Niebuhr's treatment of self-deception, *ibid.*, pp. 203-7 to Sartre's treatment of the same theme, *Being and Nothingness*, pp. 47-73. See also Barnes's commentary, *ibid.*, pp. xxviii ff.
[38] Cf. Barnes, *Humanistic Existentialism*, pp. 229-30.

turn I look at the Other, because by the very fact of my own self-assertion I constitute him as an object and as an instrument, and I cause him to experience that same alienation which he must now assume. Thus original sin is my upsurge in a world where there are others; and whatever may be my further relation with others, these relations will be only variations on the original theme of my guilt.

But this guilt is accompanied by helplessness without this helplessness ever succeeding in cleansing me of my guilt. Whatever I may do for the Other's freedom, as we have seen, my efforts are reduced to treating the Other as an instrument and to positing his freedom as a transcendence-transcended. But on the other hand, no matter what compelling power I use, I shall never touch the Other save in his being-as-object. I shall never be able to accomplish anything except to furnish his freedom with occasions to manifest itself without my ever succeeding in increasing it or diminishing it, in directing it or in getting hold of it. Thus I am guilty toward the Other in my very being because the upsurge of my being, in spite of itself, bestows on the Other a new dimension of being; and on the other hand I am powerless either to profit from my fault or to rectify it.[39]

Normal love is described, in *Being and Nothingness,* as only a conventional form of alternation between two psychotic and hateful extremes: one, of the masochist who vainly attempts to get rid of his own ineludible "nothingness" by voluntarily becoming a plaything, an object, for another; two, of the sadist who vainly attempts to hide his ineradicable "nothingness" by objectifying himself in another as the pain that he brutally inflicts and watches there. According to Sartre, human existence is impossible outside society, but never authentically human within it. It need not be this way, but it actually is characterized by mutual alienation and rapacity among its members. It is the fire of Hell that glowers

[39] *Being and Nothingness,* p. 410.

in our eyes when they accidentally catch. The Look erupts from the forgetfulness that was our pathetic attempt at conversation, and our eyes shift in order to cover our bad faith and self-deception once again. Under the surface of our workaday world there is a restless self-estrangement that establishes our every day on violence and guilt.

In *Being and Nothingness*, Sartre answers Kant's four questions in a mood that Kierkegaard would have described as "defiant despair." [40] To the question, "What can I know?" Sartre answers: only phenomena—nothing but the being of objects—and, by reflection, my own anguished lack of such being. To the question, "What am I?" he replies, in effect: nothing but an unhappy consciousness—"a being which is not what it is and which is what it is not"—an incarnation of imperfection, being-and-nothingness.[41] The question, "What ought I do?" has, in a sense, no answer. Duty is not something that exists before one chooses it. Every individual must create his duty, *ex nihilo*, every time he acts deliberately. Paradoxically, Sartre cannot even tell us, consistently with his principle of freedom, that we *ought* to act authentically. It is up to each individual to choose his own mode of existence, although, again paradoxically, if one chose in full awareness to live inauthentically (in bad faith) one's act would be authentic (in good faith). But we refuse to choose authentically. Thus, to the last question, "What can I hope for?" Sartre can at best only affirm what has been called a "reverse stoicism." [42] Each human individual is encouraged to accept his own absurd and inevitably tragic existence, taking up the burden of his life (like Sisyphus) as one doomed to do what he does not want (to alienate himself from himself and his

[40] Søren Kierkegaard, *Fear and Trembling and the Sickness Unto Death*, trans. Walter Lowrie (Anchor Books; Garden City, N.Y.: Doubleday, 1954), pp. 200 ff.
[41] *Being and Nothingness*, p. 627.
[42] Greene, *The Existentialist Ethic*, p. 206.

world) and to want what he cannot accomplish (the over-coming of such estrangement)—another instance of the anguish of courage without hope of success, and of despair when such courage fails. "Thus the passion of man is the reverse of that of Christ," says Sartre, "for man loses himself as man in order that God may be born. But the idea of God is contradictory and we lose ourselves in vain. Man is a useless passion." [43] This is the phenomenological description of "fallen man" which Sartre's atheistic existentialism describes, and across which, in proliferate mythological terms, religion draws its language of hope and its peculiar testimony of "miraculous" fulfillment.

4. Religious Implications of Atheistic Existentialism

Both Heidegger and Sartre adapt the traditional religious term "fallen man" to their analyses of the human condition.[44] Yet, the conclusion of Being and Nothingness holds little or no hope for an existentialistic equivalent of religious redemption. "I know that my Redeemer lives," cries Job (19:25), but Sartre is sure that he does not. Atheistic existentialism fully echoes the despair of our religious traditions, but not their hope. This is, perhaps, the best reason for calling Sartre's description of human existence "atheistic." His writing never leaves, and does not unequivocally express the hope that we ever can leave, the wasteland that mirrors fallen man. Even an existentialist saint, one who would achieve the ideal of authentic existence, apparently cannot hope to leave his despair behind but must learn to live with it in a world without real love or atonement. Sartre "excludes any philosophy of love," says Wilfred Desan. "Philosophical

[43] Being and Nothingness, p. 615.
[44] Heidegger, Being and Time, pp. 210-24; Sartre, Being and Nothingness, p. 263.

subjectivity, which starts with the Self and measures everything from the viewpoint of the Self, is a form of speculative
egotism, just as unselfishness is a prelude to charity. Sartre's
Pour-soi in *L'Etre et le Néant* meets an opponent at every
turn, as does the individual man in the *Critique de la Raison
Dialectique*. Since there is no *we*, but only *me* . . . we find
neither charity nor benevolence." [45]

The intra-subjective and inter-subjective forms of alienation that Sartre describes have, of course, been discussed in
other terms by sociologists, novelists, theologians, and other
students of mankind. But the all-important question of human life arises with as much urgency as ever. Is it true, as
Sartre concludes, that religion's age-old promise of salvation
goes unfulfilled?

Surely, as with the existential problem of sin and alienation, so with its existential solution: if that solution exists, its
appearance, like the appearance of the problem, is a matter
not of mere speculation but of existence. If, when it is not
encrusted with the metaphysical extravagances of some traditional theological system, the conception of original sin has
a phenomenological justification—if, in short, human existence is inevitably qualified by a condition of self-alienation
for which man himself is responsible—then, regardless of
its not having revealed itself in Sartre's phenomenological
studies, perhaps there is also a phenomenological justification for the religious conception of salvation.

On the phenomenological level, the problem of sin and
its solution is not a matter of logic or speculation, but of
sheer appearance or nonappearance. On that level it is not
important what we call the brute intrusion of the problem
and the astonishing serendipity of its solution, if it appears.
Whether we say "sin and salvation" or "alienation and inte-

[45] Desan, *The Marxism of Jean-Paul Sartre*, pp. 265-66.

gration" or something else, our vocabulary is immaterial when we confine our attention to the merely phenomenological level of bare appearance. What is important then, if it occurs, is the spontaneous upsurge of a phenomenologically adequate solution to the problem, a solution that will carry us beyond despair into "bliss" or "peace of soul," as Max Scheler, another phenomenologist, has said:

It belongs to the essence of these feelings, however, that they are either not experienced at all or they take complete possession of our being. In despair an emotional "No!" is hidden in the core of our personal existence and our world—without the person becoming thereby an object of reflection. In bliss—the deepest level of the experience of happiness—an emotional "Yes!" These feelings seem to be the correlate of the ethical value of personal existence itself. Hence they are also, pre-eminently, the primary metaphysical and religious feelings. They can only be given when we are no longer directed toward a particular region of being (society, friends, profession, state, etc.), when we no longer consider ourselves as able to modify existence or value through some act of ours (of knowing or willing), but rather as: "we ourselves alone." Only when no particular thing or value outside or inside us sensibly motivates us to this all-pervading bliss, only when its being and duration—phenomenally—does *not* appear to us as conditioned or alterable by any possible act of will, action, or manner of living—only then is bliss in the most pregnant sense present . . . These feelings are therefore the only ones which cannot be represented as producible nor even as *earned* through our efforts.[46]

The question that we must answer is this: Is Scheler right or is Sartre? Does anything appear that can properly be identified as the phenomenological content of religious salvation?

[46] Max Scheler, "Towards a Stratification of the Emotional Life," in *Readings in Existential Phenomenology*, eds. Nathaniel Lawrence and Daniel O'Conner (Englewood Cliffs, N.J.: Prentice-Hall, 1967), p. 30.

God is love, it is said. But does anything appear as such? Sartre admits the existential presence of "original sin," as he says, but he denies even the existential possibility of salvation! [47]

On what grounds?

Apparently, on all the reasonable grounds there could be: (1) that salvation is logically impossible, and (2) that it does not in fact occur. Existential psychoanalysis can at best help us to accept the terrible alienation indigenous to human existence as such, but we cannot hope through its help to transcend that condition. Yet that is the hope which the Judeo-Christian religious tradition extends.

At this point, Sartre offers several arguments to show that the concept of God is logically false.[48] Accordingly, the conception of atonement, the union or communion of God and man, is also a logical impossibility. Like the idea of married bachelorhood, atonement is, in a sense, unthinkable. Furthermore, Sartre apparently takes for granted that its miraculous occurrence—the actual appearance of the "impossible" and "unthinkable"—is a chimera. The "peace of soul" that Scheler deliberately describes in words that support Luther's description of Grace (though Scheler does not endorse Luther's metaphysical beliefs) does not occur in Sartre's phenomenological studies. To admit that it *could* would violate the logic of Sartre's thought. But, more than that, to admit that it *does* would, apparently, violate the phenomenological character of Sartre's own experience. Thus, he rejects the

[47] Some readers might wish to compare Sartre to Heidegger on this point. Heidegger acknowledges the possibility of an existential salvation outside the context of traditional religion. See John Macquarrie, *An Existentialist Theology* (London: S.C.M. Press, 1955), pp. 149 ff.

[48] *Being and Nothingness*, pp. 232, 266, 365, 538, 566, 626. See also the translator's comments, pp. xxix ff. Cf. Greene, p. 63 and H. Paissac, *Le Dieu de Sartre* (Vichy: B. Arthaud, 1950), pp. 14-18, 22-23, 31-38 *et passim.*

traditional religious promise of immanent salvation, as if this promise necessarily entails an endorsement of metaphysical theology, but, more especially, for the two reasons I have already mentioned—the first, logical; the second, phenomenological. Nevertheless, religious experience does not necessarily involve trans-phenomenological speculations, and the logical and phenomenological bases of Sartre's criticism of religion are only two Achilles heels—one for each foot—of Sartre's stand on this matter.

Insofar as his atheism is merely logical it is, as logicians sometimes say, merely "trite." Like the existence of a married bachelor, divine consciousness—"being-in-itself-for-itself," as Sartre defines it—is only impossible by definition. The self-contradiction that is involved only expresses the logical form and grammatical limitation of Sartre's lapse into rationalism, and, incidentally, the inevitable limitation of any rationalistic definition of the "feeling" that Scheler points to. The presence of God in man, the upsurge of being-in-itself-for-itself, may be impossible by definition, but this does not prove that existence will not spill over the thimble beaker of our linguistic etiquette. Whether or not it *does* run over is a matter that can be discovered only in certain of life's surprises, or by a consistent lack of them. In our philosophizing we are all frequently guilty of proceeding without heed to Nietzsche's warning: "There are schematic minds," he said, "those which hold a thought to be *truer* when it can be inscribed in previously designed schemes or tables of categories."

There are countless self-deceptions in this field: almost all great "systems" belong here. But the *fundamental prejudice* is: that order, perspicuity, system must belong to the *true being* of things, conversely that disorder, the chaotic, incalculable appear only in a false or incompletely known world.[49] . . . It is quite indemonstrable that the nature [*an sich*] of things behaves according to this recipe. . . . It requires an entirely different strength and flexibility to keep hold of oneself in an incomplete system with free, unbounded vistas, than in a dogmatic world.[50]

We should not forget that religion is essentially a mythopoeic response to life, and not a rational system, and that the function of paradox in theology and religious thought is phenomenologically related to the above observation of Nietzsche's. It is an intellectualistic prejudice that prompts us to think of God as a theologically minded system-builder, as though "he" were an omnipotent and well-intentioned graduate of a traditional seminary. Our *conception* of God must remain vague, as Peirce said, and mythologically variegated, as Nelson Pike left it, in effect, in his discussion of the theological problem of evil (although without adequate explanation, as I suggested in the preceeding chapter). This is where the enormous testimony of the world's major religions, the witness of the prophets and saints, becomes existentially relevant for us. That witness testifies to the occurrence and reoccurrence of something *Being and Nothingness* denies. It contends, against Sartre's rationalistic deviations, that what is impossible by definition, in this case, does in fact happen —"for with God all things are possible."

To the extent to which Sartre's denial of religion's promise is merely an expression of his philosophical presuppositions, we must retrace our way to phenomenology. We have all heard that the being of God is inexpressible except in self-

[49] Friedrich Nietzsche, *The Complete Works of Friedrich Nietzsche*, ed. Oscar Levy, 18 vols. (London: Allen & Unwin; New York: Macmillan, 1909), XIII, 57.

[50] *Ibid.*, p. 55. Cf. William James, *The Varieties of Religious Experience* (Mentor Books; New York: New American Library, 1958), pp. 107, 331, 369, 387 ff.

contradictory terms, but we have also heard that people claim to have encountered him, nevertheless, in a presence that is ineffable in self-consistent discourse.[51] Surely, then, it is not consonant with the alleged presuppositionless method of phenomenology to brush such testimony aside! As long as this alleged witness exists, the question of the paradoxical existence of God must either be answered in the affirmative by individual phenomenologists and pilgrims on an ancient way, or left an open question. "The phenomena that *show themselves* to one person need not necessarily show themselves to another," a contemporary student of existentialism, Fernando Molina, observes.

The granting of this point entails the significant consequence that the findings of two phenomenological existentialists need not be in agreement with each other. The reports of an existentialist, in other words, need not be expected to hold in all respects for all human beings at all times. I emphasize this point particularly because of the theoretical compatibility that it makes possible between the emphasis on the uniqueness of the individual in existentialism and the *de facto* uniqueness exhibited in the description of existence recorded by the existentialists themselves.[52]

Compare, for example, the Look as described by Sartre, to the Look that the poet, Karl Wolfskehl, experienced in the presence of Jewish philosopher-theologian, Franz Rosenzweig.

Whoever stepped over the threshold of Franz Rosenzweig's room entered a magic circle and fell under a spell, gentle yet

[51] See, for example, Rudolph Otto, *The Idea of the Holy*, trans. J. W. Harvey (New York: Oxford University Press, 1958). This book and its appendix are rich in illustrations too numerous to detail here. See also Thomas McPherson, "Religion as the Inexpressible," *New Essays* . . . , pp. 131-44.

[52] Fernando Molina, *Existentialism as Philosophy* (Englewood Cliffs, N.J.: Prentice-Hall, 1962), p. 55.

potent—in fact, became himself a charmed being. The solidity and the familiar forms of every-day life melted away and the incredible became the norm. Behind the desk, in the armchair sat, not as one had imagined on climbing the stairs, a mortally sick, utterly invalid man, almost totally deprived of physical force, upon whom salutations were lost and solace shattered; behind the desk, in the chair, Franz Rosenzweig was throned. The moment our eyes met his, community was established. Everything corporeal, objects as well as voices and their reverberations, became subject to a new order, were incorporated without strain, conscious effort, or need for readjustment, into that wholly genuine, primordially true kind of existence irradiated by beauty. It simply couldn't have been otherwise, for what reigned here was not pressure and duress, but utter freedom. . . .

It was not only that all petty human feelings, anxieties and embarrassments were wiped out. It was not only that all the paltry, complacent pity of well-being was purged away. What happened here was much more: in the presence of this man, *well* in the fullest sense, one's own welfare was assured, wholly and in accord with the spirit. Near Franz Rosenzweig one came to oneself, was relieved of one's burdens, heaviness, constriction. Whoever came to him, he drew into a dialogue, his very *listening* was eloquent in itself, replied, summoned, confirmed and guided, even if it were not for the unforgettably deep and warm look of the eyes.[53]

If we wish to be phenomenological, we cannot assume, as Sartre seems to do in much of his writing, that people like Wolfskehl in the presence of Rosenzweig—or like the apostles in the presence of Jesus—are necessarily victims of their own unlovely self-deception and continuing bad faith. Indeed, we cannot baldly accuse even the author of *Being and Nothingness* of such a failure. For the conclusion of that

[53] Karl Wolfskehl, quoted by Nahum N. Glatzer in *Franz Rosenzweig: His Life and Thought*, ed. Nahum N. Glatzer (New York: Schocken Books, 1961), pp. xxxiii-xxxiv.

work is not unambiguous, and although Sartre is certainly one of the most systematic of existentialist philosophers, the total body of his writings does not comprise a system. It is, among other things, a welter of compassionate as well as of cynical insights into himself and his fellowmen. And, if we consider the contemporary existential theologies of Rudolph Bultmann, Paul Tillich, Martin Buber, Abraham Heschel, and others, we see how difficult it is to assert that Sartre's observations and conclusions are plainly inimical to the Judeo-Christian tradition.

Sartre's quarrel with religion is not clearly delineated on all fronts. Since it is not the case that all forms of religion retreat into metaphysical reassurances or otherwise attempt to avoid existential despair by seeking a speculative way out of the human condition, it is too soon to tell how his "atheistic" existentialism will finally contradict or corroborate the "atheistic" theologies that certain existentialistic, analytical, and unconventional philosophers of religion and theologians are now developing. Current books and journals on religion are studded with such terminology as "religionless Christianity" (Bonhoeffer), "the secular meaning of the Gospel" (van Buren), "the theology of dialogue" (Buber), "the God above God"(Tillich), "the death of God" (Altizer, Hamilton, and others) and so on and on. These castigations of bad faith in religion come from commentators writing within the context of the Judeo-Christian tradition itself, for viable religion is nothing if not phenomenological, self-critical, and self-renewing. While reading Sartre and studying contemporary theological writing, one can hardly help recalling the fate of Spinoza, who was condemned as an "atheist" by the conservatives of his own day and then hailed later as a "God-intoxicated man."

I am not insinuating that Sartre will one day be hailed as a God-intoxicated man, or that he should be. Certainly, he is passionately involved in the sort of problems that are one traditional motivation of religious life, but the "forelornness" of *Being and Nothingness*—its unalleviated sense of the absence of God, or of the "silence" of God, as Buber says in correction—is due, it seems, both to the author's failure to find Him and to his failure to listen. "Let us realize," says Buber, "what it means to live in an age of such a concealment, such a divine silence, and we shall perhaps understand its implication for our existence as something entirely different from that which Sartre desires to teach us." [54] Buber maintains that the hopelessness of *Being and Nothingness* is due to its author's unacknowledged presuppositions, in violation of the phenomenological method. Sartre's conclusion is possible "because he holds the subject-object relation to be the primary and exclusive relation between two beings. He does not see the original and decisive relation between I and Thou, compared with which the subject-object relation is only a classifying elaboration." [55]

If Buber is right, Sartre is perhaps misled by his intellectual pride. He does not recognize that existence might indeed violate the logic of his thinking. He is painfully aware of the mystery of existence; the inexplicable presence of being and its peculiar relation to (its alienation from) "nothingness" all but overwhelms him; but he refuses to recognize the credibility—or, more accurately, to probe the existential

[54] Martin Buber, *Eclipse of God* (Torchbooks; New York: Harper, 1957), p. 66; cf., Paissac, *Le Dieu de Sartre*, p. 154.

[55] *Ibid.*, p. 69; cf. Erich Fromm, *The Art of Loving* (New York: Harper, 1963), pp. 70 ff. In an anthology, *Existential Psychology*, ed. Rollo May (New York: Random House, 1961), Abraham Maslow writes (p. 60) as follows: 'I do not think we need to take too seriously the European existentialists' harping on dread, on anguish, on despair, and the like, for which their only remedy seems to be to keep a stiff upper lip. This high I.Q. whimpering on a cosmic scale occurs whenever an external source of values fails to work. They should have learned from psychotherapists that the loss of illusions and the discovery of identity, though painful at first, can be ultimately exhilarating and strengthening."

sense—of traditional religious testimony regarding the single central miracle of religion: that atonement is a fact of history, experienced by both Jews and Christians, among other men. For just as the concept of original sin is not as unrealistic as we have generally come to believe, so too the traditional promises of religious salvation are not as *foolishly* other-worldly as many critics and well-meaning defenders of religion assume. It is not only the critic of religion, but the religious community itself that must acquire a more subtle understanding of the nature of sin and salvation, and of the conceptions of God and man.

You all know the witty satirist Lichtenberg (1742 1799) of whom Goethe said: "Where he makes a joke a problem lies concealed." And occasionally the solution of the problem is revealed in the joke.

SIGMUND FREUD, *General Introduction to Psychoanalysis*, 2ND LECTURE

CHAPTER III

ORDINARY WIT AND RELIGIOUS WITNESS

1. *The Problems Reviewed and a New Approach*

Philosophers have become aware, in the recent past, that ordinary language is a tangled skein of different "logics" or "grammars." [1] At one time, between the two World Wars, most British and American philosophers were not so broadminded. They were, instead, the dogmatic apes of mathematics and science. They sought to show that all cognitively meaningful discourse must ape the logical orderliness of mathematics or the experimental concreteness of science. Philosophical analysis, the "linguistic analysis" of that time, was an effort to "reduce" such grammatically misleading and semantically vague statements as frequently occur in our ordinary language to their allegedly proper logical form and to their concrete semantical referents. In this way, both strict

[1] See, for example, Wittgenstein's *Philosophical Investigations*, pp. 8-12, 38, 45-51.

logical order and perfect empirical clarity were to be impressed upon the relative disorder and vagueness of ordinary talk and thought. Today, however, most language-analysis philosophers no longer aspire openly to develop a privileged form of discourse that they can then hold up as the only or most proper form of intelligible communication. This common hope of the thirties and forties is no longer a deliberate or popular program.[2] Philosophers have now learned to observe and describe our myriad linguistic activities as they actually occur rather than to stipulate how they should occur if only man's symbolic life were neater. As a result, philosophical analysis is now drawing our attention to long overlooked peculiarities of syntax and semantics, enabling us to avoid the misunderstandings that occur when we confuse one way of thinking and talking with a subtly different way. This analysis also helps us root out the confusions that fault our thinking when we fail to see equally subtle similarities between linguistic activities that we had mistakenly assumed to be different.

With this in mind, we must now compare and contrast certain forms of ordinary speech to certain forms of religious language. We must describe, and not prescribe. But we will take one important point for granted, now: that Sartre's description of the basic relation in all symbolic activity is essentially correct. The semantic *content* (the intended referent or meaning) of every sign is partially constituted by the logical *form* of the symbolic system (clear or vague) in which it occurs; both content and form are integral elements of every communicating *consciousness*, whether in soliloquy or dialogue. What we encounter, how we express ourselves, and

---

[2] See J. O. Urmson, *Philosophical Analysis*, pp. 167 ff.; *The Revolution in Philosophy*, by G. Ryle *et al.* (London: Macmillan, 1956); *Essays in Conceptual Analysis*, ed. Antony Flew (New York: Macmillan, 1956).

who we are form a symbiotic communion—a lived relation. And whenever one of these basic elements of language becomes divorced from the others, the remaining ones will also undergo a radical change. If the original form of some symbolic activity is dissociated from its original content, the language in question will either become a dead language, a hollow shell, or it will be filled by some alien significance— an alien life. In this way, the content of relatively primitive forms of experiencing are often lost as cultures change or as new meanings replace the original contents of old linguistic forms. Traditions might then be preserved, but they are only superficially the same, and persons who live in those traditions are significantly different spirits from their ancestors.

Today many Westerners regard their religious heritage with suspicion or outright hostility. And many of those who seem to live within it are hardly more than ghosts or usurpers of the life that once animated "the Word of God." In such circumstances and in that sense, the God of our fathers is "dead" or "silent." Indeed, there is considerable sociological and psychological evidence to support the contention that at least some of modern man's sense of alienation is due to his having lost the ability (or Grace) to rejoin the mythopoeic subject whose fossil remains are our religious rituals and myths.[3] Not only is God dead, so also are his people, the individual spirits who might have been conscious of the sacred life that is the subject of religious testimony.

To enter the presence that once illuminated the prophets and saints of our Judeo-Christian faith seems to be impos-

---

[3] See Eric and Mary Josephson (eds.), *Man Alone: Alienation in Modern Society* (New York: Dell Books, 1962), esp. pp. 56-73, 166-201, 339-46, 478-505; C. G. Jung, *Psyche and Symbol* (Anchor Books; Garden City, N.Y.: Doubleday, 1958), esp. pp. 113-224; Dietrich von Hildebrand, *Liturgy and Personality* (Baltimore: Helicon Press, 1960), pp. 9-26, 66-101, *et passim*. The work of Paul Tillich and Mircea Eliade often makes the same point.

sible for many of us even if we desire it.[4] Knowledge of God by acquaintance involves a painful expansion of modern conceptions of "reason" and of "rational behavior." Pinchbeck conventions of "secular" life and hackneyed modes of "piety" must first be shattered before they can be restored in us religiously transfigured. Once again, new wine must break old bottles. Religious illumination has always been a complex and painful phenomenon in the human spirit; during its most viable periods it has always seemed like mere nonsense, or dangerous nonsense, to the dead. Religious testimony is often related to the iconoclasm of ordinary wit and to the double vision of the common pun.

My comparison of religion to wit in this chapter—and, in the next one, to punning—is an example of the "paradigm case technique": an attempt to understand symbolic behavior that puzzles us by paralleling it to certain linguistic phenomena with which we feel at home.[5] Confronted and scandalized by traditional religious utterances, the Western intellectual must keep in mind that what Goethe said of Lichtenberg may also be said about God: "Where he makes a joke a problem lies concealed." Conversely, whenever we encounter a religious problem in deep existential concern, it may be a "joke" of a painful and practical kind that we have to suffer, because, as Freud said: "Occasionally the solution of the problem is revealed in the joke."

If we appreciate the importance of something like humor in traditional religious testimony, we may see why it is so

[4] See William Hamilton, "The Death of God Theology," *The Christian Scholar*, XLVIII (Spring, 1965), 27-49; Gabriel Vahanian, *Wait Without Idols* (New York: Braziller, 1964); a convenient anthology of representative problems in contemporary Christian faith and theology is *New Theology No. 3*, eds. Martin E. Marty and Dean G. Peerman (New York: Macmillan, 1966).
[5] For a discussion of this technique in its application to philosophy of religion, see Frederick Ferré, *Language, Logic and God* (New York: Harper, 1961), Chap. 3; William T. Blackstone, *The Problem of Religious Knowledge* (Englewood Cliffs, N.J.: Prentice-Hall, 1963), *passim*.

difficult to explain the language of religion to one who does not get it. It is like trying to explain a witticism or pun to someone who, in the midst of a laughing company, fails to see the point. Thus, philosophers have often been witless spectators of religion, as indeed have all of us, even if we are not professionally committed to such seriousness. That is why a comparison of selected elements of ordinary humor and religious witness may provide both a reasonable response to the four intellectual objections to religion that I canvassed in the Introduction, and a helpful corrective to the overly simple or sententiously doctrinal interpretations of religion that are offered by some members of the religious community itself. Religious language is a tangle of prose and poetry, of liturgy and myth, of all sorts of symbolic devices; and woven through many religious expressions, influencing the whole range of the kerygma, are important characteristics that religion shares with ordinary humor.[6] This is true of both Judaism and Christianity.

Traditional religion has been accused of being silly, senseless, self-contradictory, and sick. But if we think of these criticisms again, now, we will certainly find it remarkable that the very people who castigate religion on these grounds sometimes use a form of communication—humor—which is silly, senseless, and self-contradictory, sometimes even sick ("black humor" for example), in much the same way as religion. Although they understand and prize one sort of humor, most critics of religion do not recognize or properly evaluate the other. They approach it with erroneous preconceptions.

[6] See Tillich, *Systematic Theology*, I (Chicago: University of Chicago Press, 1951), 165-200; Elton Trueblood, *The Humor of Christ* (New York: Harper, 1964), p. 25, *et passim*; Reinhold Niebuhr, "Humor and Faith," in *Discerning the Signs of the Times* (New York: Scribner's, 1946), pp. 111-31. Also *A Rabbinic Anthology*, eds. Montefiore and Lowe, see index for examples of paronomasia "including homonyms, puns, wilful mistranslations, etc."

They do not see the important logical and phenomenological similarities between wit and witness. They have never considered, or at least never understood, what Kierkegaard said: "Since an existing humorist presents the closest approximation to the religious, he has also an essential conception of the suffering in which life is involved."

The comical is present in every stage of life . . . for wherever there is life, there is contradiction, and wherever there is contradiction, the comical is present. . . . The religious individual has as such made the discovery of the comical in the largest measure. . . . The comical is always the mark of maturity; but it is important that the new shoot should be ready to appear under this maturity, and that the *vis comica* should not stifle the pathetic, but rather serve an indication that the new pathos is beginning.[7]

We are not bound to Kierkegaard's theological vision or terminology, but if his category of the comic is understood as a generic term that embraces the essential elements of both pun and wit, we will presently see that in religion, as in all of life, punning is a fairly low form of humor—but it is one that points toward the highest, which is wit. Suffering is an essential part of wit, as Kierkegaard frequently suggests, and as I shall argue phenomenologically. And the "wit" of religious witness is the ultimate wisdom of every nonidolatrous religion.

2. Witticisms Contrasted to Puns

In *The Autocrat of the Breakfast Table,* Oliver Wendell Holmes observes that "people that make puns are like wanton boys that put coppers on the railroad tracks. They amuse

[7] Søren Kierkegaard, *Concluding Unscientific Postscript,* trans. David Swenson (Princeton: Princeton University Press, 1941), excerpts from pp. 400, 459, 413, 250 in that order.

themselves and other children, but their little trick may upset a freight train of conversation for the sake of a battered witticism." [8] Holmes' use of the expression "may upset"— the fact that it implies that the upset is not inevitable—suggests both the similarities and the differences between puns and witticisms that we must keep in mind throughout the remainder of our considerations.

The most important resemblance between them is that they both depend on ambiguity to obtain their effects. There could be no puns or witticisms if it were not for the fact that the same words, pictures, movements, and so forth can be intended and interpreted in several different ways at the same time. If we think of a *sign* as a mere physical object (a gesture, mark, word, noise) and if we think of a *symbol* as a sign that is placed by some interpreter within the context of some logical system (in some "grammar" or syntax that gives the sign its logical implication and directs us toward a certain meaning), then we see how one sign can be an organic part of many different symbols. For example, the physical word "bug" can be used to designate a certain sort of insect, while at other times it is used, just as effectively, to denote a mechanical defect in one's car.

It is such semiotic versatility that both puns and witticisms exploit. Yet there is a momentous difference between them, and this difference is related in an important way to the theological distinctions between God as transcendent and God as immanent, to the difference between mystery and miracle, and to the contrast between negative and positive theology.

Consider ordinary puns. A pun is a sign that is simultaneously and *successfully* taken as a constitutive part of two or more symbols. It is like a single section of track that

[8] Oliver Wendell Holmes, *The Complete Writings of Oliver Wendell Holmes*, I (Boston: Houghton Mifflin, 1892), 12.

bears us without trouble in the direction of both New York City and Philadelphia—like one segment of track that is part of two or more different railroad lines: for example, like one track that is simultaneously a part of the New York Central and of the Pennsylvania Railroads. The meaning of a pun is easily complex because the syntax of one symbol is enough like the syntax of the other symbol so that all the meanings in which the sign is involved—at least, all with which we happen to be concerned—can be taken at the same time without too much difficulty. In puns, several different lines of thought go through the same sign at the same time, and if one of those lines of thought is religious in some heightened sense, then that pun—which might be any sort of object or event, and not a conventional sign—will be sacramental in that way.

The genius of puns, in the context of religion, is that they can carry us into the heart and mind of traditional religion while we are still deeply committed to workaday affairs and contemporary concepts. From a religious point of view they are helpfully insidious, moving us from one line of thought to another in what we can properly call a religious direction. The analogical method of reasoning that characterizes so much traditional theology—the method of reasoning by analogy that is intended to move our understanding from sense knowledge toward relatively nonsensuous apprehension of metaphysical truths—the so-called analogy of proportionality, is an example of such "punning." Analogies of proportionality describe God in various highly suggestive ways. He is said to be "loving," "powerful," "intelligent," and so on, as though he were only proportionately more loving, more powerful, and more intelligent than we are. But the concept of proportionality is not strictly applicable here, for God is said to be *infinitely* loving, powerful, intelligent, and so forth, and whatever proportional concep-

107

tion we may have of God as compared to ourselves, our concept of him is always infinitely inadequate. Yet, in order to talk about him, we are forced to keep punning.[9] The biblical technique of teaching by parables and paranomasia is another example of this fact.[10] Biblical analogies, parables, and figures of speech carry us gently in the direction that its religious teachers wish us to take. They invite us to enter a train of thought thinking that it will take us to a certain sort of conclusion, and it *would* usually—but, as a matter of fact, when we leave it this time, we are in a subtly different context from the one we had anticipated.

In his *Varieties of Religious Experience,* William James has in effect suggested that one typical variety of religious experience is an ever-deepening punlike approach to God, and that another and contrasting variety is more like an experience of wit, through violent and painful conversion. According to James, such disparate forms of religious experience illustrate a difference between "once born" and "twice born" souls.[11] Admittedly, this is an oversimple categorizing of religious types—James knew that—but it is an instructive one, and in the context of our comparison of humor and religion it throws a light on an important logical, psychological, and theological fact. Compared to witticisms, puns are

[9] See F. C. Copelston, *Aquinas* (London: Penguin Books, 1955), pp. 126-36. Copelston remarks: "We enunciate different descriptive propositions about God while at the same time we realize the lack of proportion between our [inevitable] way of speaking and the reality spoken of. . . . According to Aquinas the most appropriate name for God is the name disclosed to Moses (Exodus, 3, 14), *Qui est,* He Who is. . . . We cannot form any clear concept of what this is . . ." (pp. 135-36). Cf. Ian Ramsey's discussion of the function of "religious qualifiers," *Religious Language* (London: S.C.M. Press, 1957), Chap. 2.

[10] See Ian Crombie, "Theology and Falsification," *New Essays in Philosophical Theology,* pp. 123 ff., also Ian Ramsey, *Christian Discourse, Some Logical Explorations* (London: Oxford University Press, 1965), Chap. 1.

[11] James, *The Varieties of Religious Experience,* pp. 78 ff.

relatively tame, like a commuter's life—but witticisms are wild!

Witticisms are locutions, or more properly the wrecks of locutions, which must be taken in two or more logically or psychologically incompatible senses at once. They derail rational discourse and upset complacency at the point at which they occur. They force us to take two or more widely disparate lines of thought at the same time—but we cannot. While enjoying, or suffering, a witticism—since humor (as Kierkegaard knew) is not always an unalloyed pleasure—a person cannot occupy any symbolic system at all! Thus wit, which is the odd meaning (the "object") of any witticism, is always literally ecstatic—it stands out of every world order —literally "out of this world."

Our discussion has, in effect, changed Holmes' metaphor a bit. Instead of likening puns and witticisms to "coppers" that "may upset" freight trains of conversation, we have likened puns to places where two or more lines of thought easily join each other with only a nervous clatter to mark the ambiguity (always a point of possible disaster) where those lines intersect. Then, in contrast to puns—to which they are related as disaster is to mere danger—we have likened witticisms to tracks that are laid at logical or psychological cross-purposes to each other. Careening into such a junction, into the tangle of a logical falsity or a psychologically self-defeating action, our train of thought is thrown off the tracks of rational discourse and reasonable expectancy. Having struck a witticism, we can only laugh in shocked surprise, or in deeply serious contexts curse or pray, but we cannot proceed until we have "collected ourselves" and repaired or renounced our initial line of thought and conduct. We may, thus, use the familiar drawing on the following page as a rough visual illustration of the form of wit:

109

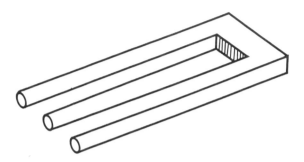

If one puts a finger over one or the other end of the "cross-over fork," it makes good optical sense. Obliterating the closed end, one looks at three rods running parallel to each other. And if, instead, one places a finger over the other end, one looks at something like a rectangular horseshoe. So far there is no problem. The trouble occurs when we take our fingers away altogether and come on the "fork" unexpectedly, as we usually do. Then our eyes automatically travel down the parallel rods and are repeatedly upset by running into the horseshoe. This is a visual witticism.

Now, it may be necessary to emphasize what has already been suggested. Witticisms do not have to be contradictory in a strict logical sense. As long as the lines they tangle are disparate or contrary enough to bring about a violent upset in our train of thought and emotions—as long as the frustration of our expectations is, thus, *phenomenologically* effective—we will be tumbled into the chaos of wit. For example, if some should demonstrate, in opposition to our argument of Chapter I that the theological problem of evil does not necessarily involve a *logical* contradiction, it would still be proper for us to use that problem as an illustration of a religious "witticism" because the existential effect of that speculative problem is peculiarly self-defeating and profoundly upsetting to intellectually fastidious but religiously

110

passionate people. It tears them apart, as Aiken says, and they cease to be what they were. They, thus, cease to be religious—or their understanding of what it means to be "religious" is changed. Here is where talk of "religionless Christianity," "the God beyond God," "the death of God," and so on is apposite. And there is an important appositeness to the suggestion that the religious person is also "dead" (but, perhaps, "reborn"), "religionless" (but, perhaps, in possession of the "kerygma") when his old religious conceptions are so undone. To experience a witticism of *any* sort, one must be committed to reason at some level—the level on which the witticism is to occur—for wit cannot be apprehended except at the expense of the existing individual. That is why Kierkegaard concludes his discussion of "the comic" by introducing a study of "pathos" and new "maturity."

In contrast to the gentle broadening of perspective that puns effect, we cannot get the point of a witticism—we cannot intuit wit—without disaster. Tragedy, even if it is nothing more than the relatively trivial consternation of ordinary wit, is essential to this catastrophic and therefore most exciting form of the comic. Witticisms are always self-destructive in some way, either by being strictly self-contradictory (like the statement, "The red barn is green all over") or by being self-defeating in some other fashion (as when a person says, "I can't speak a word of English," or attempts to deny truthfully what he firmly believes).

The essential relationship between humor and the existing individual is even more forcefully brought to our attention when we consider why some jokes so quickly lose their comic savor. Whenever witticisms lose their power through being repeated too often in the same company, it is because the intended victims of that wit can no longer be lured to ride the relevant train of thought to their destruction. A some-

111

what bored audience hears the words that introduce the familiar witticism, but being forewarned, nobody is *in* the witticism when it occurs. It happens in form, but not in existence. To experience either commonplace wit or the "wit" of religious witness—to see the point of a witticism in its full sense (nonsense)—one must have more than a merely verbal knowledge of it. One's self, one's ego, must be the freight that is run into fragments along with one's world and its conventional values. As this chapter and the next one unfold, several examples of religious "wit" will be described, and, since there are too many examples to discuss within the limitations of this book, many others will be pointed to in passing. We must work up from relatively commonplace illustrations.

Consider the following example of an ordinary witticism. Take Alexander Woolcott's quip, flung, it is said, at some bibulous companions after he had accidentally staggered off a pier into Lake Bomazine: I must climb out of these wet clothes and into a dry martini!" The laughter of Woolcott's friends indicates that they did not succeed in rattling over the ambiguities of his remark without disaster. As a train is derailed by a switch that the villain pulls while the cars are crossing, Wollcott's friends' train of thought was wantonly wrecked by him when he tricked them into entering a dead metaphor (for one thing) that he suddenly animated as they were moving through it. Let us put ourselves in their position.

We do not normally *climb* out of our clothing, and in a phrase like "climb out of these wet clothes," the word "climb" is habitually taken by us in that dead sense. Indeed, in that context, one would normally expect the metaphor "climb" to be as dead as the "legs" of a table. But Woolcott pulls a switch! We start across his metaphor in its usual dead sense—"I must climb out of these wet clothes"—only to have the word "climb" stealthily repeated in such a way that, too late to retrace our course, we are suddenly aware that we took a wrong turn—"and [climb] into a dry martini!" When the suppressed metaphor was slipped under us, we were not still moving through a hackneyed figure of speech; we were being shunted instead toward the calamity of wit. The change from one sense to another was too unexpected for us to negotiate successfully. But we were not aware of our mistake before it was too late.

The logical and phenomenological complexities of Woolcott's relatively simple crotchet is obviously even more complex. It also lures us to enter the word "dry," in a mistaken sense, as the contradictory of the word "wet" in "wet clothes" —the words "climb out of . . . into" speed us along in that direction—only to be violently dumped in the direction of a different logic of the word "dry" as the contrary of the word "sweet" in "dry martini." Once again various lines of thought are suddenly drawn at cross-purposes, and we are thrown from syntax to syntax without being able to complete a thought along any one line. So our train of thought is scattered. Our ratiocinative momentum carries us into the presence of chaos beyond our lost world order, and we find ourselves laughing, the *glossolalia* of ordinary wit, in shocked surprise.

3. The "Wit" of Religious Witness

Compare this sort of occurrence with the religious "wit" that many earnest people experience when, for example, they strike against the theological problem of evil in their religious pilgrimages. The only proper answer to the theological problem of evil, the only religious solution to a person's consternation in that predicament, is conversion or turning—*metanoia* (Christian) or *teshuvah* (Jewish)—an upset and a revision of a person's religious understanding and of his apprehension of self. After experiencing disaster on a certain theological and conceptual level, and a simultaneous or subsequent awakening of one's mythopoeic and existential awareness, that person may "never be quite the same again."

It is noteworthy that events which effect such "wit" do not have to be theological or religious in any obvious way. A Sartre-like apprehension of the ultimate absurdity of one's inauthentic existence might, for instance, be the occasion of such a painful and "witty" awakening. It might startle a worshipful mode of existence quite unlike conventional forms of religiosity, and yet be more passionately responsive to "the God above God," as Tillich says, than more familiar forms of devotion.[12] Whether the witness becomes the prophet of a new cult or only of an entirely private form of existence, or merely takes his place as a member of some traditional religious community, whenever he is turned from problem-solving on one level to worship on another, something like a painful experience of wit will probably be involved. The only other road from the profane to the sacred is by way of "punning" in a certain direction—by way of an analogical dilation of consciousness, an "approximation process"—which, however, might never lead to religious "wit." [13] We will discuss this approximation process in the next chapter.

What we must realize, now, is that one can grow even in the deepest reaches of religious "wit." An intellectual who has wrestled with the problem of evil may, for example, suddenly experience one depth of that religious "witticism" after

[12] Tillich, *The Courage to Be*, pp. 186-90.

[13] My juxtaposition of punning and wit parallels Ian Ramsey's juxtaposition of "qualifier" and "disclosure"; see *Religious Language*, pp. 51 ff. Crombie's notion of "the logical father of religious belief" may also be likened to my notion of religious punning in important respects; see *New Essays . . .*, 116 ff. Although I disagree with Crombie's eschatological conclusion, I think that "logical father," "qualifier," and "pun" are mutually supplementary models.

another, like a theater audience that laughs and laughs again at what might be called the same joke. As Jacob, wrestling with God, received a broken hip before he could walk with the Lord (Genesis 32:24-31), so, in our inauthentic and fallen existence, we must be repeatedly disjointed in order to make progress in love and wisdom. The Word of God is, thus, a paradoxical stroke of joy and pathos, but not a philosophical system. Yet, it can be properly converted into a "system" if we keep in mind that such systems must be systematically incomplete (philosophical theology's "death by a thousand qualifications"), or systematically self-destructive (crisis theology's "Moment of Truth"). The way of death by a thousand qualifications is the way of theological "punning." The other road, with its Moment of Truth, is the way of theological "witticism," aimed at a continuous repetition of "wit" in those who take theology seriously.

There are, as consequents, at least two important reasons why many people think that religious language is utterly senseless. The first is that they think its proper meaning is *further* from their everyday experience than it really is—as though common puns and witticisms were not akin to the Word of God—and the second is that they think it is *closer* than it really is—as though the humor of religious testimony, especially its "wit," were not a continuous confounding of Babel in our workaday worlds. If Sartre is right, that God is an absurd project of every man, it is because human fulfillment can never be encompassed like a bird in hand. God is not an object or condition to be possessed. But that is no good reason to give way to despair rather than cling to hope, to rebel against the human condition rather than accept it, to describe human life as an unmitigated tragedy rather than a promise of triumph. As our existential problem is one of choice, our philosophical problem is largely one of arranging the language of our lives along lines of "hope" and "redemption" rather than of "despair" and "alienation." So human life may follow the course of a redeemed perspective, out of perdition, and constitute a religious witness in itself.

The simple identification of laughter and religion that we occasionally encounter must always be qualified.[14] What we have been calling the "wit" of religious witness is paradoxically wedded to the ethico-religious anguish that Aiken expresses, the pathos of Kierkegaard's thought, the "salvation through self-despair, the dying to be truly born . . . the passage into *nothing*" which William James describes:

> To get to it, a critical point must usually be passed, a corner turned within one. Something must give away, a native hardness break down and liquefy. . . . This is certainly one fundamental form of human experience. Some say that the capacity or incapacity for it is what divides the religious from the merely moralistic character. With those who undergo it in its fullness, no criticism avails to cast doubt on its reality. They *know*; for they have actually *felt* the higher powers, in giving up the tension of their personal will.[15]

If we compare ordinary wit to religious witness, we must be quick to recognize that, in the fundaments of religious life, we are thrown further and scattered more radically than in the comic. And yet, a helpful model of religious Truth is common wit.

4. Wit as Intuition and as Object

Considered as an object of intuition, wit is a difficult topic to discuss because it is not a thing or event or meaning in

[14] See Havelock Ellis, quoted by William James, *The Varieties of Religious Experience*, pp. 54-55. Notice James's criticism of Ellis' lack of qualification in the latter's simple identification of humor and religious consciousness. How emphatically Kierkegaard avoids that mistake! Notice that we do, too.

[15] *Ibid.*, p. 99. Cf. Max Scheler, "Towards a Stratification of the Emotional Life."

any usual sense. It is instead a sudden absence of the old expected sort of things before anything new appears to take their places, or before the old world order is reaffirmed by us. Wit is the momentary disappearance of all particularity along with the loss of all grammar, the disappearance of a world in an explosion of syntax.

Yet, although it is true in one sense that there is no rational form or intuitable object in wit, there is another sense in which every instance of wit has an odd "form" and is also an intuition of a strange kind of "object." It is not the case that wit is just emotion. The total phenomenon of wit includes emotion, but every instance of wit is more than that. It is also an odd kind of knowledge. It is the sort of intuition that can profitably be compared to man's awesome apprehension of God, as traditional religion often describes that confrontation, and to man's painful intuition of himself as that apprehension is understood by existentialist philosophers like Sartre.

Ordinary wit is not wholly devoid of the "ontological shock" that some existentialists call "awareness of the abyss." [16] Nor is everyman's occasional encounter with the witty absence of world order completely unrelated to the biblical allusion to "the deep" over which "the Spirit" moved, and still moves, in the mythical "beginning" (Genesis 1:1-2).[17] According to the Bible (Genesis 2:19-20) and to Sartre's and Heidegger's account of "fallen man," language continuously evokes cosmos out of chaos, continuously fashions a world order that each language-user seeks to maintain as the necessary and sufficient basis of his own temporal existence.

[16] See, for example, Reinhold Niebuhr, "Humor and Faith," in *Discerning the Signs of the Times*, esp. pp. 125 ff. Cf. Heidegger, *Being and Time*, pp. 192-94, 354-58; Kierkegaard, *Concluding Unscientific Postscript*, pp. 159-60, 243, 258-59, 404, 447, 464, 489.

[17] Cf. Paul Tillich, *Systematic Theology*, I (Chicago: University of Chicago Press), 178-82.

Ordinary wit is, therefore, a breath of "whirlwind" (Job 40: 6) akin to the destruction of historical time that primitive man experienced in his repeated participation in, in his repeated enactment of, "the Word of God." [18] Thus, wit is phenomenologically related to Sartre's understanding of destruction, which we discussed in the preceding chapter. In his relatively mundane flashes of wit, even the inauthentic "mass man" of the existentialists has an inkling of the "abyss" within him whose demonic presence stirs his dreams and is inadequately kept in check during his hours of wakeful anxiety.[19] In wit we encounter nonbeing, "one of the most difficult and most discussed concepts," as Tillich declares.

It is implied in Aristotle's distinction between matter and form. It gave Plotinus the means of describing the loss of self of the human soul, and it gave Augustine the means for an ontological interpretation of human sin. For Pseudo-Dionysius the Areopagite nonbeing became the principle of his mystical doctrine of God. Jacob Boehme, the Protestant mystic and philosopher of life, made the classical statement that all things are rooted in a Yes and a No. In Leibnitz's doctrine of finitude and evil as well as in Kant's analysis of the finitude of categorical forms nonbeing is implied. Hegel's dialectic makes negation the dynamic power in nature and history. . . . Recent Existentialists, especially Heidegger and Sartre, have put nonbeing (*Das Nichts, le néant*) in the center of their ontological thought; and Berdyaev . . . has developed an ontology of nonbeing which accounts for . . . freedom in God and man. These philosophical ways of using the concept of nonbeing can be viewed against the background of religious experience of the transitoriness of everything created and the

[18] On primitive man's experience of chaos and destruction, and the primitive's method of escape in myth, see Mircea Eliade, *The Sacred and the Profane* (Torchbooks; New York: Harper, 1961), pp. 29-32, 42, 47-50, 55, 64, 116. Also, by the same author, *Cosmos and History: The Myth of the Eternal Return* (Torchbooks; Harper, 1959), pp. 9-20, 54-71, 88.

[19] See Tillich, *The Courage to Be*, p. 36.

power of the "demonic" in the human soul and history. In biblical religion these negativities have a decisive place in spite of the doctrine of creation. And the demonic, anti-divine principle, which nevertheless participates in the power of the divine, appears in the dramatic centers of the biblical story.[20]

The last three sentences, Tillich's remarks about the inter-relationship of the demonic and the divine, are particularly relevant to our present considerations. Biblically as well as psychologically, Satan is akin to God. There is, for example, a strong tendency in the Old Testament to represent Satan as one of the heavenly court. And recently Carl Jung has argued as a psychologist, but also on biblical grounds, that Satan is the "brother" of Christ, that Satan is a psychological and religious symbol of God's and man's "dark side." [21]

Now our phenomenological description of wit suggests that it too is an experience—similar in certain important respects to the agony and ecstasy of the "twice born" soul—in which both creative and destructive forces, the divine and the demonic, vie in the soul of man for his eventual allegiance. In both ordinary wit and religious witness, creative insight is linked to a momentary destruction. The phenomenological character of the "object" of that intuition is, thus, a function of the response to it of the one who finds himself suddenly stripped of ego and world order before it.

Although some philosophers and theologians think that the alleged concept of nonbeing is merely empty and utterly meaningless,[22] I suggest—with Sartre, Kierkegaard, James, Heidegger, Tillich, and many others in addition to the ones

---

[20] *Ibid.*, pp. 32-33.

[21] Jung, *Answer to Job*, pp. 64-74, 97-102, 138.

[22] See, for example, Ronald W. Hepburn, "Demythologizing and the Problem of Validity," *New Essays* . . . , pp. 227-42; Paul M. van Buren, *The Secular Meaning of the Gospel* (New York: Macmillan, 1963), pp. 79, 83.

the latter has mentioned—that an apprehension of nonbeing is a common denominator in many sorts of otherwise disparate experiences. Tillich cites Aristotle, Plotinus, Leibnitz, Kant, Hegel, Heidegger, and Sartre. But of course, Tillich's lumping together of such different systems of thought is much too casual and unqualified. We must, for example, recognize the vast difference between Aristotle's conception of "matter" and Sartre's conception of "nothingness"—indeed, they seem almost to be contradictory concepts—and yet we must seriously entertain Tillich's implicit suggestion (typical of phenomenologists) that what is vastly different in differently *interpreted* experience may often be the same "object" on the more primitive phenomenological level. We can make up our minds on this score only after we have conducted a careful analysis of the quality of our own raw apprehension in the areas of experience under discussion. Then, even if we are critical of such incautious conflations of philosophical conceptions of nonbeing as Tillich has engaged in, nevertheless we may find that his comparison is helpful in suggesting the kind of basic intuition we are to look for when we try to understand certain parallel elements in the conceptual systems he has mentioned.

Accordingly, my present task has two related aspects. The first is to persuade those who think that the alleged concept of nonbeing is a pseudo-concept that they have actually glimpsed the phenomenological "object" from which this philosophical concept derives. The second is to show that the philosophical conception of nonbeing is dialectically inherent in its contradiction, the philosophical conception of being, and that together, as being-nonbeing, they direct our attention to the phenomenological basis of the mythopoeic figure of the Creator. But how is the traditional philosophical conception of being related, phenomenologically, to the traditional philosophical conception of nothingness? And how are such philosophical concepts related to the much more ancient biblical images of God?

These questions have been answered obliquely already. The many biblical names of God—"the thousand names of God"—are so many *mythopoeic* responses to the phenomenological "object" we brush against in common wit, and which all but overwhelms some people at times—in mystical intuition and religious conversion, for example. Subsequently, appearing much later in the history of man, the *philosophical* conception of being-nonbeing functions as a vain attempt to conceptualize that paradoxical "object" adequately.[23] Now, to appreciate this complex historical fact properly— particularly since the advent of existential phenomenology —we must never forget that one element of every intuited object, even of the intuited disappearance of all conventional objects, is the knower himself. This is as true of religious intuition as it is of wit, or of any other sort of knowledge. Speaking phenomenologically, staying within the experiential limits we have agreed upon, whatever is known, however "objective" it is, is also a part of the subject, the knower, and *vice versa*. Every man is himself an aspect of being-and-nothingness revealed in wit and in religious witness. His problem, when he becomes fully aware of this, is to respond to this revelation in his own way—to choose his response to this new and most disruptive intelligence. Thus, each pole of the following polarities is to some extent, and in various capacities, an instantiation of one's own individual existence: in wit, frustration and laughter; in existential awareness, despair and authentic response; in religion, Satan (the Adver-

---

[23] See Ernst Cassirer, *Language and Myth*, trans. S. K. Langer (New York: Harper, 1946), pp. 79-83; Martin Heidegger, *An Introduction to Metaphysics*, trans. Ralph Manheim (Anchor Books; Garden City, N.Y.: Doubleday, 1961), pp. 111, 170 ff.; Tillich, *Systematic Theology*, I, 211 ff.; Jacques Maritain, *A Preface to Metaphysics* (Mentor Books: New York: New American Library, 1962), Chap. 4.

sary) and our saving God. God-as-known—at least, the God of every nonidolatrous religion—might well be thought of as a phenomenological *relationship* rather than as an object.

The philosophical conception of being-nonbeing and the religious conceptions of God and Satan are so many examples of man's traditional response to the paradoxical "object" revealed in various forms of witty apprehension. One side of such dialectical opposition reveals the fact that the "object" of wit includes the awesome presence (being-itself, God) in which all beings stand before us. The other side of the polarity underscores the fact that the same "object" of intuition includes a conscious absence (nothingness, Satan) of all the beings, of the world order and conventions, under whose sway we had fallen. In the moment of wit, man experiences a vertiginous apprehension of his own absolute freedom in the midst of a historically conditioned world. In the moment of wit he is once again given the opportunity to determine how he will constitute himself within the subject-object relation that is the inescapable basis of his personal existence. A careful analysis of religious consciousness reveals that (if we may speak in terms of myth) Satan's work is a part of the divine activity that also involves man as a partner in God's continuous creativity. As the Book of Job illustrates, the demonic works with the sufferance of the divine. As, in wit, frustration is a part of laughter, so, in the more painful reaches of religious consciousness, the Adversary's temptations and tests are a paradoxical aspect of God's mercy, of our miraculous, painful, and joyous deliverance from bondage to the world in which we repeatedly enslave ourselves. Like ordinary wit, religious consciousness witnesses a sudden subversion of the world's seriousness and makes it possible for us to possess our world orders once again rather than to be possessed by them. In the profoundly suggestive terms of the Jewish and Christian myths, our Adversary (Satan) works

122

with our Redeemer (God) to undo and deliver us from our own egos and our egocentric world orders. We are, thus, given another chance to establish a healthy relationship with our historical selves and our environment.

In *The Idea of the Holy*, a classic example of the phenomenological study of the paradoxical "object" of religious consciousness, Rudolf Otto has expressed these same points in a more abstract and academic terminology. This scholarly description is, perhaps, more difficult to understand than the comparison of ordinary wit to religious witness that I have been making. But in his professorial fashion, Otto is saying much the same thing. He is describing the disruptive and dilating effect of religious "witticism" on the self-consciousness of the person (Otto's mystic) who is undone (brought to "nothingness") in a flash of "wit" (Otto's "immeasurable plenitude of being") which, compared to any conventionally describable state of being, is "wholly other."

We said above that the feeling of the 'wholly other' gives rise in mysticism to the tendency to follow the *'via negationis'*, by which every predicate that can be stated in words becomes excluded from the absolute Numen—i.e. from Deity—till finally the Godhead is designated as 'nothingness' and 'nullity', bearing in mind always that these terms denote in truth immeasurable plenitude of being. Now this is also the origin of that tendency to let the conception of *personality* and the personal also be submerged in the same 'nothingness', a tendency which is in appearance so irreligious. We need not dispute that the denial of personality to God does often in fact denote a wholly irreligious attitude; mostly it is simply a disguised form of atheism, or betokens a desperate attempt to equate faith in God with belief in natural law and with naturalism. But it would be a huge error to suppose that anything of this kind is in the minds of the mystics when they

123

set themselves to oppose the idea of personality in God. We shall be in a better position to understand what they are contending for if we take mysticism—following our previous definition—as meaning the preponderance in religious consciousness, even to the point of one-sided exaggeration, of its non-rational features. What we have, then, is a sort of antinomy, arising from the inner duality in the idea of the divine and the tension of its more rational and its more non-rational elements. (The non-rational assumes thus an apparently *irrational* character.) It is the 'wholly other' aspect of the numen, resisting every analogy, every attempted comparison, and every determination; so that it is here really true that '*omnis determinatio est negatio.*' [24]

When, despite their obvious differences, we are made aware of certain logical and phenomenological similarities between ordinary wit and religious witness, it enables us to understand the important truth contained in the frequently repeated suggestion that, regardless of their formal dissimilarities, all major religions voice the same fundamental insight: encounter with the ineffable "object" of nonidolatrous worship. Appreciation of the similarities between wit and witness also helps us understand why God is traditionally described as both immanent in, and wholly transcendent to, the world. God is like wit in this respect. We have seen that the point of every witticism, its wit, is out of this world—wit is a transcendent "object" in that sense—and yet every experience of wit, every epiphany of wit, is also an event in time. We have also seen that every occasion of wit is a crossing, in some individual existence, of chaos and cosmos—an intersection of the timeless with time—and such "crossing," as T. S. Eliot has observed, "is an occupation for the saint." [25] Witticism

[24] Rudolf Otto, *The Idea of the Holy,* trans. John W. Harvey (New York: Oxford University Press, 1958), p. 197.
[25] T. S. Eliot, *Dry Salvages* (London: Faber & Faber, 1941).

is "the word," so to speak, and wit is its "spirit." Thus, witticisms resemble theophanous events.

Stories of theophanous events illustrate the sort of personal upset, insight, and change of character that is characteristic of wit when the destruction of wit approaches tragic proportions. We will discuss the experience of Job and the author of Ecclesiastes (Koheleth) in detail in Chapter V, but now consider the following few examples in passing. Take, for example, the story of Abraham's experience while sacrificing his son on the mountain called "The Lord Will Provide," or "See" or "He Will Be Seen" (Genesis 23:10-14). Think of Jacob's mutilation by, and victory over, God at Peniel, and of the significance of Jacob's change of name to Israel, "He Who Strives With God" (Genesis 32:24-31). Consider the story of Simon Bar-Jona, the most erratic and vacillating of Jesus' original twelve, who nevertheless became the exemplar of Christian insight and constancy—Peter, "The Rock" (Matthew 16:13-20)—heated and hardened by the very experiences that also demonstrated his original undependability and faithlessness (for instance, in Matthew 14:28-31; 26:69-75). Ponder the classic example of Saul, the Pharisee, "breathing threats and murder against the disciples" (Acts 9:1-9) who, when he encountered the supreme object of his hate on the Road to Damascus became—and who could have expected it?—the author of the hymn to Love (I Corinthians 13) and the Epistles of Paul. Consider the story of each one of us who, if he is to find the infinite and eternal meaning of his life, must find it in the depths of his temporal existence (being), in a passionate willing of his own death (nonbeing) as the paradoxical price he must pay for his authentic human existence (being-nonbeing), for *life* within life. Consider how like a witticism a world is in which the body and blood of God—or what will be consecrated as such —is baked and brewed through the rude instrumentality of

125

men and nature, a world in which priests, though their eyes may be riveted on Heaven, must try on their hats before they buy them! [26] If there is something inescapably tragic, there is also something just as consistently hilarious about human life as such, and religious consciousness is aware of both.

Every theophanous event is an oxymoron; it has radically opposite sides: wise and foolish, positive and negative, joyous and tragic, divine and human. Thus, if the response to a witlike apprehension is "religious," its subsequent theological "clarification" may well stress, for example, the immanent and effable side of that paradoxical experience. It may emphasize the historicity of the object revealed and the historical symbols used to describe it. It may develop a certain religious "grammar," enscribe a certain "theological circle," and foolishly take that way of speaking as the one true form of divine revelation. On the other hand, the theological interpretation of the original revelation may stress the transcendent and ineffable aspect of the experience, emphasizing its ahistorical content in terms that are strangely self-contradictory or self-defeating. As a matter of fact, when kept within their limitations, both forms of theology are helpful, and I have alluded to them both already. The first is typical of "positive theology," which purports to describe God in analogical terms: God is "wise," "loving," "creative," and so forth—but not quite in the same way as men sometimes are. The second is typical of "negative theology," which adds a "No, no!" to everything that positive theology declares: thus, God is "omniscient," "infinite in love," "omnipotent," and so on—in short, we cannot understand him, even in analogi-

[26] Cf., Ludwig Wittgenstein, *Lectures and Conversations on Aesthetics, Psychology and Religious Belief*, ed. Cyril Barrett (Berkeley and Los Angeles: University of California Press, 1967), pp. 53 ff. "During the war, Wittgenstein saw consecrated bread being carried in chromium steel. This struck him as ludicrous."

cal terms.[27] Every religious community involves both kinds of theology, but different religious traditions are characterized by different stresses—for example, in the East by negative theology, in the West by positive theology; in Roman Catholicism by positive theology, to which, in its emphasis on crisis, Protestantism adds a strong tincture of negativity. The theological amplification of the Word of God is perpetually torn between dialectical opposites, fluctuating between the theology of the once born and that of the twice born soul, for every religious person is, perhaps, a bit of both.

"If the meaning of the negative divine is that no predicates are attributable to God, the meaning of the positive divine is that the religious consciousness nevertheless attributes predicates to Him," says W. T. Stace. "The most general characterization of the negative divine is that God is Non-Being. The most general characterization of the positive divine is that God is Being." [28] This is our answer to the question we asked ourselves concerning the relation between the philosophical concepts of being and nonbeing. It is also our answer to the question of the relationship between the religious conception of God and the philosophical conception of being-nonbeing.

Although the theological intellect . . . endeavors always to arrange its propositions in a self-consistent system, yet, in regard to the most fundamental and ultimate religious insights, this cannot be done. The first principle of logical reasoning is the law of contradiction, namely, that two propositions which contradict each other cannot both be true. Theology can follow this principle in its peripheral and subordinate assertions, those which are mere

[27] For clear and brief discussions of the functions of positive and negative theology, compare F. C. Copelston, *Aquinas*, pp. 126-36 to Ian Ramsey, *Religious Language*, Chap. 2.

[28] W. T. Stace, *Time and Eternity* (Princeton: Princeton University Press, 1952), p. 50.

implications of its central core of insights. But this central core itself does not yield to this logical treatment. When we seek to logicize it, we find in it irreducible self-contradictions.

We may be inclined to express this by saying—as has often been said—that at the heart of things, in the very nature of the Ultimate itself, there is contradiction. We may make use of this mode of expression without objection. But it is not strictly accurate. For the Ultimate itself cannot be either self-contradictory or self-consistent . . . for both of these are logical categories. It is neither logical nor illogical, but alogical. What we should say, rather, is that the contradictions are in us, not in the Ultimate. They arise from the attempt to comprehend the Ultimate by logical concepts. The Ultimate rejects these concepts, and when we seek to force them upon it, the only result is that *our thinking* becomes contradictory.[29]

In this passage, Stace summarizes what we have been saying about the wit of religious witness. Because of the "witty" nature of its basic revelation, there is a paradoxical need in religion both to speak out and to be silent, a need that is expressed, for instance, in the laugh-provoking parables and questions (the *koans*) of Buddhism: 'What is the sound of one hand clapping?" But paradox and contradiction are also to be found in biblical testimony—for example, in the Old Testament juxtaposition of God's unspeakable name, the tetragrammaton (YHWH), and his speakable name, the Lord—in the Lord's combined refusal and readiness to be named (Exodus 3:14-15). The Lord's name is Nameless, but it is also "the Lord, the God of your fathers, the God of Abraham, of Isaac and of Jacob." [30] He is the Nameless One, the "Wholly Other," who nevertheless acquires many names when he enters history—when, as he baptizes those in whom

[29] *Ibid.*, p. 153.
[30] Erich Fromm, *Psychoanalysis and Religion*, p. 116; cf. Martin Buber, *I and Thou*, trans. R. G. Smith (New York: Scribner's 1958), pp. 111-12.

he appears, he is himself baptized, or when he is called after the holy places he has sanctified.

5. *Ordinary Wit Contrasted to Religious Witness*

Upset in relatively trivial conversation while pursuing ends that are comparatively unimportant to our personal existence, we laugh in ordinary wit, like demigods, amused at our "merely human" pratfalls. That is common wit. But, wrecked in the course of our most passionate concerns, unable to extricate ourselves easily from the chaos that then surrounds us, we may—like Paul, Augustine, Luther, and many lesser persons—experience the "wit" of religious revelation. In common wit we laugh in trivial tragedy, a little giddy from our upset. Our egos are not too badly damaged. But in religious "wit" we pray or curse—to withstand a harder fall and a more difficult return to some world order we can call our own.

To distinguish ordinary wit from the "wit" of religious witness we must take both the antecedents and the consequents of the moment of wit (or witlike Moment) into account. Such moments are like musical notes in one respect. A moment or note may be just like other moments or notes of the same witlike quality or pitch when they are compared out of context, but in the concrete contexts in which they occur, those same moments or notes may be egregiously dissimilar. A blast on a hunter's horn is a very different thing from the same noise sounded in a symphony; and instances of wit that are almost identical in themselves will be profoundly different from each other when they are considered in the existential situations in which they occur as moments of ordinary wit or as Moments of religious witness. Different lives have different themes—in our freedom we must each compose our own score—and if we could compare occurrences of wit in different people, those occurrences would be seen to have profoundly different existential values. The religious value of a moment of wit depends on where it occurs, in whom, and how it is scored. A note of wit may occur as a somewhat cynical element in ordinary humor, or it may only deepen a mood of existential despair. On the other hand, it may change the dominant key of an individual existence from despair to religious consciousness.

But for the earnest project that it upsets and the prayerful response that follows it, any moment of religious "wit" might have been but a moment of common wit in a workaday world. Witness is distinguishable from wit, not only by the relatively greater importance, in some person's life, of the logic that the experience of religious "wit" overturns and empties, but also by the language and life to which the subject returns. Whoever experiences a knowledge of divinity by acquaintance—as Jacob encountered the Lord, and Saul met Christ—has experienced the Truth that the Lord declared to Moses: "Man shall not see me and live" (Exodus 33:20). Whoever experiences the relatively trivial upset of ordinary wit is not so deeply involved in disaster, and after the "ontological shock" that evokes his laughter, he responds to the experience by returning once again to the conventions that were, for but a moment, wittily suspended.

Before picking up the pieces of his former world, the one who experiences the "wit" of religious witness must prophetically create or re-establish a religious vocabulary, no matter how unorthodox or "profane" it may seem. That prayerful act is what places his experience of "wit" in a religious context and makes him a religious person. From then on (as we shall see in the next chapter), he may enact a sort of "pun" through all his days, every mundane moment being taken in both a common and extraordinary sense, and the commonplace be sacramental.

The meaning of every witticism, its wit, lies in a *threefold* chaos that mingles our dead egos, our scattered logics, and our momentarily ruined worlds of facts and values.[31] If any sententious soul, exhibiting the witless spirit of all heresiarchs, presumes to make "good sense" of such disaster—should he, to take a trivial example, presume to cure Mr. Woolcott's linguistic malaise by "making sense" of that nonsense—he may "translate" Woolcott's witticism into an uneventful conjunction of two logically respectable sentences ("I must climb out of these wet clothes, *and* I must drink a dry martini") and reap the pedantic applause of some tidy minds, but he will get no prize for understanding wit! That is why analyses of religious language have so often been applauded by philosophers while the same efforts have been scorned by those who actually live in the language that has been "explained."

Since it affects both Jews and Christians, we have already discussed the theological problem of evil as an example of a religious "witticism." We have also alluded to several biblical and non-biblical examples of the "wit" of religious witness. But let us now consider one more illustration: take Christianity's Trinitarian Dogma as another instance of a religious "witticism." All attempts to make good sense of it have been pronounced heretical. After centuries of rationalistic bustle, this locution still remains a paradoxical expression of *Mysterium Tremendum*. As a scandalous crotchet, this dogma endlessly deepens the "wit" of the community that repeats this "witticism" to itself in its liturgical life: " . . . one God in Trinity, and Trinity in Unity . . . The Father incomprehensi-

---

[31] See Buber on the three "spheres in which the world of relation is built," *ibid.*, pp. 101-2; also Philip Wheelwright, *Metaphor and Reality* (Bloomington: Indiana University Press, 1962), Chap. 1. A classic treatment of the relationship between sign, symbol, and interpreter is C. S. Peirce, "The Principles of Phenomenology" and "Logic as Semiotic: The Theory of Signs," in *The Philosophical Writings of Peirce*, ed. J. Buchler, pp. 74-119.

ble, the Son incomprehensible, and the Holy Ghost incomprehensible." [32] This dogma spells salvation for the Christian, but only because it also spells his undoing. The verbal precision of the dogma conceals its cognitive vagueness, and any attempt to make its cognitive content less vague runs one into self-contradictions on the one hand, or heresy on the other.[33] The Church ("by the Grace of God") has had the genius to resist all attempts to convert its central dogmas into common sense. By this intransigence it preserves its "other-worldly" potency while remaining peculiarly relevant to every world order, a revolutionary instrument ticking in the middle of our conventional culture.

"The Church tries to formulate a mystery which still evades complete understanding," a fairly recent handbook on the Catholic faith declares. "Trinity in Unity and Unity in Trinity cannot be explained in human language." [34] And most Protestant theology concurs: "While one may be in danger of losing his soul by denying [the doctrine of the Trinity], he is in equal danger of losing his wits in trying to understand it." [35] From the point of view of common sense and logical consistency, the saving barque of Christ is in fact a shipwreck! It avoids the conceptual vagueness of Scylla only to run aground on the self-contradictions of Charybdis. But such wrecks are the occasion of sudden Grace.

In my lengthy quotation from Stace, he pointed out what must always be the case when we "attempt to comprehend the Ultimate by logical concepts." Judaism, Unitarianism, and other religions may avoid the Trinitarian scandal of

[32] The Athanasian Creed according to the English *Book of Common Prayer.*
[33] See Ian Ramsey, *Religious Language,* pp. 168-70.
[34] N. G. M. Van Doornik, S. Jelsma, and A. Van de Lisdonk, *A Handbook of the Catholic Faith,* ed. John Greenwood (New York: Image Books, 1956), pp. 160-61.
[35] Cyril C. Richardson, *The Doctrine of the Trinity* (Nashville: Abingdon Press, 1958), p. 15.

Christianity, but all nonidolatrous religions are involved—like Judaism in the Book of Job, Ecclesiastes (Koheleth), and elsewhere[36]—in one equally disastrous crotchet after another. Atheistic Buddhism and death of God theology are, of course, no exceptions.

Obviously, the problem of religious meaning must not be solved according to the typical methods of well-meaning rationalists, nor should that problem be lightly left unsolved by the complacent faithful. We must *try* to solve our religious and theological problems as we stand in them—and fail in order to succeed. Most discourse is conventional and self-preservative, but religious language is meant to lure us to disaster. "The moments of the *Thou* appear as strange lyric and dramatic episodes, seductive and magical," says Martin Buber, "but tearing us away to dangerous extremes, loosening the well-tried context, leaving more questions than satisfaction behind them, shattering security." [37]

The meanings one finds in the basic testimonies of religion are not usually what one expected, no matter how long one has moved within the "theological circle." Even those who choose to live within a certain religious tradition must keep in mind that a truly religious life involves either a relatively gentle shunting from track to track on a broad mythopoeic format, or a more violent progress through one derailment after another. Only the spiritually dead find what they always expect. Thus, knowledge by acquaintance of God in his transcendence—the "wit" of religious witness, the immanent transcendence of God—can occur only in the continued sacrifice of religious *logos* and return to it renewed: "The Father loves me," says the Christ of John's Gospel,

[36] See Solomon Schechter, *Aspects of Rabbinic Theology* (New York: Schocken Books, 1961), chaps. 1, 2, 9; also A *Rabbinic Anthology*, pp. 20-25.

[37] Buber, *I and Thou*, p. 34.

133

"because I lay down my life, that I may take it again" (John 10:17).

No matter what its cultural context might be—whether it is Christian, Jewish, or something else—if it is to continue to address the living God, the Word of God must continually be both lived in and broken. It must be a "witticism" and its point be "wit," a compound of joy and pathos—as when Dostoevsky was led to his Christian faith in spite of, and because of, his failure to solve the theological problem of evil—which is no laughing matter.

Nevertheless, every religion is indeed a "comedy" insofar as that word still retains the connotation it derives from its Greek source, *komos*—the feast of Olympic victors in honor of Bacchus. As opposed to the classical conception of tragedy, in which the hero always dies, the classical conception of comedy entails a happy ending. The hero of comedy goes through paradoxical and comic purgation—the clown goes through disaster into wisdom. So, even in the context of modern civilization, viable religion must always be a divine comedy in honor of God. Dante's great poem is, for example, aptly named. In the *Divine Comedy* we are taken through Purgatory, in a series of versions and conversions, to a vision of Heavenly Joy in the end. But the poet speaks for us all, in the first stanza, by rudely awakening us in Hell:

> Midway in our life's journey,
> I felt myself astray from the right path,
> and having lost the road
> I woke to myself, alone, in a dark wood.

The Lord said to Abraham, "Why did Sarah laugh and
say, 'Shall I indeed bear a child, now that I am old?' Is
anything too hard for the Lord?"
... And Sarah conceived, and bore Abraham a son
in his old age. ... And Sarah said, "God has made
laughter for me; every one who hears will laugh over me."

Genesis 18:13-14; 21:2, 6.

CHAPTER IV

PUNS, PARONOMASIA, AND MYTHOPOEIC EXISTENCE

1. *Myth, Metaphor, and Pun Compared*

The technical theological term for the puns and punlike expressions in the Bible is "paronomasia." The Bible and its theological elaboration in Judaism and Christianity not only contain "witticisms" of the kind we have been discussing, but also a gentler type of ambiguity. Puns, I have said, are tame compared to witticisms. Puns are merely metaphors of a sort. Yet, we usually distinguish them from other kinds of metaphors because, although we can successfully take a pun in several senses simultaneously, nevertheless they are ordinarily more surprising and psychologically difficult to negotiate than most ambiguous expressions. Puns are very *live* metaphors, but they are usually somewhat different from other vivid figures of speech. For one thing, they are ordinarily more exasperating. We will, for example, excuse a difficult

135

poetic ambiguity—indeed, we invite such trouble from poetry—but we do not anticipate it in workaday prose or suffer it quietly when it occurs there. When we are going about the world's business, the uninvited nuance of the common pun seems frivolous, as Holmes observed, and that lack of worldly seriousness is important to our considerations. When we find it also in the punlike devices that are all but concealed in what we take to be serious biblical accounts of historical events or in apparently serious religious narratives, we will have entered the profounder ambiguity, the more critical "punning," which is characteristic of art, existential philosophy, and religious myth. Uninvited nuances disturb a prosaic passage.

Puns, paronomasia, and poetry are related in various ways, and no superfine distinctions can be drawn between them; there would always be exceptions to such rules. The poetic features of religious testimony and the religious character of much fine poetry are fairly evident. They have been the subjects of many studies. But the similarity between ordinary punning and certain kinds of religious testimony has generally been overlooked, and this is philosophically unfortunate. In some respects, ordinary humor is a better model than poetry of religious life. Today at least, humor is apt to occur more spontaneously than poetry, and although poetic inspiration and comprehension are as mysterious as the giving and receiving of Grace, our generally more intimate acquaintance with humor may make it, rather than poetry, a more effective bridge from prosaic life into at least a philosophical appreciation of religion.

Puns are related, logically and phenomenologically, to the character of witticisms, which we have already discussed. A good pun brings us to the brink of disaster, close to the abyss of wit. And although all metaphors have some of the dilating characteristics of good puns, most metaphors, being more dead than alive, lack the shock and challenge of the latter. An ingenious pun will amaze us, while a dull one— failing so miserably in its attempt to introduce the interesting unexpected—will only make us groan. We pass over "feeble" puns with, at most, a polite smile of sufferance; but a good one will arrest our passage for an instant, as though our minds were rocking on a point.

There are puns, or punlike expressions, that seem to conflate countless lines of thought and being. They are ambiguous signs that carry an apparently limitless symbolic freight, signs that appear to require a simultaneous comprehension of innumerable nuances if we are to understand their seemingly inexhaustible multiple significance. The kind of religious statements that I have been describing as cognitively vague, in their run-on ambiguity, are examples of such punlike pronouncements. Traditional theology's analogical description of God is a notorious instance, but, as we shall see, a more neglected example is biblical paronomasia.

The meanings of these biblical and theological statements are vague—hopelessly so in the opinion of some critics of religion—because the ambiguity of these statements is self-defeating in a narrowly conceptual sense. We never arrive at a conceptually adequate understanding of these expressions because, like the tales of Scheherazade, they are endlessly connected one with another, each qualifying the other ambiguously. Yet, such symbols lure us to follow them along the paths that they suggest so wantonly; and to characterize the seductive function of such endlessly ambiguous signs as "death by a thousand qualifications"—as though the suggestiveness of those expressions becomes more empty as qualification continues—is a typically unromantic mistake. It lacks passion and imagination.

What for one person is nothing but an exasperating evasiveness is for another an exciting enrichment of plural signif-

137

icance and promise. That is why the meaning of such statements as "God is love" can function punlike, can expand their pluralistic meanings, indefinitely—or suddenly burst in a shower of "wit." The statement, "God is love," is an expression that is meant to suggest that God loves us like a father, but it says so in an indefinitely ambiguous way. Apparently, God also loves us like a mother, and like a suitor too—even as a child loves its parents, a teacher a student, a person himself, a judge the accused, an executioner the condemned. But we cannot accommodate such a welter of overlapping, gradually contrary, and (perhaps) eventually contradictory meanings in one complex thought. The result is an exciting dilation of sense, and, maybe, depending on the passion and persistence of the individual involved, eventual "death" by a thousand ambiguities. But this is not an impotent collapse of significance. It is, rather, an exploding overabundance of simultaneous meanings. Even comparatively trivial puns can be enormously complex conceptually and profoundly revealing existentially, and the more they are, the more likely they are to affect us—after leading us gently on—with the sudden violence of wit.

The excitement of punning is partly due to the proximity of pun to wit. But it is also the thrill of unexpected discovery in a more ordinary sense. When we experience a good pun we enjoy a sudden dilation of understanding without being overturned by it. And one advantage of puns over witticisms is this: that a complex but successfully traveled conceit may initiate our comprehension along several lines of thought at the same time. Puns succeed in communication where, in a sense, witticisms fail utterly.

In contrast to witticisms, which are nonsense in the sense that they scatter the values that a person is affirming at the moment he is overthrown by wit, puns are an enrichment of values and meanings. Puns make a plural sense, which accounts for their occasional fathomless depth. They not only may communicate several senses of the same logical type simultaneously, they may also communicate several different logical types of senses in the same instant, as when a slapstick soldier in a comedy show repeats the command he has been given by the General in a way that both asks a question and voices a criticism of his superior: "Charge?!"

Puns and punlike expressions can conflate imperatives, questions, assertions, exclamations, *non sequiturs,* and so on in one breath. So, if we think of the Bible not only as a collection of loosely connected "witticisms," but also as a series of punlike expressions—if we think of it as a scattering of all sorts of conscious and unconscious, deliberate and inspired ambiguities on the part of the people who wrote it—then we cannot naïvely expect to interpret it properly as a series of straightforward assertions. Like other religious scriptures, the Bible scores its points the way a billiard player does, by careening each shot off several cushions, from different sides. The cumulative meaning of the Bible is, thus, integrally related to the logical and phenomenological meaning of each of its differently directed nuances, and the meaning of each of these nuances is reciprocally determined by the fantastic conceptual complexity and the spreading phenomenological significance of the whole. As a word that is intimately related to man—particularly to man in Western society—the Bible is not only the "witty" disaster or the series of "witty" disasters that follow one another whenever we cannot perform the multiplication of meanings that it demands of us, it is also (since we sometimes do enjoy a relatively prosaic expansion of insight in response to it) a punlike expression or series of such "puns." We are titillated by the Word of God, and properly so, whenever we begin to suspect the humor that lies at the center of its serious exterior. Thus, we begin to catch a glimpse of the questions it is asking when it states

139

facts: we realize that its talk about God is also about us and *vice versa*; we are uncomfortable as we suspect that a story about another is a biography of ourselves; we see that the Word of God says one thing, incidentally, in order to communicate another that is essential to it. Ironically, what is meant is often hidden in what is said.

For example, when commentators point out that the Hebrew word for laughter sounds like the name of the son whom Sarah miraculously conceived in her old age, they are suggesting to us that the story of her laughter is really a "pun" with a religious dimension.[1] If we read that story in Hebrew, or read it in translation with this in mind, we may understand it as a re-enactment of a mythological event into which we ourselves may be drawn. Sarah ridicules Abraham's foolish faith; she is too sensible to believe the impossible. But, ironically, her skeptical laughter—"Isaac . . . Isaac"—is the very conception in her of the occasion of which she despairs. The joke is on her, and yet she soon learns to laugh at herself. In Sarah, a realistic skepticism becomes the environment that originates and nourishes the community of faith that the Jewish Bible enshrines, and the Christian Testament continues in its own way. The religious skepticism of both Jews and Christians may echo with religious possibilities when they read of Sarah's surprise. We may laugh at Sarah with a literary enjoyment of her story, but our laughter may end in reflection and join hers. "God hath made me to laugh," the King James translation has Sarah say, "so that all that hear will laugh with me" (Genesis 21:6).

The Bible is a mythopoeic response—a continuously repeated drama of human errancy and restitution to Truth—in which, for their own soteriological benefit, the generations

---

[1] Cf. Samuel Sandmel, *The Hebrew Scriptures* (New York: Knopf, 1963), pp. 358-59; also Bernhard W. Anderson, *Understanding the Old Testament* (Englewood Cliffs, N.J.: Prentice-Hall, 1957), p. 178.

of mankind are invited to participate. Thus, Exodus and Calvary are neither merely historical events, nor, soteriologically speaking, primarily historical events. The deliverance from human bondage that the Judeo-Christian Scriptures describe again and again, in different ways, with different figures, consists of myriad temporal occasions that have been transfigured by the alchemy of "the Holy Spirit" into one mythic happening. The Bible is a myth, itself a trans-historical event that marks the ubiquitous intersection of absolute value ("the Eternal") with the merely relative values of history. The Bible's promised deliverance is from death in life to life in life—a vague conception, but an existential fact according to witnesses. The Bible is an expression of God and man—a collection of historical reports, poems, songs, "shaggy dog" stories, witticisms, puns, and so on. It is a myth, magnificent and messy, the product of many tongues and hands, and profoundly true in the way of mythic illumination: we must *enact* it in order to catch its sense. Its meaning is in its rehearsal, not in its script. To understand it in a religious fashion, we cannot remain in the conceptual environment (Buber's "I-it") of pragmatic consciousness. We must *enter* the myth the way we enter a dance or take part in a play, for we ourselves are *dramatis personae* in the events ("I-Thou") that are described.

To be truly religious, not only formally so, one must be more than merely modern man. One must also be the primitive who conceived him and to whom we must occasionally return, if, like prodigal sons, we wish to mend the estrangement that exists within ourselves, among ourselves, and between ourselves and nature. This, in short, is the mythopoeic answer to alienation.[2] Men once walked with God "in the

² See Mircea Eliade, *Cosmos and History*, Chap. 4; *The Sacred and Profane*, pp. 14-18, 201-13; Erich Fromm, *The Art of Loving*, pp. 26 ff.; Martin Buber, *I and Thou*, pp. 24-33, 39-46; C. G. Jung, *Psychology and Religion*,

141

cool of the day" (Genesis 3:8), but now, at high noon, God is "dead," "an absurd project," "silent," and we are without access to the Garden. As one group of well-known anthropologists have acknowledged, "all the fundamental difference between the attitudes of modern and ancient man as regards the surrounding world is this: for modern, scientific man the phenomenal world is primarily an 'it'; for ancient —and also primitive—man it is a 'Thou'."

Myth is a form of poetry which transcends poetry in that it proclaims a truth; a form of reasoning which transcends reasoning in that it wants to bring about the truth it proclaims; a form of action, of ritual behaviour, which does not find its fulfillment in the act but must proclaim and elaborate a poetic form of truth.[3]

The religious task that faces modern man does not call for the abandonment of reason, but only for a recognition of its limitations and a subsequent enlargement of consciousness to include those reaches of personality which most of us have more or less neglected. At least we must not, by discarding our imaginative ability to enter myth, throw away a valuable means toward our own total self-fulfillment, even though to retain this means is to invite trouble of a sort that characterizes moral and spiritual development. To understand religious statements we must not only experience the occasional "witty" revelation of reason's limitations, we must also come to embody a relatively gentle, but often still annoying pun-like dilation of meaningfulness—a mythopoeic experience of God-man-and-nature such as that which characterizes the world of the Bible. The purpose is not to supplant science with myth, but only to supplement our technological world

Chap. 1; Gregory Zilboorg, *Psychoanalysis and Religion*, pp. 113-16; Rudolph Bultmann, *Jesus Christ and Mythology*, pp. 83-85.
[3] Henri Frankfort, *et al.*, *Before Philosophy* (London: Penguin Books, 1951), pp. 13, 16.

view with the numinous personification of nature and the naturalization of self that is essential to the Jewish notion of *shekinah* and the Christian ideal of the "indwelling of the Holy Spirit."

2. Ambiguity and Truth-Value in Religious Statements

Every human individual must—to use a mythopoeic metaphor—cross his own wilderness. Each must find himself, in a spiritual and moral sense, as he would an oasis. This fact introduces another feature of religious "puns" and punlike expressions (paronomasia) that makes them especially important to religious life. If such an expression is only partly understood by each of the individuals who respond to it, each may understand it quite properly in a different sense, according to his character or the momentary limitations of his spirit. A successful pun may evoke ribald laughter in the maid while at the same time it is deepening the theological sensibilities of the bishop. Consequently, if the miracle stories that are part of every major religion have a punlike character, as many theologians in effect suggest,[4]

[4] For example, Friedrich Schleiermacher writes: "Miracle is only the religious name for event. Every event even the most natural and common, is a miracle if it lends itself to a controllingly religious interpretation. To me all is miracle," *Speeches on Religion* (London: K. Paul, Trench, Trubner and Co., 1893), p. 88. For Schleiermacher, the liberal Protestant 19th-century theologian, as for Jacques Maritain, the conservative Catholic 20th-century theologian-philosopher, all natural events are punlike signs with "metahistorical" ambiguities. Maritain says (*Approaches to God*, p. 73), "The word event itself is therefore ambiguous." Schleiermacher read natural events as "puns" with a metahistorical significance in addition to their natural meaning. On the other hand, he also read miracle stories (like that of the virgin birth, for instance) as punlike descriptions of natural events. See John Dillenberger and Claude Welch, *Protestant Christianity Interpreted Through Its Development* (New York: Scribner's, 1954), Chap. X, for convenient descriptions of how liberal theologians have typically handled miracle stories. Consider Bultmann's present day juxtaposition of "historical" and "historic" meanings in both miracle *stories* and "miraculous" *events*: R. Bultmann, *Kerygma and Myth*,

then as men grow in their own religious understanding, they may respond to such stories in one sense at one time and in another sense later. This will be the case both within the private lives of individuals and in the public lives of religious communities and cultures. The wisdom of myth is eternal— it forever enshrines the Truth for every human individual —only because it is temporally and subjectively relative to the understanding and maturity of each individual in himself.

The long tradition, in Judaism and Christianity, of allegorical exegesis in biblical studies and of analogical reasoning in theology, is an example of this fact. We may smile, now, at some of the allegorizing of Philo Judaeus (first century) or Maimonides (twelfth century), and we may sigh impatiently over certain of the analogical arguments of a Thomas Aquinas (twelfth century) or a William Paley (eighteenth century). Nevertheless, today when we read the Bible we must often substitute our own culturally conditioned analogies—from existentialism, psychoanalysis, and so on—and we must also allegorize spontaneously in terms of our own experience. This is not reprehensible. A religious understanding of any scripture calls not only for exegesis, but also for eisegesis—not only for a reading out of but also for a reading into the tradition. Reading the Bible, for example, is a creative act. The meaning of Scripture is not something that exists in the Book independent of its being read, but something that occurs as an existential relation between the reader with his peculiar questions, and the text. The voice of God is this repeated experience.

---

ed. Hans Werner Bartsch (Torchbooks; New York: Harper, 1961), pp. xi-xii, 10 n., *et passim*. See also Paul Van Buren's interpretation of the Easter Story, *The Secular Meaning of the Gospel*, pp. 126-34. Ian T. Ramsey's *Christian Discourse*, Chap. I, is an especially helpful description of the logic of miracle stories.

Contemporary studies in mythology, depth psychology, linguistics, phenomenology, and biblical criticism have renewed man's awareness of the fact that there is no one obvious or one true theological interpretation of religious testimony. In its fluid significance—because it belongs to the ages—religion is more like folk art than it is like science. And even though institutional religion, like academic art, can become doctrinally rigid, nevertheless both religion and art are essentially personal in a profoundly intimate and potentially revolutionary way. Religious institutions sometimes want to possess the Truth they are only meant to cherish, but they cannot do so indefinitely. "What harm is it to me, I ask again," Augustine wrote, "if I think that the writer had one meaning, someone else thinks he had another?"

While therefore each one of us is trying to understand in the sacred writings what the writer meant by them, what harm if one accepts a meaning which You, Light of all true minds, show him to be in itself a true meaning, even if the author we are reading did not actually mean that by it: since his meaning also, though different from mine, is true.[5]

The existential freedom that we encounter here in Augustine is an echo of the same free spirit that the early rabbis prized and practiced in opposition to the formalistic excesses of fanatic pharisaism. Within both the Jewish and Christian traditions, there is early recognition that many sorts of deeply personal meanings run through each religious symbol and that, in an important sense, some are intended today especially for me. It is my personal and private predicament that must be transfigured by the Word. And it is extremely important for modern man—so narrowly confined to his current intellectualistic misconceptions of religion—to have

[5] Augustine, *Confessions*, trans. F. J. Sheed (New York: Sheed and Ward, 1943), p. 303. See also pp. 305-6.

145

his attention called to this fact. In the drama of religious myth there are as many doors as there are those who knock, and for each person there is a door on which his own name is starred. Thus, in principle, any man can still enter his own religious tradition without having to identify himself with the dead options of the past or, with what are for him, the existentially irrelevant options of his neighbors. He may become part of the drama of salvation without being intellectually faithless to his own century.

In comparing puns and witticisms to certain pecularities of religious language it is important to keep in mind that witticisms are irrelevant to truth and falsity in the usual propositional sense. Being strictly self-contradictory, or at least self-defeating in practice, witticisms do not describe any state of affairs. They are presentational rather than representational. Although they may sometimes look or sound like assertions about something or other—since their logical form is deliberately misleading—actually witticisms function not as assertions, but more as exclamations that precipitate the witty insight they intend.

In contrast, puns are conflations of expressions any number of which may be assertions that are either true or false in some fairly prosaic fashion. The complex concept of religious truth has, therefore, at least two important and somewhat dissimilar aspects, one relating to the sort of Truth that witticisms evoke when we get their point, the other loosely related to the sort of truth that characterizes verifiably assertible propositions about matters of fact. Nevertheless, since they are extremely complex "puns," the punlike expressions of religion are only very loosely related to this latter sort of truth because most attempts to make the vague and ambiguous meanings of religious language absolutely clear and distinct will precipitate the kind of logical and psychological upset that we have characterized as religious "wit." The meanings of religious "puns" are thus not only ambiguous but also—since their ambiguity is so rich and each meaning in turn ambiguous—incessantly vague. Such run-on punning really leads us away from prosaic truth-values in religion toward the existential Truth—personal and presentational, rather than representational—of religious "wit." [6]

Modern biblical exegesis, the history of religion, religious confessions, art, poetry, and so on are so crowded with examples of ambiguous symbols and punlike experiences that it is almost misleading to illustrate this fact with a few random examples. Those which one person will choose are bound to seem less apt than those which especially affect another. But whoever ponders the riot of meanings that Judeo-Christian civilization has cast abroad in biblical terms —"in the beginning," "the spirit," "the deep," "Adam," "the tree," "the fall," "Israel," "Egyptian bondage," "the passover," "the law," "the day of the Lord," "the Son of Man," "Jerusalem," "virgin," "Jesus Christ," "death," "the new being," "the last judgment," and so on—may well suspect that, when such a punlike symbolic heritage becomes hackneyed or appears to be irrelevant to human existence, it is because its heirs are callously burying their spiritual inheritance along with their poetic imagination. In this connection, it is important to observe that although some of the Bible's punlike expressions cannot be appreciated unless we understand the ancient tongues in which the Scriptures in question were originally composed, or unless those puns are skillfully explained by those who translate the Bible for us, nevertheless the "puns" with which we are here primarily concerned are not those which depend upon special knowledge of ancient languages. People who must read the Bible in translation are yet able to understand vague ideas and

[6] Ian T. Ramsey, *Religious Language*, Chap. 2; notice esp. pp. 90-91.

overlapping images like "the tree," "Egyptian bondage," and "virgin birth," for example—ideas and images that come through in translation and that function in a punlike manner as multisignificant *images* rather than as multisignificant words. Thus, although someone had to know Hebrew in order to appreciate the pun about Sarah's laughter or to know that "Adam" means "man," no one has to understand Hebrew in order to appreciate the punlike function and multiple religious significance of the miracle stories that are told in the Jewish and Christian testaments. Take, for example, the raising of the dead and the feeding of the multitudes that are performed both by the prophet Elijah (I Kings 17:20-22; 17:10-16) and by Christ (Matthew 9:18-25; 15:30-38; Luke 7:11-16 and elsewhere). Think of the miraculous frustration of the deaths of Elijah (II Kings 2:11-13) and of Christ (Matthew 27:45-54; 28:5-7 and in the other Gospels). Consider the odd account of Enoch's "death" or disappearance (Genesis 5:24). What is the religious significance of these stories? What is the fullest meaning we can discover in the Jews' invitation to Elijah during every year's Passover celebration, and of the Christians' resurrection story each Easter? Every interested student of religion must ponder the multiple meanings of such images and acts if he is to expand and deepen his own-most religious awareness.

Using the concepts of pun and punning, as we did the ideas of wit and witticism, only as hermeneutical devices— for we are not making a simple identification of ordinary humor and religious experience—we may now see that religious "puns" are especially important to religious understanding for at least two reasons. First, because signs that can be read simultaneously in both a "secular" and "sacred" sense can give our daily lives a sacramental dimension. In the presence of such signs the human condition—my individual existence—may acquire the significance of a vague, precious, almost self-validating promise of existential fulfillment. In the presence of such sacramentals we are not confounded as we are when we experience a religious "witticism." Instead, we respond with relative quiet to a vaguely apprehended Mystery in some present event.

This is the typical refreshment of the once born soul in religion. He lives in a punlike sacramental world. To draw attention to this fact is not to deny that, as opposed to mere "sacramentals," what some Christian communities define as "sacraments" (not "sacramentals") are more like witticisms than puns in their theological complexity. According to Roman Catholic theology, for example, we should perhaps make the following analogy: sacraments (the seven special mysteries of Baptism, Eucharist, and so forth) are to sacramentals (lesser blessings) as witticisms are to puns. But we need not go into an extended discussion of this tangential theological nicety; it would neither add to nor take away from the substance of what I have already said. Our central concern at present is only with the sacramental features of religious life, and this brings us to the second function of religious "punning" that we want to discuss: namely, that religious "puns" act as bridges of a sort.

Ordinary objects and events that acquire a sacramental sense are especially helpful to those whom William James characterized as "twice born" souls. The ambiguity of the commonplace is not only an occasional source of emotional and intellectual disaster, it is also the means of returning from such disaster to a new beginning in the world. Through religious "punning" we are able to invest the very marks and happenings that brought us to despair with new and healing meanings. Falling back from chaos to cosmos, passing once again through "the beginning" with an enlivened sense of one's personal immersion in that creative Mystery, the significance of one's daily rounds spreads wider than formerly and moves more deeply than before through ambiguous signs whose unexpected acquisition of plural meanings is the sudden serendipity of the miraculous in all religious narratives and in religious history. The essential but often unnoticed miracle in every miracle story is a punlike epiphany in which the commonplace acquires a value that is uniquely important to human existence. A new meaning enters a hackneyed situation, and a punlike excitement enters human life at that point.

3. The Religious Meaning of Miracles

Puns that are relatively dull are, at best, only clever; but they show us how religious puns and punlike symbols operate. Thus, to take a commonplace example, Horace Walpole could say of *The Beggar's Opera*, which was written by John Gay and produced by John Rich, that "it made Gay rich and Rich gay." Here the clatter of ambiguity as we pass over one homonym after another—as new meanings are introduced to old sounds—is loud and alarming. Each repetition of the same sound—"Gay . . . rich . . . Rich . . . gay" —noises the introduction of an unexpected syntactical network. Walpole's dull pun is like the miracle story of Sarah's laughter in that respect. In each case we arrive at the destination vaguely indicated by the initial logic of our terms, but we end up traveling on a trunk line full of unlooked-for ambiguities introduced by unexpected connections between disparate systems of discourse and experience. This is, of course, the essential characteristic of puns that causes them to be closely related to, though not the same as, witticisms.

Notice, in Walpole's punning, that although one understands the suggestion in passing, one is not altogether taken in by the insinuation that one man actually became another. We can say that the pun was true in the sense in which we believed it, false in a sense to which we refused to commit ourselves. We took it in two different ways. We had only a formal and speculative understanding of one meaning, but we were and still are existentially involved in the other.

If we use this example as a model of the way religious "puns" function, it suggests that it is one thing to see the several meanings of an ambiguous sign, quite a different thing to take them all as of equal religious value. Yet this is the mistake of many critics and would-be defenders of traditional religion.

Take, for instance, those Orthodox Jews and conservative Catholics and Protestants who insist on the religious importance of what is sometimes called the literal meaning of religious testimony. They act as though its mythopoeic originators would have recognized the distinction, drawn much later, between "literal" and "symbolic" language. These modern Jews and Christians act as though it is obvious that the mythopoeic originators of religious testimony could properly have classified their religious utterances as literal *if* they had known the modern meaning of this term. This is certainly iffy thinking on the part of the moderns in question —and it can properly be challenged as anachronistic and misleading. Indeed, while they sometimes condemn contemporary existential and symbolic interpretations of primitive religious utterances as "radical" and "dangerous," our present-day Protestant and Jewish fundamentalists and Catholic conservatives are probably themselves employing much more modern, much less primitive hermeneutic principles than those they reject as innovations. If (as is not always obvious) such modern-day literal-minded defenders of tradition are aware of the ambiguous symbolic character of biblical testimony, they too often seem to forget it. Thus, either deliberately or unwittingly, they confuse our religious discussions by skewering biblical testimony on the relatively

151

unambiguous thrust of some rationalistic philosophy or on the sort of steno-language that is characteristic of science and practical affairs. Although they may have a theoretical appreciation of the fact that one cannot understand the religious testimony of the Bible without experiencing such mythopoeic nuances as I have alluded to, nevertheless they insist that commitment to the stenographic meaning of religious testimony is just as important as a reawakening in us of the sacramental and mythopoeic senses that once danced within the flickering light of those signs.[7]

Workaday meanings of some sort are always present in religious testimony, and it may be that modern man must always understand his cultural inheritance in his own characteristic conceptual fashion. But taken alone, such literal meanings are not sacramental, and there is no need for a contemporary man to limit himself to the semiotic characteristics that distinguish both him and his secular age. In both Judaism and Christianity, what is commonly called literal-mindedness is often a form of religious illiteracy. The "faithful" who are literal-minded in this fashion believe what is merely silly to common sense and relatively immaterial to spiritual maturity. Confusing *credulity* with faith, they confound even the critics of religion. Thus, many a passionate individual of deep religious despair and high intellectual integrity refuses to be silly, and, mistaking his *incredulity* as a relevant criticism of biblical religion, becomes either morose or himself a strident obstacle in the way of the life he is looking for. Neither these critics nor those who unintentionally lead them astray are sufficiently appreciative of the punlike character of the religious testimony that confronts them. In the presence of those "puns," all are misled by the spirit of seriousness. Both the faithful and the faithless are too blind-

[7] See, for example, *The Honest to God Debate*, ed. David L. Edwards (Philadelphia: Westminster Press, 1963), Chap. III, "Some Readers' Letters."

ed by "the world," too firmly stuck in its characteristic meanings.[8] Confronted by traditional religious testimony, all act like dullards in the midst of a hilarious company: the credulous believing, the incredulous not believing what in any case is not the point.

The fact that modern biblical criticism has shown that most if not all of the miracle stories of the New Testament are relatively late accretions to the Gospel accounts of Christ's life and ministry supports my argument. It was not a historical interest that dominated the Gospel writers, says Rudolph Bultmann, "but the needs of Christian faith and life."

> One may designate the final motive by which the gospels were produced as the *cultic* (that is, the needs of common worship) . . . its individual episodes being composed for purposes of edification. . . . It is not only pious fancy which is at work here, but also apologetic interest . . . the whole narrative has been composed from the point of view of faith and worship. . . . The Resurrection Narrative has been composed in the interest of faith and under the influence of devout imagination. . . . The later evangelists add further legendary features, e.g., the story of Peter's miraculous draught of fish (Luke v. 1-10) and of his attempt to walk on water (Matt. xiv: 28-32). . . . In John the original meaning of the gospel comes out in fullest clarity, in that the evangelist while making free use of the tradition creates the figure of Jesus entirely from faith.[9]

Twentieth-century "form criticism" has shown that the miracles that are central to the Jewish faith are also conflations of various Hebraic and non-Hebraic traditions, imaginative embellishments of historical and legendary narratives for

---

[8] See Sartre's discussion of "the sticky": *Existential Psychoanalysis*, pp. 137 ff.; also Heidegger, *Being and Time*, pp. 219 ff.

[9] Rudolph Bultmann and Karl Kundsin, *Form Criticism: Two Essays on New Testament Research* (Torchbooks; New York: Harper, 1962), Chap. VI, *passim*.

cultic purposes. The Passover was "already an established institution at the time the Israelites came out of Egypt," says Theodor H. Gaster. "Religious institutions rarely go back to one single motive," he remarks.

As a rule, they reflect a whole congress of thoughts, emotions, impressions, and insights, which fuse and blend not logically but naturally and which alternate, at different times and under different influences, as overtones and undertones of a resultant symphony. A given rite or practice may therefore possess more than one meaning or complexion, depending upon the particular prism through which it happens to be viewed.[10]

Religious faith does not consist in believing what must seem silly to the common sense of contemporary man, no more so than, in my example of an ordinary pun, we were required to believe that Rich became Gay.[11] The Jew who thinks that anthropological and sociological explanations of the Exodus event jeopardize his religion is badly confused. The Christian whose faith would be shaken by the thought that the empty tomb might not have shown up as such in a photograph is no better off. Neither is the critic of religion who disparages miracle stories because he assumes that their essential significance contradicts the principles of common sense and science. All that religion contradicts is the pinchbeck insistence of "tough-minded" individuals that experimental explanations somehow supersede and replace the need for, and propriety of, myth. If we keep in mind that understanding a miracle story is not like following a news-

[10] Theodor H. Gaster, *Passover: Its History and Tradition* (Boston: Beacon Press, 1962), p. 21.
[11] My point, here, is similar to Braithwaite's distinction between understanding the literal meaning of religious stories and believing them in that sense. See R. B. Braithwaite, "An Empiricist's View of the Nature of Religious Belief" in *The Existence of God*, ed. Hick, pp. 242-50.

paper report, but rather like appreciating a pun that has happily enriched our conventional understanding of common affairs without replacing it, then we will not make the mistake of assuming that what is essential to religious belief can ever be superstitious. This, of course, is in substance what Rudolph Bultmann and like-minded theologians have been saying in various ways for a number of years.

Although Bultmann's discussion of myth has often been confused and confusing, he and other students of myth are now trying to correct our medieval and modern tendencies to interpret primitive mythopoeic utterances along logical or technological lines. The mistaken transposition of Judeo-Christian revelation into rationalistic philosophy in the medieval period and into science in the modern period changed an expression of religious Truth into a patchwork of inadequate cosmologies. Now philosophers tell us, as David Hume did in the eighteenth century, that "religious" beliefs are either senseless or silly;[12] through the eighteenth, nineteenth, and twentieth centuries, "religion" has become more and more divorced from modern life. The result is that today, despite the attempted retreat of some intellectuals into a medieval conceptual framework (the typical defense of Thomistic theologians against both "modern" thought and biblical "radicalism"), the Judeo-Christian religious traditions are faced with a climactic either/or. Religious Jews and Christians must either preserve their rational integrity as members of twentieth-century technological culture by giving up their religion, or they must preserve religion in a secular world by giving up their rational integrity. The only way to pass between the horns of this dilemma is to see that our conventional conception of religion is in need of a "witty" upset and return to its beginnings. Fortunately for us all, the

---

[12] David Hume, *An Enquiry Concerning Human Understanding*, Sec. X; cf., Patrick Nowell-Smith, "Miracles," *New Essays* . . . , pp. 243-53, esp. 249.

slogans of contemporary radical theology—"the death of God," "religionless Christianity," and so on—signalize such a renaissance of the religious spirit. In an ecumenical and radical age, the religious community will not be impaled on its either/or. Instead, it will move on to a more sophisticated level of religious consciousness that includes both the myth-opoeic imagination that is typical of biblical religion *and* the technological reasoning that is the typical genius of contemporary secular life. We should not be surprised that as the human race grows older, the spirit of man that we each exemplify feels growing pains. The ordinary paroxysm of wit and the extraordinary paroxysm of religious witness require us not to give up our logical and technological techniques, only to be less serious about them, less stuck in the particular values that are the defining and confining ideals of our day.

What bothers some contemporary philosophers so much about traditional religion is that the community of faith does not acknowledge that any state of affairs *could* falsify its mythopoeic beliefs.[13] But this is not really a compelling indictment of those beliefs when we realize that the basic statements of religion consist of "puns" and "witticisms" in the context of cultic behavior. The run-on ambiguity of religious "puns" lead us indefinitely in a sacramental direction, through one fairly prosaic set of nuances after another, unless (or until) we stumble into a sudden paroxysm of "wit"—of "witticisms" that are so patently self-defeating in their conceptual difficulty that they act as a repeated "last judgment" against our conventional way of looking at things, and a repeated invitation to make a more adequate "beginning."

The most important philosophical question now is whether or not we recognize that in addition to the expla-

[13] See Antony Flew, *New Essays* . . . , pp. 96-99. The entire "Discussion on Theology and Falsification," which follows, is obviously relevant.

nations and descriptions of contemporary common sense and science, there is also a proper and necessary place in human existence for myth and liturgy. It is not a question of either/ or—either common sense or religion—but of both/and. To believe in a God whose unique existence can be revealed only in religious "wit" and "pun" is quite a different sort of belief from one that is merely superstitious. It is neither a silly belief, contrary to science, nor does it fly in the face of common sense except as a comic rebuke of our intellectual pride.

Of course, we do not always get the point of "witty" and punlike expressions in religion. Sometimes the only meanings that we are able to detect at the time are straightforward and spiritually unilluminating. Such dullness of spirit is as common in religion as it is in art. But in religion as in art, it is not necessarily unreasonable to have faith in symbols to which we cannot presently respond except by waiting. Such commitment—a movement of passion that may carry with it the sort of anguish that Aiken expresses—is often the necessary condition for the sudden illumination of religious "wit" or the gradual sacramental enrichment of religious "punning." As we sometimes get the point of a joke only after we have joined in the laughter it provokes in others, so in religious life, if we wish to understand eventually what is opaque to us today, we may have to join in the appropriate public response and wait for private illumination. Whoever wishes to know what is hidden in the language of the prophets and saints must commit himself to their language before he can understand it. This is the significance of the well-known theological formula, *credo ut intelligam*, which so often offends us: "I believe in order to understand."

Since every religion is essentially a myth that transfigures the commonplace, there is both a very public and a very private aspect to religious life. Religion originates as a cry of astonishment in the presence of some of the ordinary things

157

that confront us: the sound that is heard is merely human; the event that is witnessed, however unusual, can be expressed in terms of common sense or science; but the prophetic meanings of these signs are ambiguously human and divine—mythopoeic—incommunicable except by indirection. The meanings of miracle stories—and, in a sense, the whole Bible is such a story—are to be found not in those stories by themselves, but only in their relation to us. Properly read, the story of the Bible is a mythical enactment of everyman's struggle to traverse the dreadful freedom of his human existence. And although Sartre (for example) has described that condition primarily from a mere wilderness, a merely solitary and despairing perspective, individual Jews and Christians can walk as members of their respective religious communities in the light of a fantastic promise. For every devout Jew looks from the miracle of Sinai toward that same accomplishment in him, and every faithful Christian is similarly related to Calvary. Miracle stories are "puns" that reflect the people who confront them, and, in this respect, what Lichtenberg observed is true: "If an ape looks into a mirror, no apostle will look out." [14]

[14] Quoted by Søren Kierkegaard, *Concluding Unscientific Postscript*, p. 254 n.

*The fox knows many things, but the hedgehog knows
one big thing.*

ARCHILOCHUS, QUOTED BY ISAIAH BERLIN,
The Hedgehog and the Fox

CHAPTER V

THE EXISTENTIAL SIGNIFICANCE OF RELIGIOUS SALVATION

1. Knowledge and Self-knowledge

Lichtenberg's ape will often have much in common with the fox of Archilochus. In a society of mass education and communication, the ape, like the fox, will know many things. We are all apes and foxes in various proportions, and the problem for each of us is to cultivate the cleverness of the fox while avoiding the limitations of the ape. One is reminded of the Bible's figure for expressing this fact: that we must master the cleverness of the "serpent" (Matthew 10:16) as well as the Lord's wisdom.[1] Unfortunately, at present, Western civilization seems to be more adept at the first than the second.

[1] Cf. Genesis 3:1; Luke 10:3; 16:8; Romans 16:19-20; also Reinhold Niebuhr, *The Children of Light and the Children of Darkness* (New York: Scribner's, 1944), Chap. 1 ff.

The more things we know, the more we need also to grow in knowledge of the one big thing that is the hedgehog's wisdom; we need self-knowledge that is more than merely well-informed. All religions say this, but in view of the general contemporary disparagement of traditional religion—particularly in view of the fact that many intellectuals believe that religious beliefs and practices necessarily violate the canons of good reason that are taught by our colleges and universities—it is imperative repeatedly to consider the relationship between education, religion, and the good life.

Whether it is formally or informally acquired, a liberal education is not only a knowledge of many things, not only a mastery of facts and research techniques, but also a perspicuous knowledge of self—the sort of self-knowledge that we have all occasionally sensed in someone else as a kind of self-possession. This ideal includes the idea not only of intimate self-awareness, but also of self-acceptance of a liberating and liberalizing sort. Man is not merely a rational animal; he is, paradoxically, both more developed and more unfinished than the brute. Because he is uniquely able to reflect on his own nature, he inherits a moral and spiritual vocation and preoccupation. Every human individual must find a reason to live and a reason to die, or live a life of obvious despair or poorly concealed self-forgetfulness. The problem is one of finding infinite value (nothing less will do) in an existence that is temporally bounded at both ends by nothingness and haunted every moment in between by a sense of that same vacancy. Any candid and clever person can see that his life is a tale told by an idiot. The central problem of every human individual's existence is to transfigure the story, or to have it transfigured. What most of us almost succeed in doing is to forget our life-problem entirely, but such behavior is inimical both to the spirit of existential philosophy and to traditional religion.

Unfortunately, it is not inimical to what usually passes as "liberal education." Our books, file cards, laboratories, and museums not only open our minds in some ways, they shut them in others. We catalogue, itemize, and file away our childhood sense of mystery along with the world order we are busily bringing into being. While discovering the world, we lose sight of its ambiguous depths and of our own submarine involvement in them. We move like fish through an ocean of signs, in schools that protect us from unexpected significance; and if intellectuals are not to become prisoners of their own dazzling facility, as sharks have become captives of their own magnificent speed, clever men must be torn apart and reconstituted periodically.

That is one essential function of viable religion. We encounter it in our first brush with the theological problem of evil, and we run into it again and again when we try to understand what it is that our great world religions are saying. The central dogmas and principles of all nonidolatrous religions have a critical, upsetting, and revolutionary function. At least they do as long as they keep faith with the prophetic spirit of their origins, before they become matters of pious prattle in houses of comfortable worship or scholastic cant in schools of philosophy. If the word "dogmatic" is taken to signify blind allegiance to narrow and illiberal formulas, we see that nothing could be more contrary to the prophetic spirit of, for example, the Judeo-Christian tradition. Properly understood, religion is a safeguard against all stultifying dogmatism. And although the religious community often loses sight of its own central character, or only begins to be aware of its essential genius after centuries of revealing and painful experience, it is not unique in this respect. Other communities—scientists, scholars, politicians, merchants, artists, and poets—have no more cause to boast in that regard. All have made mistakes, and all must learn from such experience.

161

If we use the word "dogmatic" in its common pejorative sense, we should recognize that, although it is often false to its prophetic origins, religion is essentially anti-dogmatic. What, for example, is Christian dogmatic theology but a body of dogmas to the effect that all dogma is misleading and false, Christian dogma included, if we presume to think that we have more than an unfathomably ambiguous or self-contradictory understanding of such symbols? "As we survey the developments of Christology and Trinitarian doctrine, what is evident," says Ian Ramsey, "is how often the heretics run some model or other—sometimes a highly sophisticated model—to death, in a passionate desire to understand."

Opponents then come forward with other models which show the inadequacy of the first, but they too develop them beyond necessity, and court fresh heresies at the next move. . . . The struggle to understand God can never come to a satisfactory end; the language game can never be completed. . . . Orthodoxy . . . has invisible assets—mystery—of which the models take no account. . . . Christian doctrine can only be justified on an epistemology very different from that which lay behind traditional views of metaphysics. In no sense is Christian doctrine a "super-science." Its structure, and its anchorage in "fact" are much more complex than that parallel would suggest. . . . The point above any other that I would like to emphasize is, then, the logical complexity of doctrinal assertions. . . . We sympathize with Augustine's view that doctrine only "fences a mystery"; and we express ourselves doctrinally only because we cannot live and keep silent.[2]

We have already had cause to observe that Christian dogma enters a negating no (negative theology) after every affirmative yes (positive theology). So do the rabbinical and cabalistic writings of Judaism. Dogma is only the conceptually self-defeating "grammar" of some particular theology, the

[2] Ian T. Ramsey, *Religious Language*, pp. 170-72.

syntactical "wrapper" that must be thrown away to get at the substance it protects. And yet we cannot do without such wrappers. We have seen that the significance of theological statements must be endlessly ambiguous and therefore excessively vague (conceptually meaningless), or else be excessively precise and therefore eventually self-contradictory (logically false). We have seen that theology is myth straining to conform to rationalistic canons, condemned to be unsuccessful in order to make its point. We know why philosophers, as such, cannot understand religious language, and why those who do understand it, but not as philosophers, cannot make it any clearer to the philosophical fraternity.

Neither Jews nor Christians can escape this humorous situation, and that is why religious testimony is so full of "wit" and "pun," paradox and paronomasia. It is the reason that religion, properly understood and practiced, is an invaluable critical component in any truly liberalizing education. Although the "grammars" of different religions differ from each other in various ways—as they reflect the different cultures they suborn—what Tillich called the "Protestant principle" might also be called the essential critical principle of every religion that eschews idolatry in itself and systematically overturns the idolatrous tendencies of the culture it confronts. This principle is "not exhausted by any historical religion," said Tillich, and is not identical "with a religious form at all. It transcends them as it transcends any cultural form."

The Protestant principle . . . contains the divine and human protest against any absolute claim made for a relative reality, even if this claim is made by a Protestant church. . . . It is the guardian against the attempts of the finite and conditioned to usurp the place of the unconditional in thinking and acting. It is the prophetic judgment against religious pride, ecclesiastical arrogance, and secular self-sufficiency and their destructive consequences.[3]

One special function of prophetic religion—as of every form of comic consciousness—is to be iconoclastic. And we have noticed that the first icon to be shattered by every authentic wit is himself. Religious consciousness must move through the comic to uncover a nonidolatrous answer to the question: What am I? In keeping with the ideal but infrequently realized accomplishment of liberal education, a truly religious individual will have a knowledge of the one big thing that the hedgehog knows—a *negative* knowledge of himself—a vivid existential awareness of his own speculative, moral, and ontological limitations.

2. *The Pluralistic Implications of Religious Experience*

The significance of Tillich's so-called Protestant principle is the significance of self-contradiction and endlessly compounded ambiguity in all nonidolatrous religion. In spite of the efforts of some philosophers and theologians to make theology completely systematic and relatively prosaic, the original mythopoeic form of religious revelation ultimately defeats such intellectual neatness. When we examine the Bible's answers to the fundamental questions of human existence—when we look at the answers it gives to Kant's four questions, for instance—we either find ourselves tumbling, sense over sense, in an abyssal ambiguity, despite the concrete imagery of the language, or we are thrown violently against contradictions between statements whose meanings seem

[3] Tillich, *The Protestant Era* (Chicago: University of Chicago Press, 1957), pp. 163 ff.

clear, precise, and probably true in themselves, but which are logically false in conjunction with each other. Thus:

1. What am I? "You are dust, and to dust you shall return" (Genesis 3:19). Yet God has made me "little less than God" (Psalms 8:5).[4]

2. What must I do? "You shall love," we are commanded (Mark 12:30-31), and yet "it depends not upon man's will or exertion, but upon God's mercy. . . . He hardens the heart of whomever he wills" (Romans 9:16, 18). This is the testimony, not only of Paul, but of the author of the Book of Exodus (Exodus 7:3-4; 10:1-2, 27; 11:9-10).[5]

3. What can I know? "You may freely eat of every tree in the garden; but of the tree of the knowledge of good and evil you shall not eat" (Genesis 2:16-17). Yet that very tree is "to be desired to make one wise" (Genesis 3:6-7).

4. What can I hope for? Job asks this question, and he answers for both Jews and Christians: "I know that my Redeemer lives, and at last he will stand upon the earth; and after my skin has been thus destroyed, then without my flesh I shall see God" (Job 19:25-26).[6]

These familiar quotations from the Jewish and Christian testaments can easily provoke almost equally familiar exegetical debates, not only between Jews and Christians but within each of those groups itself. The ambiguity of such imagery and the paradoxes that these myriad meanings lead us into are too well known on the one hand and too recondite and scholarly on the other to encourage recapitulation in this place. No biblical scholar worth his salt will deny that it is improbable that these passages, and hundreds of others like them, will ever be given a clear, consistent, and final exegesis. Nor need we hope for such a thing—i.e., that the Word

[4] Cf. Genesis 1:26-29.
[5] Cf. Matthew 22:36-40; Deuteronomy 6:4-5.
[6] Cf. I Corinthians 15:35-38.

of God will become the property of any group of academicians.

Religious revelation has given rise to the various formal and informal dogmas that characterize Judaism and Christianity and their various sub-branches. But what is true of the original biblical testimony is also true of its formal and informal amplification in the various religious traditions it supports. Where we might expect our theological or rabbinical analyses to lead us to clear and distinct conceptual interpretations (in traditional rational theologies, for instance), we are always given instead an answer that is more or less ambiguous or somehow paradoxical.

Although Judaism and Christianity are sometimes called "philosophies of life," it is not so often realized that they are philosophies of *life*, existential testimonies and practices, only because they are philosophies of a peculiar sort. They are witty subversions of all world views that take themselves too seriously, or endlessly compounded punlike dilations of all attempts to provide a self-contained or humanly adequate description of reality. An essential aspect of religious life is prophecy, and that is essentially an openness to upsetting insight and new values that cannot be contained in any one system.[7] Thus, religion is a critic not of science, but of scientism as well as of Marxism, Thomism, Hegelianism, and so on—even of Judaism, Catholicism, and Protestantism —whenever their adherents think they have "the last word." Historically—from the primitive church to the Protestant Reformation, from Protestant Scholasticism to Protestant Liberalism, from Liberalism to neo-orthodoxy; from the "fortress" theory of the Catholic Church as expressed in Vatican I to the "leaven" theory as expressed in Vatican II—the "new being" has repeatedly burst the staves of static Chris-

[7] Cf. Henri Bergson, *Two Sources of Morality and Religion* (Anchor Books; Garden City, N.Y.: Doubleday, 1954), pp. 215-16.

166

tianity. And what is true of Christianity in this respect is analogously true of Judaism.

The death of God theology which has recently shocked religious conservatives and fired the imagination of some religious "radicals" can best be understood as a contemporary manifestation of the old-time death-of-theology God, the "Ancient of Days" whose name is Nameless and whose spirit transcends every isolated ego and precious truth. The death of God theology is a dirge for the passing of an idol, or, more exactly, a dirge for the passing of an idolatrous perversion of prophetic religion. But it is important to notice that idols can be secular as well as religious—the "secular city" is full of them—and tough-minded men are as ready as any others to make and worship images that reflect their own egoistic confinement. That is why the "witty" language of traditional religion, and a venturesome commitment to that way of speaking, are valuable correctives, not only of overintellectualized theology, but of every other form of intellectualism whose successes in some area have encouraged its practitioners to lose sight of that method's limitations and of their own bondage in it. "Religious experiences . . . plainly show the universe to be a more many-sided affair than any sect, even the scientific sect allows for," said William James:

> What in the end, are all our verifications but experiences that agree with more or less isolated systems of ideas (conceptual systems) that our minds have framed? But why in the name of common sense need we assume that only one such system of ideas can be true? The obvious outcome of our total experience is that the world can be handled according to many systems of ideas . . . science and . . . religion are both of them genuine keys for unlocking the world's treasure house to him who can use either of them practically. Just as evident neither is exhaustive or exclusive of the other's simultaneous use. And why, after all, may not the world be so complex as to consist of many interpenetrating spheres

of reality, which we can thus approach in alternation by using different conceptions and assuming different attitudes . . . Primitive thought, with its belief in individualized personal forces, seems at any rate as far as ever from being driven by science from the field today. Numbers of educated people still find it the directest experimental channel by which to carry on their intercourse with reality.[8]

Religion is in principle, though often not in practice, an integral aspect of what we call the "liberal mind"—also of what we might call the "radical mind." The prophetic spirit will not be tamed, and its influence affects science and philosophy as well as theology and morals. "The formulation of the highest truth needs constant revision," says a spokesman of Jewish Reform, "and even more surely do the forms in which that truth is clothed. . . . A liturgy that cannot expand, that cannot absorb the best religious teaching of the age . . . is a printed page, not a prayer book for the supplicant's heart." [9]

It is not genuine religion, with its central principles of "witty" destruction and ambiguous dilation, but all self-consistent and tidy philosophies that threaten liberal education and open-mindedness. Once we become content with, or frightened into a schematism to which everything must conform, then the life of the mind (not to mention the heart) begins to wither. There are scores of competing "philosophies of life," some of which are properly famous (like Thomism and Marxism) and others which are properly obscure (like Ayn Rand's ridiculous mélange), but all are false to the extent that their disciples manifest a spirit of dull seriousness in their single-minded adherence to the respec-

[8] William James, *Varieties* . . . , pp. 107-8.
[9] Israel Abraham, quoted by David Philipson, *Reform Movement in Judaism* (New York: Macmillan, 1907 and 1951), p. 421; cf. Martin Buber, *The Prophetic Faith* (Torchbooks; New York: Harper, 1960), pp. 35 ff.

tive norms that distinguish each of those perspectives from the others. In that way, what were once prophetic insights become hardened into mere speculative and moral prejudices.[10] Unless they contain some inherent safeguard against it, our philosophies and our religious institutions are only extensions of our egos through which we try to possess our worlds, our selves, and (alas) our fellowmen—only to lose that knowledge of ourselves, the intimate self-awareness and sense of responsibility, which is essential to an authentic humanity.

It is important for scholars *as* scholars, and for religious individuals as *truly* religious, to keep this constantly in mind. For the concept of a pluralistic universe to which we have been led includes pluralistic possibilities of describing the deepest agony and the sublimest happiness that man is heir to. It is, for example, perfectly proper to describe an individual's transition, from a pervasive agony of despair to a general attitude of joy and peace, either in secular "atheistic" terminology or in the mythopoeic language of traditional religion. Although one of these forms of consciousness may lead an individual into more riches of spirit than the other, this is a question of fact that each individual must discover for himself, for no one else can legislate for him in such matters.

3. Authentic Existence and Religious Salvation

Although Sartre is more effective than Heidegger at describing the despair of "fallen" and "inauthentic" man, it is Heidegger who has given us the better description of "atheistic" conversion from inauthentic to authentic existence. Much more clearly than Sartre, Heidegger believes in the

---

[10] Bergson, *Two Sources* . . . , Chap. 3.

169

possibility of authentic existence. His description of the human condition explicitly includes an account of salvation that avoids the use of the word "God" and makes one think of Bonhoeffer's suggestion that this word be avoided in a world "come of age." [11]

Heidegger's discussion of salvation begins with the recognition and acceptance of the "nothingness" of human consciousness of which both he and Sartre have labored to make us aware. Being the hollow man that I described in my second chapter, fallen and inauthentic man tries in vain to identify himself with his ego and with other objects in the world. He is, thus, "scattered" and filled with concern for things over which he has no ultimate control. His values are conventional; he is in bondage to the world. Only his own death can free him from this plight, it would seem. Yet he flees from that ultimate oblivion, and his pervasive anxiety is in fact an amorphous sense of his own personal finitude. He longs for joy and peace of mind in place of his uneasy emptiness, but they escape him. Nevertheless, as Heidegger sees it, there is hope in the pit of this sort of despair. If one's inauthentic pretence of security and one's boast of being at home in the world are shattered, conscience may show one the way to "salvation." [12]

According to Heidegger, the authentic hearing of con-

---

[11] See Dietrich Bonhoeffer, *Letters and Papers from Prison*, ed. Eberhard Bethge, trans. R. H. Fuller (New York: Macmillan [1953]; Paperback ed., 1962), pp. 95-96, 165. We are not forgetting Bonhoeffer's criticisms of liberal theology, particularly of such existentialistic efforts as we find in Bultmann's adaptation of Heidegger to Christian theology, see *ibid.*, pp. 167, 195, 211 *et passim;* but Heidegger's conception of *dasein* is not a traditional conception of man, nor even of *homo religiosus.* Like Bonhoeffer himself (*ibid.*, p. 165), Heidegger points to a mystery at the "center" of the world, and it is worth noticing that despite Bonhoeffer's criticism of liberal theology he wanted to incorporate some of its insights into his own "modern" theology. *Ibid.*, p. 235.

[12] Heidegger, *Being and Time*, pp. 312-48.

170

science is always heard as a call to guiltiness. The first step on the way from inauthentic existence to a new beginning—to possible authentic existence—is to acknowledge one's own absolute responsibility for (one's free choice of) one's fallen condition, even though, in one obvious sense, one has not yet possessed the power to avoid it. Thus (to lapse into Sartre's phraseology) one's inauthentic existence starts as a "spontaneous upsurge" of which one is not fully conscious, not self-conscious, until (as Heidegger puts it) one hears the *authentic* call of conscience. This is a call to admit one's total responsibility for—i.e., to see oneself as the sole cause of—one's inauthentic life of despair. The propriety or impropriety of this paradoxical description of human existence (that one is helpless and yet wakes to oneself as totally responsible) can be determined only by making the painful descent into one's own existence that the existentialists call for, beneath the surface of conventional self-deceit. Then, according to Heidegger, the authentic hearing of conscience will occur in the penitent as an unhappy consciousness. This is not the same as the conscience of fallen man, the "mass man," whose conscience is *utterly* conditioned by conventional morality. It is a new and revolutionary call that is already the first step in the direction of authentic existence.[13]

Authentic hearing of the call of conscience is defined, according to Heidegger, by authentic action—action that one undertakes as the sole originator of one's acts, in full conscious responsibility. Such freedom involves: first, a deliberate revolt against the tyranny of the crowd; second, a commitment to one's resurrected conscience; third, a resolve to live *for*, not in flight from, one's own individual death.[14] As a primitive king did when he acknowledged his *moira* and

13 *Ibid.*, pp. 317, 322 ff.
14 *Ibid.*, pp. 349-58; cf., John Macquarrie, *An Extentialist Theology* Chap. 6,

ritually sacrificed himself that others might live more abundantly according to the myth—plunging the knife in himself and founding his whole life on this last grand act of freedom—so may we choose our own deaths, each as a separate individual, and by "living toward death" be freed from the tyranny of the world.

Heidegger's thought is helpful to the contemporary religious thinker at this point. We too, it should be noticed, may accept our *moira* in both ritual enactment and historical deed. We may turn the king's blade on ourselves only in dramatic imagination, but we can nevertheless involve ourselves as he did in both mythopoeic and historical existence. We may do so by allowing each aspect of our lives (the religious and the secular) to be a commentary on the other, waiting for both perspectives to intersect within ourselves as authentic individuals. Then, not by the depth of a blade but rather by the profundity of our acceptance of our individual finiteness, each of our lives may be given that others may live more abundantly. Although priestly immolation is a symbol for them all, there are other forms of sacrifice than ritual death. There is, for instance, really selfless service that expresses the essence of both traditional religion and the contemporary existentialist ethic; there are acts that express existential "commitment" as well as "divine love."

Heidegger does not concern himself with the preservation of any particular form of religious expression, but in his unorthodox fashion he wishes to recall us once again to the chthonian wisdom of the old myths. Thus, for example, by "living toward death" one lets go of neurotic anxiety and opens to life within the limitations of one's own situation in the world. One becomes the king of a domain that is, for the first time, one's own. The individual, returning from his flight from death, like an heir who flees the responsibility of his inheritance before accepting it, is surprised by joy; he

172

enters an abundance of life that Heidegger carefully distinguishes from mere indifference to the world. The individual is now free, we may assume, really to love the world unselfishly—free, for example, to love his neighbor by helping to liberate him from the tyranny of "mass man," that Egyptian bondage which we all impose on each other in our inauthentic relationships. We can, so to speak, transfigure the Look in our eyes that Sartre describes with horror, and, like mirrors that have been miraculously resilvered with a different kind of light, reflect an image of the other, to the other, of the freedom we now enjoy in our inmost subjectivity.

It is just as foolish for religious commentators to disparage the possibility of such occurrences outside the context of formal theism as it is for rabidly atheistic commentators to disparage the actual occurrence of "grace" (Christianity) or "divine mercy" (Judaism). In either case, the occurrence of conversion is a matter to be determined phenomenologically, and such firsthand testimony as we have strongly suggests that it occurs in both atheistic and theistic contexts. Atheism has its saints as does theism, and only the deaf and blind in our culture must keep debating such feckless conundrums as the problem of the existence of God, as though divine immanence and transcendence were any more paradoxical in conception, or any less obvious phenomenologically, than, as Sartre puts it, the "being" of man conjoined with his simultaneous and puzzling "nothingness," or, as Heidegger expresses it, the "being-in-the-world" of man (*Dasein*) coupled with his "being-alongside-the-world." [15] The language of religious myth and traditional biblical theology has had an enormous moral effect on individuals and communi-

[15] Heidegger, *Being and Time*, pp. 415 ff.; Sartre, *The Transcendence of the Ego*, pp. 93, 98 ff.

ties that have used that language in the past, and it has also had an uncanny semantical reference for them; nevertheless, in principle, it is possible to say essentially the same things in a style that is vastly different in form from that of biblical faith, and it is possible that such a seemingly nonreligious (even "irreligious") restatement may be closer to the spirit of biblical revelation than the relatively ossified expression of conventional religious institutions and conventional religious thought. It is important for us to remember that biblical faith is not necessarily identical with—in fact, it is apparently often lost from—the "theism" and "religious philosophy" that has been developed by various schools of theology. Thus, once we accustom ourselves to defining biblical testimony phenomenologically, by reference to our own intimate experience of personal existence, then we will appreciate the fact that the Bible has something of importance to say to contemporary men, whether or not they call themselves "theists" or "atheists," "religious" or "nonreligious." Take the lesson of Ecclesiastes as an example.

The author of Ecclesiastes, *Koheleth* (in Hebrew), provides us with as passionate an expression of the vanity of human existence as does any contemporary existentialist, and yet Koheleth celebrates life. No one has written more poignantly of man's desire to be God, of man's hunger to possess the world and live forever, than has Koheleth; and no existentialist is more convinced of the nothingness of man and of the vanity of every man's hope to save himself without giving up any of his pride or ego. No one, it seems, has wanted more to possess wisdom, to possess the good life; and apparently no man has been more bitterly disillusioned with what passes for wisdom than Koheleth, or has known better than he that human existence is absurd. Nevertheless, out of Koheleth's despair comes a magnificent paean to the excellence of wisdom and the intrinsic goodness of human life: "Cast your bread upon the waters, for you will find it after many days" (Ecclesiastes 11:1).[16]

Paradoxically, it is only when the preacher sees that what he had sought as wisdom is vanity, it is only when he accepts that fact without resentment, that he experiences the quality of religious wisdom that is not in vain. What is revealed to Koheleth, after he has written that "there is nothing new under the sun," is the same as that which is revealed to the author of the Book of Revelation: "Behold, I make all things new" (Revelation 21:5). Koheleth continues to affirm that "all that comes is vanity," but his values are no longer those of the mass man. Thus, the final wisdom of Ecclesiastes is a classic description of authentic existence in the context of religious faith.

> For if a man lives many years, let him rejoice in them all; but let him remember that the days of darkness will be many. All that comes is vanity.
>
> Rejoice, O young man in your youth, and let your heart cheer you in the days of your youth; walk in the ways of your heart and the sight of your eyes. But know that for all these things God will bring you into judgment. (Ecclesiastes 11:8-9.)

The author of Ecclesiastes knows from personal experience that a man can have wealth, honor, and wisdom of a sort, "yet God does not give him power to enjoy them" (Ecclesiastes 6:2). Nevertheless, Koheleth comes to know a wisdom that "makes his face to shine, and the hardness of his countenance is changed" (Ecclesiastes 8:1). The remarkable fact is that this change is effected only when he no longer tries vainly to possess that wisdom, or to possess himself, or even to pos-

[16] See, also, Ecclesiastes 11:1-10.

sess his "possessions." Speaking existentially—since we have now left theory and illusion behind—the good life (religious wisdom) is a matter not of possessing, but of letting go; a matter not of getting, but of giving; a matter not of receiving justice, but of rendering it. "No man has power to retain the spirit, or authority over the day of death," says Koheleth. "There is no discharge from war, nor will wickedness deliver those who are given to it. . . . Man lords it over man to his hurt" (Ecclesiastes 8:8).

The difference that one student of Koheleth, Robert Gordis, claims to see between Job's discovery (according to Gordis) that the world "was a rational and just world-order, though on a scale incomprehensible to man," and Koheleth's "tragic realization" (according to the same commentator) "that the all-inclusive Wisdom of the universe was also unattainable," does not seem to make a real, that is to say, a phenomenologically distinguishable difference.[17] The contrast between an alleged "world-order" that is nevertheless "incomprehensible to man" and an "all-inclusive Wisdom" that is "also unattainable" seems to be purely verbal. Rather, it seems to me that although there are obvious differences between Koheleth's story and Job's, nevertheless those two authors walked parallel roads to arrive at much the same destination. Koheleth's final wisdom, like Job's, is a para-doxical solution to the question that Job asks for all of us— and that he punctuates with a suggestion that is mindful of Heidegger's "living toward death."

> "Whence then comes wisdom?
> And where is the place of understanding?
> It is hid from the eyes of the living,
>   and concealed from the birds of the air.

[17] Robert Gordis, *Koheleth—The Man and His World* (New York: The Jewish Theological Seminary of America, 1951), p. 82.

Abaddon and Death say,
'We have heard a rumor of it with our ears.' "

(Job 28:20-22)

It is probable that this passage is a relatively late addition to an earlier version of the Book of Job. But even if we cannot totally ignore questions of textual provenance, they are not central in our attempt to understand the religious sense of that book as it now stands. The understanding of Job that I am advancing is one that can be recommended on several grounds. It conforms to my treatment of the theological problem of evil in Chapter I, and, indeed, it is an interpretation of Job that is supported by the exegesis that Moses Maimonides advanced in the thirteenth century.[18] It is a reading that makes the best philosophical and religious sense of that book, and it is still exegetically defensible in the light of modern scholarship.[19] Maimonides calls our attention to the fact that, in spite of Job's conventional virtues and fine character, wisdom is not ascribed to him in the beginning of that story. Wisdom is a quality of human existence that he does not attain until the end. In the beginning, Job's values are those of inauthentic man in every age and station. In the midst of his misfortunes, Job thinks that he deserves better than he gets, and, indeed, according to every canon of rational justice, he does. But life is not the creation of a system-builder, as Job eventually learns; and although a religious person may mistakenly suppose that he is seeking a super-philosophy, he is not. Nor, as a person who acknowledges the sovereignty of God, is he seeking a way to avoid the human condition as such. Indeed, the passion to be God is

[18] Moses Maimonides, *The Guide for the Perplexed* (New York: Dover, 1956), Chaps. 22-23.
[19] See H. Joel Laks, "The Enigma of Job: Maimonides and the Moderns," *Journal of Biblical Literature*, LXXXIII (Dec., 1964), 345-64.

man's primary sin. What the religious man recognizes as the Truth, when he turns to it, is to be reconciled with what he is, with what he has or will have, and with what he must endure if human existence is (what it seems to be in the light of rational standards) a tragedy—a moment in the sun. Thus, for example, Maimonides describes Job as one who is searching for religious Truth, but Maimonides argues that it is Elihu—philosophically the shallowest of Job's advisers—who ultimately prepares him for his encounter with God in the whirlwind. Then, paradoxically, in that dreadful encounter —while witnessing a response to his questions that is completely inadequate philosophically—Job is filled with the wisdom that passes all conceptual understanding.

"He was without wisdom," writes Maimonides, "and knew God only by tradition, in the same manner as religious people generally know him. As soon as he had acquired a true knowledge of God, he confessed . . . felicity . . . and no earthly trouble can disturb it." [20] We must not confuse conventional knowledge with wisdom, says Maimonides, for "the pious do everything out of love and rejoice in their own afflictions." [21] In its phenomenological purity, what Job discovered—the "object" of the intuition to which Maimonides directs our attention—is the same as that which prompted Paul's magnificent paean to love (Paul's "more excellent way"), which is described in I Corinthians 13: "If I speak in the tongues of men and of angels, but have not love, I am a noisy gong or clanging cymbal. And if I have . . . all knowledge . . . but have not love, I am nothing" (vss. 1-2).

The point is not, of course, to make a sentimental defense of suffering. Pain of any sort is some kind of evil. The purpose of Job's story, according to Maimonides, is to show that divine wisdom is not so much like the knowledge of philos-

[20] Maimonides, *The Guide for the Perplexed*, pp. 297-300.
[21] *Ibid.*, p. 303.

ophers and practical men as it is like falling unaccountably in love. The story of Job describes a representative man's "miraculous deliverance" from a life of spiritual death to a love of spirited life in the midst of pain and tragedy. In the end, Job suffers the sort of upset and transvaluation of values that I have compared with certain aspects of our common experiencing of witticisms and puns, and with the sort of whirlwind that Heidegger describes as the authentic hearing of conscience. "In modern terms," says a twentieth-century commentator on Maimonides and Job, "rendered in the patois of the existentialist, pain may be viewed as the sense of nausea, manifested by aimless insignificant, purpose less existence."

It is the veritable mask of Cain, stamped on human existence, the consciousness of an everwidening gulf of guilt and despair. There is the quality of morose incapacity to confront oneself and honor one's Creator. It is only in the felt presence of the Divine that the sense of liberation, of true realization of human potentiality, is experienced. . . . Ultimately, it is the way of life of a person, his perceptiveness of God and enjoyment of the blessed state, that constitutes the evidence of good or evil.[22]

The result of Job's casuistical attempt to understand the meaning of life is that he found what he did not expect: no philosophical answer—and that, "answer" enough, existentially. The answer to the problem of evil in the Book of Job is not a new cosmogony, but a "new being" in Job. The religious miracle that is expressed but never explicitly mentioned in that miracle story is that his despair led him not to some form of theological self-deception, nor to ultimate hatred of life and to suicide. He did not take his wife's advice to "curse God and die" (Job 2:9). Nor did he develop a

[22] Laks, "The Enigma of Job," pp. 362-64.

philosophical theology to hide what he had discovered. Instead, he stumbled into wisdom as the equivalent of love in the face of moral and theological absurdity.

Both Job and Koheleth discover the ironical truth contained in at least one of the remarks that Job's "comforters" make: "He delivers the afflicted by their affliction, and opens their ears by adversity" (Job 36:15). Thus, Koheleth also comes to see that the vanity of his existence is due to his loving the world, his neighbor, and himself not too much, but too little—too little to have their mere existence (and his own) worth the passion and death that is the intrinsic cost of human life. "So I hated life," he says.

He comes to glory in it only after he has seen through it to the bottom—after he is stripped of illusion and is able to accept his own existence and death responsibly for the first time. In that moment he valorizes all he encounters by the care he bestows on its evanescent flowering—giving it infinite value in the light of his passion and the eventual price of his own senescence and death. What he discovers is that without such love lavished on what must die, by one who must die himself, the world is valueless at best, and at worst is hateful. What he discovers is a reason to live and a reason to die—and that reason is his philosophically unjustified love. It is not a theory he discovers, nor an explanation—not a "philosophy of life" in the usual sense—but a state of being. It is a value that the world acquires as an immediate consequence of his own tragic payment for it. It is (in terms of the myth) God's miraculous redemption of the world in him, the establishment, now, of the kingdom of God in the heart of an existing individual.

It is noteworthy that Koheleth's salvation is not mere Cyrenaicism; it is not "eat, drink, and be merry, for tomorrow we die." It is deeply faithful to the mythopoeic Judaic awareness of God and trust in his promises. Koheleth's final wisdom is a typically religious attitude. There is a mystery in existence that inspires his fear and reverence. Even the power to enjoy life, which he eventually experiences, is treated as a mysterious gift. Thus, Koheleth becomes a lover, and not a cynic; a bestower, rather than a proud possessor; and the world wears the colors of his love. But, to use a mythopoeic mode of speaking, that love is not his own accomplishment.[23]

Koheleth and Job are brought from the common morality of fallen man, of mass man, to full religious consciousness —that is to say, to authentic existence. They do this by experiencing the call of consience that Heidegger describes and by answering that call authentically in what Sartre calls a "spontaneous upsurge." They turn (teshuvah) or are converted (metanoia) from the despair (sin) of inauthentic existence. And how we shall describe or explain this conversion, whether mythopoeically in terms of Judaism or Christianity, or phenomenologically in terms of existential philosophy, is also the result of a spontaneous upsurge or of "prophecy," depending on how one chooses to speak.

4. Morality and Myth

Judaism and Christianity have each two basic and parallel components. Each of these religions is, first of all, a mythic description or series of descriptions of the damnation and salvation of man. And the central myths of both Judaism and Christianity involve historical facts. There are Exodus and Calvary, for example, and there are all the soteriological events—some of them partly rooted in history and others almost entirely founded in cultic imagination—that tell a story of man's deliverance from bondage to his own sinful

[23] Cf. H. Louis Ginsberg, *Studies in Koheleth* (New York: The Jewish Theological Seminary of America, 1950), pp. 3-4; Gordis, *Koheleth—The Man and His World*, pp. 136-88.

self. Both Judaism and Christianity involve myths, elaborate examples of what Jews call *Aggadah*, stories of God's mighty acts on earth, which men are invited to enact and re-enact liturgically. Each religious community repeats and repeats its myths to itself, in words, in dramatic actions, in dance and in song. In religious calendars myth has the temporal shape of the changing seasons, but each week, each day, and each liturgical celebration reiterates the same story, like identical narrative wheels that are turning inside of one another. A single gesture may tell the whole story to someone who can read it, like a précis of the spiritual history of mankind, and the drama of the whole year repeats the same action in slow motion.

Second, each religion involves a moral discipline or law, which, in the context of the rabbinical tradition, Jews call *Halacha*. Each community is an ethical community defined by rules that go beyond cult practices to determine the manner of the members' behavior with one another and with the rest of God's creatures. In this respect, the Judeo-Christian tradition may be viewed as a cultural evolution of various systems of conduct, each of which is intended to engraft the members of its community into the saving event (Exodus or Calvary) that, in the deepest sense of community, is humanity itself and the divine life. For example, both Jacob (Israel) and Christ (the new Israel of Christians) are archetypes of—mythopoeically identifiable as—the very communities that are founded in them (Genesis 35:9-12; Romans 11: 1-12; Hebrews 12:5-8).

The total phenomenon of every nonidolatrous religion includes a myth for man to enter imaginatively, and a disciplined way of life that is the pragmatic definition of the myth but that does not exhaust its indefinite plural significance. The saving event of every religion is thus a complex phenomenon in which ontological insight and moral discipline, the community and the individual, God and man, time and eternity are all imaginatively constituted as elements of each other. Recognizing the metastable nature, in every isolated individual, of his ontological awareness and moral resolve, cultic observances and moral laws are designed by a religious society to hold its members to a course. Their lives are held to a path, like a pendulum swing, that takes them again and again through certain cultic practices and ethical actions in which insight and commitment may be repeatedly renewed. As a string becomes a candle by being re-repeatedly dipped in wax, so individuals in a "saving community" may be transformed by a rule of life that is calculated to enlarge them in heart as well as mind. Traditional religions have developed rules of cultic and practical life because the spirit of God is not only an object of revelation *in* man, but an act *of* man. All forms of Judaism and Christianity are so many ways of life. There are the various communities of Torah and the various communities of Christ.

Christian and Jewish religious communities have to develop rules of one sort or another to cope with the shifting and meandering course of human life. But such communities will be true to their essential character only if they refuse to absolutize any but the one ambiguous moral precept of the Judeo-Christian tradition. That precept carries religious morality beyond the area of casuistry—where pride and prejudice flourish—into the center of religious (authentic) morality where men can never presume to be righteous. This fact is illustrated for both Jews and Christians in the Gospel according to Mark, and again in Matthew, by the answer spoken from the heart of Torah that Jesus declared to be the supreme commandment of the Law.

"The first is, 'Hear, O Israel: The Lord Our God, the Lord is one; and you shall love the Lord your God with all your heart, and with

all your soul, and with all your mind, and with all your strength.'
The second is this, 'You shall love your neighbor as yourself.'
There is no other commandment greater than these." (Mark 12:
29-31.)[24]

In these commandments the letter of the Law and the
spirit of the Myth flow together in a punlike confluence.
This flowing together of morality and myth expresses the
essence of both Jewish and Christian ethics; it is also repeated
constantly as an important element in the cultic practices
of both communities. Jesus' answer—the central confession
(the *Shema*) of synagogue worship, and an essential element
in the Roman and Eastern Orthodox Masses, as well as of
many Protestant services—is the supreme moral imperative
for all Jews and Christians: the primary mythico-moral law
that determines the religious worth of all other laws. Judaism
and Christianity, in all their forms, are merely pragmatic
and inspired elaborations of the "law of love"—or violations
of it. "Thou shalt love," the members of those religious communities are told, not merely by observing the rules of justice
that society develops, but in a way that addresses the other,
the neighbor, as the personification of infinite worth, the very
person whose story is told by the myth and enacted by the
cult.

If we do not confuse the supreme value of the primary
law with derivative value of all lesser moral laws—if we do
not allow ourselves to become self-righteous or compulsive
exponents of some casuistical system—then, in our own responsible and anguished decisions, we will always be faced
with the problem of translating the law of love into everyday
action. Even the most inauthentic and mechanical interpre-
ters of their faith cannot entirely escape this necessity, nor

[24] Cf. Deuteronomy 6:4; Matthew 22:37-40; Luke 10:27.

184

can the most antinomian. No amount of casuistry can be specific enough to eradicate all the mental and emotional distress involved in deciding, in one exigency after the other, exactly how one can best enact one's love of God and neighbor. Nor can one love responsibly by ignoring moral principles altogether.

We should notice, first, that the more detailed our rules become, the more they tend to replace the inwardness of love with the superficiality of moralistic zeal. Thus, Christian casuistry has earned an unpleasant reputation, and a parallel zeal in Judaism has often caused it to be written off as "legalistic." Second, we will gradually discover that human existence is so complex that it is frequently impossible to avoid using some persons as means or tools to acquire the ends we project. We depersonalize our neighbors and ourselves even when we are strenuously trying to respond to the voice of conscience authentically. We exist as "fallen" in both the atheistic and theistic senses, and it *may* be that, in fact, only a *religious* miracle—the continuous re-enactment in us of a redemptive myth—can wash away the guilt of our awakened consciences. In any case, it is up to each awakening individual to decide whether or not he will do without the help of traditional religious practice and instruction.

Inasmuch as the concepts of murder, adultery, stealing, lying, and so on are so far from simple (since they are each ambiguously involved with all sorts of other moral conceptions and qualifications) and because the skein of human life is such a tangle of conscious and unconscious intentions and consequences, not one of us can even begin to keep the moral law in its purity. Indeed, our moral ideals are so vague, our ideas so inconsistent that it is impossible to say with confidence that religious morality, that the "pure heart" is possible even in principle. Certainly, try as they may to avoid it, both Jews and Christians are always guilty of breaking

185

their most basic moral law. Human life is a moral dilemma, and for the awakened conscience it often seems that there is no practical way out of despair except to go back to sleep, or to scatter oneself in the distractions of the "rat race," or— by turning to one's religious tradition—to invite the liturgical salvation of myth.

Note well that a truly religious person can never be self-righteous. Furthermore, his need for forgiveness (his sense of sin) is not unrealistic, merely neurotic or foolish. Whatever rectitude he may have in the public eye, whatever approbation he may win from mass man, he knows that his person is at best a snarl of good and evil. Anyone who has seen past the surface of human life may experience a miraculous deliverance from the pit, but he will also encompass a profound sense of his own human iniquity. "There is the phenomenon of feeling guilt for something that one has done or thought or felt or for a disposition that one has," says Norman Malcolm. "One wants to be free of this guilt. But sometimes the guilt is felt to be so great that one is sure that nothing one could do oneself, nor any forgiveness by another human being would remove it."

One feels a guilt that is beyond all measure, a guilt "a greater than which cannot be conceived." Paradoxically, it would seem, one nevertheless has an intense desire to have this incomparable guilt removed. One requires a forgiveness that is beyond all measure, a forgiveness "a greater than which cannot be conceived." Out of such a storm in the soul, I am suggesting, there arises the conception of a forgiving mercy that is limitless, beyond all measure. This is one important feature of the Jewish and Christian conception of God. . . . One may think it absurd for a human being to feel a guilt of such magnitude, and even more absurd that, if he feels it, he should *desire* its removal. I have nothing to say about that. It may also be absurd for people to fall in love, but they do it. I wish only to say that there *is* that human phenomenon of an unbearably heavy conscience and that it is importantly connected with the genesis of the concept of God, that is, with the formation of the "grammar" of the word "God." I am sure that this concept is related to human experience in other ways. If one had the acuteness and depth to perceive these connections one could grasp the *sense* of the concept. When we encounter this concept as a problem in philosophy, we do not consider the human phenomena that lie behind it.[25]

These remarks summarize several of the points I have been trying to establish in this chapter. They illuminate the fact that, in morals as in speculative reasoning, no discipline could be more conducive to liberal-mindedness than religion when it remains true to its prophetic beginnings. In the sphere of moral action as in the area of contemplative vision —since it arises as a prophetic expression of authentic existence—religious testimony cannot free itself from self-contradiction and ambiguity. No philosophy of life can be more hostile to parochialism in education and morals than prophetic religion is, while nevertheless being free to appreciate the truth expressed by every narrower view and less reflective behavior. The regular practice of one or another of the historical forms of Judaism or Christianity should make us fanatic in the defense of freedom of thought and action in others as well as in ourselves. The influence of traditional religious discipline on one's daily life will usually be indirect and unconscious, but it should nevertheless inculcate two liberating dogmas: first, that no tongue, no matter how correctly it speaks within its tiny province, speaks a privileged grammar of truth; and second, that no human being can justifiably claim to be the moral superior of any other, except on the relatively superficial level of public morality where an

[25] Norman Malcolm, "Anselm's Ontological Arguments," *The Philosophical Review*, LXIX (Jan., 1960), 60-61.

individual's subjective relation to the supreme moral law cannot be observed.

Life forces us to judge the *actions* of people according to practical moral principles; in this context we cannot reasonably equate a Hitler and an Albert Schweitzer, for example. But, whoever is acutely aware of the logical disorder of his moral principles and the conflicting motivations of his commitments and behavior will have neither rational nor psychological cause to judge *people*. We must punish and reward individuals in order to alter their characters in a practical sense, but this is not the same as judging their persons. In the workaday world, we must treat people *as if* they were nothing but their public actions, but this only re-emphasizes a point I have already made: that human life is a moral dilemma and that all men are guilty of violating the sanctuary of the human spirit. Traditional religion and contemporary existentialism have tried to make us aware and keep us aware of these facts.

In theory, all nonidolatrous expressions (all authentic expressions) of self-knowledge are on the same footing, whether they are theistic or atheistic. Dispassionately considered, no one of these expressions is phenomenologically superior to the others. In practice, of course, they may constitute very different sorts of options for the existing individual. Traditional religious expressions will strike some people dumb while giving tongue to others; the jargon of contemporary existentialism will be a barrier to one and a way in for the next. Thus, if traditional religious myths have died (if God is dead in that sense) then those who have let him die, and feel the loss, will have to animate the language of existentialism or of art or of some new cult with authentic existence —or remain forlorn. The alternative would be that modern man would come to understand the essential nature of religious myth and be able once again to enter one, not unreflectingly as did primitive man, but now as a completely responsible person engaged in a thoroughly free and deliberate act. Then, once again putting on the mask of the Son of man, or once again binding the frontlets to his forehead, men might continue to eat the flesh and drink the blood of the Eternal Word, or enshrine within themselves the Everlasting Spirit of the Law.

Whoever comes to know "grace" or "mercy" in this fashion will experience what might be called an imaginative encounter, as a person does who is taken up in the life of a poem; but this does not make the object of his intuition unreal—nor does it guarantee that we can each be successful. If we choose to enter the traditional Word of God, we must cast our bread upon the waters (waiting empty, as Koheleth did, is part of the salvation drama also), but unless we sincerely put on the action of cultic behavior we may never encounter the untrammeled spirit that animates the "saving community." Even if we are taken up, it will be by surprise from a direction we had not at all or not completely expected; for the Word must always be ambiguous—leading and misleading —self-contradictory or, in some way, self-defeating.

At the end of the *Tractatus Logico-Philosophicus*, Wittgenstein makes a remark about the significance of his work that might also be used to describe the function of traditional religious language. "My propositions are elucidatory in this way," says Wittgenstein, "he who understands me finally recognizes them as senseless, when he has climbed out through them, on them, over them. (He must so to speak throw away the ladder, after he has climbed up on it.) . . . He must surmount these propositions; then he sees the world rightly." [26]

The same sort of thing can be said about the prophetic

[26] Ludwig Wittgenstein, *Tractatus Logico-Philosophicus* (New York: Harcourt Brace & World, 1922), par. 6.541.

utterances and theological elaborations of Jews and Christians. If a Jew comes to understand Torah, he will, in a sense, have risen above it and can then throw it away. This is what happened to Paul, but it also accounts for the antinomian lightheartedness of Martin Buber's deeply Jewish piety. Likewise, when Christians come to understand Christ they will no longer need to cling to him as, literally, the only way to the Truth.[27] This, among other things, is what the so-called death of God theologians have discovered. The meaning of the Law and the Prophets (which is fulfilled in Christ, for Christians) is self-destructive: it transcends the language and the historical events in which it occurs, like the meaning of a witticism; and whoever understands it has himself been raised above the things that evoked his laughter. But who can laugh without provocation? Who can enter the spirit without the word?

Human existence is described by existentialists as a lived relationship of a very special sort, a kind of symbiotic union of brute phenomena, human consciousness, and the language of interpretation. In this context, "authentic" existence is characterized by its wide-awake and deliberate acceptance of the creative responsibility that this symbiotic union of man-word-and-world places upon each human individual. "Inauthentic" existence is characterized by a deliberate or unreflective refusal to accept such total responsibility. Thus, the authentic individual must (1) accept responsibility for what he has made of himself and his world in the *past*, attending the call of conscience and acknowledging his guilty choice of one inauthentic mode of life after another in his past performance. He must (2) accept the *present* moment as a moment of portentous decision, as the instant of choos-

---

[27] The same point is being made today even by some Roman Catholic theologians. See, for example, Karl Rahner, *The Christian of the Future* (New York: Herder and Herder, 1967), pp. 94 ff.

ing his future self and future world from the limitless number of possibilities that every moment presents to a man within the overall historical situation into which he has been thrown. He must also (3) acknowledge his *future* self and future world, now, as the particular lived relationship that he is presently projecting, and—if he is really determined to find the paradoxical self-possession and wholeness that characterizes authentic existence (and religious wisdom)—he must choose his own death now (let it come when it may) as the final act of his life, as the price he freely pays for his time in the sun.

Traditional religions each have their idiosyncratic ways of describing authentic existence and the passage to it from everyday inauthentic life and its repressed despair. Authentic existence is described mythopoeically, in Judaism, as a lived relationship between God, man, and Torah;[28] it is expressed in the drama of Christian salvation as a lived relationship between God, man, and Logos.[29] The differences between these ways of speaking are not unimportant. Different modes of discourse affect us differently and lead us toward different experiences and nuances of understanding. But there seems to be no way of recommending one mode of discourse above another without foolishly prejudging the question of religious truth, or falling into the mistake of treating essentially punlike and witty language as though it were a collection of fairly prosaic assertions. One must struggle to hold oneself to one's own mode of authentic existence, for if one is not content to lose himself inauthentically, vainly

[28] We may think of the scroll that Ezekiel was commanded to chew and digest, before he could proclaim the Word of God to the People of the Book, as Torah (Ezekiel 2:7-10; 3:1-4), and we may think of Torah as Israel's God-given wisdom (Deuteronomy 4:6-8); cf. Jeremiah 31:33-34.

[29] John 1:1-5; 14:14-27; 21:1-19. In Christianity, Jesus is accepted as the ultimate value of Torah, the "fulfillment of the Law and the Prophets" which is present whenever the Lord's Supper is celebrated.

trying to flee from responsibility and death, vainly trying to be God instead of man, one's way of talking must be deliberately sustained as an act of creative freedom and self-determination. The authentic individual must be a poet of a sort, as Heidegger suggests[30]—he must be a person who speaks the creative word responsibly, as though he were interpreting the world for the first time—a sort of prophet who heralds his own symbiotic union of man-word-and-world in which he himself will come to live and die.

[30] Heidegger *Existence and Being*, ed. with introduction by Werner Brock (Chicago: Regnery, 1949), pp. 293-351; also by the same author, *An Introduction to Metaphysics*, trans. Ralph Manheim (Anchor Books; Garden City, N.Y.: Doubleday, 1961), pp. 143-44, 155-56.

Myth and language are subject to the same,
or at least closely analogous, laws of evolution. . . .
For, no matter how widely the contents of myth and language
may differ, yet the same form of
mental conception is operative in both.

ERNEST CASSIRER, *Language and Myth*

CHAPTER VI

PROPHECY, THEOLOGY, AND PHILOSOPHY

1. *Their Symbiotic Relationship*

By describing the relationship between prophecy, theology, and philosophy as symbiotic I wish to illuminate three phenomenologically ascertainable facts: first, that traditional Western concepts of God and man are mutually related and help both to define one another in theology and to sustain one another in fact; second, that this is nowhere more apparent than in the way prophecy, theology, and philosophy are essentially and existentially involved in one another in our culture; and, third, that this mutual involvement is intimately related to the symbiotic relationship of man-word-and-world that we were discussing in the preceding chapter.

The idea of a symbiotic relationship is, in its literal sense, a biological conception that connotes such mutually dependent accommodations between living things as that which exists between the heart and the lungs of a living animal.

In a symbiotic relationship each organ or organism related is a necessary living aspect of every other thing in that relation. They are mutually dependent on each other for their concrete existence. This is the sort of thing I am saying in this chapter about prophecy, theology, and philosophy when I describe their relationship as "symbiotic." They are, in a way, *living* (symbiotic) aspects of one another.

Previously in this book, I have occasionally used another word—"semiotic." This word connotes a semantical or logical, not a biological, conception. It refers to the way signs and symbols are logically related to one another in order to make meaningful wholes. But the very existence of semiotic (or semantic) elements in a significant situation will also involve a sort of symbiotic (existential or living) interrelationship between various constituents of that total meaning. Every significant situation is a merging of logic and life in a way that is relevant to our present discussion. There is a meaningful aspect to every human situation, a sort of semiotic (logical and semantic) character in every event, that will also be involved in our discussion of prophecy, theology, and philosophy. They are *logical* aspects of one another.

Furthermore, now that we have compared and contrasted religious language with certain other forms of discourse—to witticism, puns, poetry, and drama, for example—still another purpose of this chapter is to show that religious language is really related, in many ways, to every kind of symbolic activity. Every use of signs is, in an important sense, religious. "Religious language" is not a category of speech, or category of behavior or art, that can be neatly isolated from other sorts of signification. Human consciousness is an atmosphere of drifting fragrances and forms. It is not a nest of boxes. And, although the title of this chapter is made up of three labels, its contents flow together and seep into every other form of life. Many critics of "religion" lose sight of this fact. Consequently, they are not aware that the object of their criticism is similar to their own characteristic forms of consciousness, even with respect to the characteristics they find most objectionable in religion. Many champions of religion also forget that religion is not a pigeonhole distinct from ordinary life. And their defenses of religion often rudely emphasize a separation between the "sacred" and the "profane" that makes their conception of "religion" irrelevant to "practical" affairs. This, of course, does not mean that there is no good reason for distinguishing a Sabbath from a weekday. But they must also run together.

No three aspects of Western civilization are more important historically than those which are named in the title of this chapter. Taken together, they suggest the extent to which Western culture is a product of Judeo-Christian prophecy, classical Greek theology, and the general philosophical critique of traditional beliefs and attitudes that has accompanied the rise of modern science. Perhaps for that very reason prophecy, theology, and philosophy are also among the characteristics of our culture that are most misunderstood. Even scholars are generally ignorant of the fundamental natures of prophecy and theology; unaware of the profound nature of their involvement in traditional and contemporary philosophy; oblivious to the similarity of certain basic characteristics of prophecy, theology, and philosophy to parallel characteristics in every intelligent response to the brute intrusions of life. The more we can clarify our understanding of the three activities with which this chapter is concerned, the better we will comprehend certain ubiquitous characteristics of our culture that—perhaps because of their pervasiveness—often go unnoticed. If we can throw an especially penetrating light on the phenomenological characteristics of prophecy, theology, and philosophy, the same illumination will reveal certain important

195

family resemblances in all areas of creative innovation and in every mode of discourse.

Common nouns like "prophecy," "theology," and "philosophy" have many kinds of uses, and as many shades of meaning as different uses. This adds not only to our philosophical perplexities but also to the richness of our experience and the intellectual enlargement of our lives. Meanings of all sorts, in a palette profusion, are one of the chief riches —indeed, in a sense, the only value—of culture. So, if we do not wish to invent "clear and distinct ideas" as academically neat substitutes for the smear of overlapping concepts we are trying to see more clearly, we must focus our attention carefully on the kinds of activity and experience that our culture has called prophetic, theological, and philosophical. We will then find that these three kinds of activity and experience are as intimately related as, and no more clearly distinguishable from one another than, let us say, the ostensive meanings of such words as "blue," "green," and "yellow."

Imagine that each foot of a certain yardstick has been painted a different color: one blue, one green, and one yellow. The foot in the center is green—obviously green in the very middle, but shaded toward yellow in one direction and toward blue in the other. One extreme end of the stick is obviously yellow, the other just as plainly blue; yet both end sections blend into the green foot in the middle. When our eyes pass over the stick from left to right, we first see vivid blue, then (through imperceptible changes) greenish-blue, bluish-green, green, yellowish-green, and finally brilliant yellow. Now, if we take this yardstick figuratively as the measure of Western culture, the three feet in this yard as three aspects of that culture—prophecy (blue), theology (green), and philosophy (yellow)—we will have a fair analogue of the mutual interpenetration of these three activ-

196

ities. We will have a chromatic image of their symbiotic relationship.

When we study the histories of prophecy, theology, and philosophy we find that although it is usually easy to distinguish between prophets, theologians, and philosophers in a rather brash way, nevertheless it is never possible to say that any one of these vocations is entirely free of the most distinguishing charactcristics of each of the others. Even Moses was a philosophcr to some degree, as A. J. Ayer was to some extent a prophet. Examination shows that the sort of activity that accounts for the fame of either one of these men contains a small tincture of thc contrasting kind of activity, which accounts for the fame of the other. There is something of the prophet and theologian in every philosopher, something of the philosopher and theologian in every prophet, and something of both extremes in every theologian. Analogous to the green section of our yardstick, theology occupies a middle position bctwcen two fairly obvious extremes. Consequently, if we can highlight the distinguishing characteristics of these extremes and show how they are blended in the middle—how, in addition, each extreme soaks to the extreme reaches of the other—then we will have increased our understanding of the three cultural functions with which we are here expressly concerned. Moreover, we will have avoided the common mistake of prescinding each one from both of the others and then supposing that that is how they occur in life.

2. Prophecy

Philologists tell us that the English word "prophet" is derived from the Greek word "*prophetes*," which in turn is a translation of the Hebrew word "*nabi*," meaning "to speak for another." The prophets in the Jewish Bible spoke for the

197

Lord. "Thus says the Lord," they said, and their mouths were filled with the Word of God.[1] They were inspired by God's presence as their response to some event—the way they responded was itself the presence of God in their world—and the history of the religious community that was thus established has verified that response in the only possible and only appropriate way: in the religious life of the community that that Word established.

In this connection it is of vital importance to keep the ineradicably triadic character of any language, including the Word of God, in mind. I have already commented on this peculiarity of language several times, but it is of such central relevance to the present discussion that I will add this brief reminder: Whenever a meaning is revealed, some person must take something as a sign of something else. The *person* who takes the sign, the *sign* that is taken, and the *meaning* of that sign for that person are all symbiotically and semiotically related.[2] Every meaningful situation is a living sign or symbol. This is especially true of the symbols of religion, mythology, art, and folklore. But any meaningful occurrence (and what experience is not intelligible in some sense?) is, so to speak, a word (a sign) that is taken to have the meaning (the symbolic value) which that experience thus acquires for that interpreter. Circumstances may eventually force him to change his interpretation; but he cannot avoid interpreting the event, which intrudes on him, as some sort of sign. Every meaningful situation is a logical organism of which no part can be eliminated without simultaneously eliminating all the other parts of that particular event. That

---

[1] Cf. Martin Buber, *The Prophetic Faith* (New York: Harper, 1960), p. 57; also Exodus 4:11-12; I Samuel 3:19-20; Jeremiah 1:2, 9.

[2] Cf. Justus Buchler (ed.), *The Philosophical Writings of Peirce*, pp. 74-119. See also Martin Buber, *I and Thou*, pp. 3-4: 'Primary words do not describe something that might exist independently of them, but being spoken they bring about existence."

is why every actual meaning has more than a merely logical character: it has both a biological and spiritual *life* in the life of the host of that meaning. "Every sign *by itself* seems dead," said Wittgenstein. "*What* gives it life?—In use it is *alive.*" [3]

If we eliminate any one of the triadic elements of meaning —for instance, if we take away either the prophet or the historical event he interprets or the religious meaning that he takes that event to signify—then the other two elements of that meaning are likewise eradicated phenomenologically. Where one appears, all appear; and where one does not, none does. The Word of God unites both the world and the beloved community as logical and existential constituents in the being of God.[4] It is as senseless to talk about God in abstraction from his continuous revelation as it is to talk about the existence of physical objects abstracted from all actual and possible experiences of them. As, in the latter case, the term "physical object" would not make customary sense, so, in the former case, we would not be talking about God. We would not be talking about *the* God of the biblical prophets; and the God of whom we are speaking here is the God of that specific revelation: a peculiar, enormously complex, continuous historical fact and transcendental promise —the God of our fathers. Listen, for example, to the words of Jeremiah:

Now the word of the Lord came to me saying, "Before I formed you in the womb I knew you, and before you were born I consecrated you; I appointed you a prophet to the nations." Then I said, "Ah, Lord God! Behold, I do not know how to speak, for I am only a youth." But the Lord said to me, "Do not say, 'I am

[3] Ludwig Wittgenstein, *Philosophical Investigations*, p. 128; also pp. 132 ff.

[4] Cf. Josiah Royce, *The Problem of Christianity* (New York: Macmillan, 1913), Lectures 2 and 9-12.

199

only a youth'; for to all to whom I send you you shall go, and whatever I command you you shall speak. Be not afraid of them, for I am with you to deliver you, says the Lord." Then the Lord put forth his hand and touched my mouth; and the Lord said to me, "Behold, I have put my words in your mouth. See, I have set you this day over nations and over kingdoms, to pluck up and to break down, to destroy and to overthrow, to build and to plant."

. . . The word of the Lord came to me, saying, "Go and proclaim in the hearing of Jerusalem, Thus says the Lord. . . . Hear the word of the Lord, O house of Jacob, and all the families of the house of Israel. Thus says the Lord. (Jeremiah 1:4-10; 2:1-2, 4.)

Notice that the prophet's Word, the Word of God, is also the Word of the people who accept it. It is the myth in which they live. They became and have remained, however inconstantly, the "people of the Word." [5] Israel is described as Yahweh's bride, under him and filled with him.[6] God is *in* his Word, and his Word is in his people. It is this fact, for instance, which explains the Protestant Reformers' concern with the Word, both as a written testament and as the Spirit which, in the presence of faith, that testament contains.[7] God is both the form and the content of his people's experience when they keep his Word, and that mythopoeic experience includes their whole world and their own persons. In the biblical sense of prophecy, a prophet is anyone in whom some event is suddenly apprehended as "a mighty act of God," and who announces the presence of the Lord in that event. The event is now taken as a sign of God, and, accordingly, he comes to live in it as its fundamental meaning. His presence embraces both the sign and the prophet

[5] Exodus 20:1-20; 34:1-10; cf., also John 1:1-15.
[6] Hosea 2:16 ff.
[7] Cf. Dillenberger and Welch, *Protestant Christianity Interpreted Through Its Development*, pp. 45-53.

who takes up the sign in its sacred significance. Man and God are joined sacramentally in the sign, and the prophet has *mana*. The interpenetration of man and divine in this extraordinary manifestation of meaning and power has been much commented upon by students of anthropological linguistics.[8]

In the Judeo-Christian tradition, the absolute source of all worship and theology is prophecy—the spontaneous appearance of the myth. The life of the cult is rooted in a knowledge of God by direct acquaintance even though his "fullness" is never revealed, except as it is (in a sense) in religious "wit." The traditional contention, from Augustine to Karl Barth, that Christian theology is a bona fide form of knowledge is properly based on experience of God by direct acquaintance. At the same time, the traditional Protestant emphasis on the primacy of faith has its proper though sometimes exaggerated relevance. God is both hidden *and* revealed, like Heidegger's "being."[9] Prophecy is thus like a cry one utters when one is struck by surprise. In the moment of being struck one knows, but does not fully know, what it is that strikes. As a cry of surprise is the logical form of a shock, so the Word of the prophet is the logical (or mythological) form of God. Prophecy is a spontaneous response to some situation, often to some threat or disaster, which unexpectedly transforms that event—the conventional purport (the merely secular character) of that class of events— into a precious new significance, a revolutionary meaning that transfigures a whole people's life—past, present, and future.

[8] Cf. Ernst Cassirer, *Language and Myth,* pp. 63-80; *The Philosophy of Symbolic Forms* (New Haven: Yale University Press, 1955), II, 57; also Mircea Eliade, *The Sacred and the Profane,* pp. 126-27.

[9] Heidegger, *Being and Time,* pp. 51-58; *Introduction to Metaphysics,* pp. 16, 87-98, 111-12, 141-42.

Spontaneity is thus as important a characteristic of biblical prophecy as is the fact that the prophets "speak for another." To understand what biblical prophecy is, we must first keep two main points in mind: first, that God's intention is revealed to the prophets unexpectedly; second, that "the other" for whom the prophets speak is God and his people conterminously. Prophecy is the *ingodding* of a people mythopoeically, imaginatively, and it is this fact which projects the Old Testament prophets into theology. For the sometimes challenged conception of "biblical theology" is not, after all, an illegitimate notion.

3. Dogmatic Theology

Not counting pastoral theology, which is priestcraft (important, but related to the rest of theology the way engineering is related to theoretical science), traditional theology is divided into two main branches: dogmatics and apologetics. In its formal textual aspects, dogmatic theology is closer to the original biblical prophecy than is apologetic theology. Whereas biblical prophecy shades into Christian (or Jewish) dogmatics in the course of time, apologetic theology shades into philosophy as theologians and rabbis attempt to relate the "old-time religion" to new forms of talk and thought. This is nicely illustrated by contemporary Protestantism. Both crisis theology and Protestant fundamentalism are dogmatic, notably animated by certain biblical attitudes and forms of discourse, while "liberal theology" (against which both crisis theologians and fundamentalists so often inveigh)[10] is much closer in mood and method to philosophy. In contemporary Judaism, Orthodoxy is relatively dogmatic while Reformed Judaism is relatively apologetic. Theology

[10] Cf. H. E. Brunner, *The Theology of Crisis* (New York: Scribner's, 1929), p. 104.

always exists in tension between the historical forms of biblical prophecy and the non-biblical terminology of philosophy —between the surprising appearance of the Word of God initially and the need to interpret that Word to other systems of discourse eventually.

Keep in mind that we have already noted the two most important characteristics of biblical prophecy: (1) that it is a spontaneous appearance of an unexpected meaning; and (2) that it is the Word of another in a sense of "other" that embraces both God *and* his people. Together these facts make it necessary for every prophet after Moses, and even for Moses, to *interpret* the existing Word to the very people who live in it and to whom, in one sense (since they are integrally a part of it), it need not be explained. Yet, the community forgets, or times change, and the people can no longer read the word with which the Lord, as the saying goes, once "circumcised their hearts." Then the prophet has to speak again.

And Moses summoned all Israel and said to them: "You have seen all that the Lord did before your eyes in the land of Egypt. . . . but to this day the Lord has not given you a mind to understand, or eyes to see, or ears to hear. . . . For this commandment which I command you this day is not too hard for you, neither is it far off. It is not in heaven that you should say, 'Who will go up for us to heaven, and bring it to us, that we may hear it and do it?' Neither is it beyond the sea, that you should say, 'Who will go over the sea for us, and bring it to us, that we may hear it and do it?' But the word is very near you; it is in your mouth and in your heart, so that you can do it." (Deuteronomy 29:2-4; 30:11-14.)

Moses' recall of his people to the word in which they stand, and his interpretation of that word for them, is the sort of amplification of an original prophecy that is repeatedly necessary in every religious community. Thus, in the Chris-

203

tian community, for example, Paul acts not only as a prophet of Christ but also as one who must repeatedly amplify the "grammar" of the divine Logos.

Now I would remind you, brethren, in what terms I preached to you the gospel, which you received, in which you stand, by which you are saved, if you hold it fast—unless you believed in vain. For I delivered to you as of first importance what I also received, that Christ died for our sins in accordance with the scriptures, that he was buried, that he was raised on the third day in accordance with the scriptures. . . . Otherwise, what do people mean by being baptized on behalf of the dead? (I Corinthians 15:1-5; 29.)

It is important to notice that whenever the prophets and apostles (the prophets of Christ) are exegeting the Word of God to the people who are already standing in that Word, it is not prophecy in the restricted sense of prophecy (as the original appearance of the Word) that the prophets and apostles are doing. Instead, they are entering the area of dogmatic theology, moving dialectically in the direction of apologetic theology, but not there as yet. Thus, not only do prophets interject wholly new signs into their religious traditions (prophecy in its narrowest sense), they also expand the meanings of old signs—an almost imperceptible way of creating somewhat new symbols—by juxtaposing the old marks of their respective traditions in new ways. In this fashion, they act like theologians who are interpreting the Word by correlating cultic formulas, sacred history, current affairs, and so forth in order to bring out (or create) nuances inherent (or nonexistent) in the already existing traditions.[11]

[11] Notice the developing conception of Yahweh from Exodus through Job; also the changing conception of "the day of the Lord," from one of joy before Amos, to one of judgment afterward; remember that the conception of "the Messiah" is different in the New Testament from what it is in the Old; and within the New Testament, the concept of Christ varies in certain important respects.

The result, when this expanded "grammar" is applied to life, is a corresponding expansion of the Sacred as it is encountered in human existence, an increase in verbal facility that, being genuine speech and not idle chatter, results in a widening disclosure of that which was uttered by the original language of revelation. God crowds into human life at this point, living water pours from an old sign or set of signs, like blood from a wound, and spreads over all those signs as a new baptism of meaning.

This amplificatory function, an analytical clarification of a certain kind, is the chief characteristic of dogmatics. Dogmatic theology takes the already existing Word of God and makes the *implicit* relationships between its term *explicit*. It clarifies the Word, not by introducing new signs, but by illuminating obscure relations between the more or less familiar old signs of the tradition. It is, therefore, dogmatic in a sense that can easily become pejorative. It speaks only in the existing terms of the tradition and is, as a consequence, opaque to all who do not speak that language. Such uncomprehending people stand—as Karl Barth (a good example of a dogmatic theologian) has said—outside the "theological circle."

The implicit meanings that dogmatic theologians make explicit are old meanings only in the sense that, *when* they are apprehended by the people of the Word, *they are taken* as the meanings that *were* all along implicit in the ancient tradition. After all, it is the continuous experience of the people of God that provides both the development as well as the clarification and the verification of religious beliefs. To know the meaning of such beliefs is to have experienced their meanings. Not to know what they mean is to live in faith, believing what one does not understand [12]—or to live

[12] Cf. John Henry Newman, *An Essay in Aid of a Grammar of Assent* (London: Longmans, Green & Co., 1885), Chaps. i-iii, vi-vii.

without faith (and perhaps without interest) in the face of terms that are opaque.

Religious meanings are defined by the corporate life and language of religious communities. A community whose ancient Word is confronted by questionable doctrines, which are intended to amplify it, is alone in a position to determine which of such doctrines is true or false. False prophets are unmasked by the people who "in the inspiration of the Holy Spirit," ultimately reject those prophets' teachings, and whose very rejection (that people's negative response to those doctrines) defines and determines those prophets' errors. Heresies—like Christianity within Judaism and Protestantism within Roman Catholicism—initially mark new outbreaks of prophecy, and eventually themselves grow into contradictory dogmatic systems in the manner I have been describing. They raise problems within the broad Judeo-Christian tradition that must now wait on "the fullness of time" [13] (and the ecumenical spirit) for their resolutions.

Religious truth, like religious meaning, is a continuous historical development involving both prophetic spontaneity and its dogmatic amplification.

In the secular sciences the closest analogue of dogmatic theology may be mathematics—in a manner of speaking, *the* "dogmatic theology" of modern science. For, if we omit the fairly recent appearances of completely new mathematical systems that burst prophetically upon the nineteenth century, then we can say of mathematics that it too makes progress, like dogmatic theology, only by pointing to overlooked relationships among terms long familiar but not wholly clear to those who moved among them. In this sense, neither

[13] "The fullness of time" has two theological senses, one emphasizing a present fulfillment, the other a future fulfillment. I am using the phrase primarily in the latter sense.

mathematics nor dogmatic theology adds new terms of knowledge to their respective traditions.[14] They both, rather, unfold the implicit meanings of old terms, although this too is a kind of intellectual accretion to their respective modes of discourse. As mathematicians illuminate other mathematicians, so dogmatic theologians illuminate the people of the Word merely by amplifying the Word *in its own terms*. In short, like mathematics, dogmatic theology is a kind of amplificatory analysis in which a social product—a language—is developed, albeit still within a certain recognized conventional schematism.

4. Apologetic Theology

In contrast to dogmatic theology, apologetic theology clarifies the Word by performing an odd sort of translation, which is really no translation at all in the usual sense. Whereas a dogmatic theologian is like a poet who deepens and clarifies the life of an already poetic people by addressing them in the language they already speak, an apologetic theologian is like a literary critic who must explain to those who only understand prose what poetry is all about. He tries to mediate the Word to those who are not yet of its community.

The apologetic method may vary from that of Thomas or Anselm to that of Bultmann or Tillich, or from that of Maimonides to that of Buber, but it is always intended as a bridge from one way of thinking (from one mode of consciousness) to another that is markedly different. In relation to those who do not already hold the preconceptions that make the conclusions of Thomas or Anselm or Maimonides logically necessary or probable, these arguments are at best only oddly persuasive—more *seductive* than inductive or

[14] Cf. A. J. Ayer, *Language, Truth and Logic*, p. 79.

deductive.[15] As apologetics, these arguments work (when they work) to put those to whom they are addressed—those outside the "theological circle" occupied by Thomas, Anselm, or Maimonides—into the state of mind in which the Thomistic, Anselmic, or Maimonidean "conclusions" may be seen to be necessary in some sense. Traditional "intellectualistic" apologetics are like teeter-totters, which, *if* you get on them will surely raise you to the height that the person on the other end has anticipated. Once on them, you will find yourself where they are designed to raise you. But, strictly speaking, it is not the teeter-totter, not the *logic* of the argument, that puts you on it. That only raises you to a new perspective after you are already in position for it. What puts you in this position, why a certain apologetical argument suddenly seems persuasive, cannot be explained merely in terms of logic or reason, although it can be explained in many different ways: in the terminology of theology, for instance (as the action of "Grace"), or in psychological language (as an act of "wishful thinking") or in the jargon of cynical appraisal (as "mere foolishness") and so on. For the explanation will reflect the philosophical presuppositions, experience, and prejudices of whomever describes what has caused the argument to be convincing.

In this regard, what is true of traditional apologetics is also true of the apologetic theology that has been practiced in contemporary times by such theologians as Bultmann, Tillich, and Buber. For despite their differences, the apologetics of these men are similar in certain very important respects. All are often engaged in something that looks like a *mere* translation of traditional religious and theological terminology into the relatively new terminologies of existen-

---

[15] See Norman Malcolm, "Anselm's Ontological Argument," *Philosophical Review*, LXIX (Jan., 1960), p. 62; cf. Karl Barth, *Anselm: Fides Quaerens Intellectum*, trans. I. W. Robertson (Cleveland: World, 1962), esp. pp. 16 ff.

tialism, psychoanalysis, and German philosophical idealism, but that, more often than not, is *not* mere translation in the sense that English can be translated into German.

The term that Tillich often uses to describe what he is doing is both corrective and clarifying. He is "correlating" one mode of discourse and its inherent realm of being with another.[16] In order to enable men who are rooted predominantly in the secular words of the mid-twentieth century to attain a position from which they might also strike root in the "saving Word," Tillich lays one mode of discourse after another (depth psychology, existentialism, art, and so forth) over the Word of the prophets and saints, like laying various map transparencies on one another, hoping that we will come to see in depth through one language map into the next. Where contrasting maps draw contrary lines through what might in a sense be called the same point, some people at such points, for whom the religious perspective may have been opaque, may now come to see through their accustomed orientation into the existential meaning of religious terms, entering the Word and presence of God merely by reading the "terrain" through the language of traditional religious revelation, which now begins to make sense to them. Of course, the problem of "seeing through" is actually much more complicated than this analogy suggests. It is more as though the whole *plane* of the religious transparency were on a different axis from the planes of all the other transparencies, and yet intersected each of the other planes at every point so that one must look along the proper axis at any point if he is to enter the Word of God from the word in which he stood. The method of correlation works, when it works, by perpetrating a series of deliberate "puns," suggest-

[16] Paul Tillich, *Systematic Theology*, I, 34.

ing (for instance) that "existential anxiety" is more or less like "original sin," and so forth.[17]

The main problem of all apologetic theology is to establish correlations without suggesting that they are matters of translation in the usual sense. And yet, when correlations work—when they actually mediate the Word of God to those who have been stuck outside the Word—then, although it is more like "translating" painting into music than translating English into French, nevertheless it is a *kind* of translation that is effected. One crosses from one language on one plane to another language on another plane, which, like straight lines that intersect, are often "worlds apart." It should be noticed, however, that the difference between ways of talking and thinking can usually be easily overstressed. Ordinary language is such a maze of intersections, of punlike nuances and subtle switches, that there is probably no mode of discourse that does not blend into many other kinds. Thus, there are myriad affinities between religion, humor, poetry, drama, and so on.

Tillich and certain other contemporary theologians sometimes describe what they are doing as "philosophical theology," and whether or not they are always doing it well, they are right in adopting this description. Whatever is not prophetic in theology *is* philosophical. Dogmatic theology is really a *prophetic* amplification of—a subtle accretion to—the original Word. Apologetic theology, however, is a *philosophical* mediation between the Word of God and the words of man. One activity (dogmatics) amplifies; the other (apologetics) correlates. And together, but for the omission of pastoral theology, they comprise the whole substance of theology. Of course, there is some shade of prophecy, some touch of creative addition, in *all* theology, even in the least

[17] *Ibid.*, pp. 188-89; cf. also Ian Ramsey, *Religious Language*, Chap. 2.

prophetic. Thus, while dogmatic theology (more prophetic than philosophical) abruptly announces the linguistic rules (*logos*) of the Word, apologetic theology (more philosophical than prophetic) artfully correlates the *logos* of religion with the *logoi* of our day-to-day discourse.

At this point we may see clearly that every world view and intellectual discipline has its prophetic, dogmatic, and apologetic aspects. Accordingly, our consideration of the functions of biblical prophecy and traditional theology leads us ineluctably into a consideration of the philosophical aspects, not only of prophecy and theology, but also of philosophy itself, and of the ways in which every branch of culture and every area of experience involve the essential methodological characteristics of prophecy, theology, and philosophy.

5. Philosophy

Whenever philosophy is carried on within the limits of some restricted or esoteric discipline it may profitably be regarded as a form, perhaps a nonreligious form, of dogmatics. Dogmatic theology is only the dogmatics of some religion. But science, art, law, commerce, and so forth are all dogmatic—though not necessarily in a pejorative sense—when their practitioners are engaged in clarifying the concepts of their respective disciplines to the very experts who are already familiar with these modes of discourse. Furthermore, every intellectual discipline has its apologetic side. Thus science should not be contrasted with religion and theology in the parochial spirit of evangelical scientism, as is so often done, as though modern science does not elaborate a dogmatic of its own. Rather, dogmatics of every sort—theological, scientific, jurisprudential, political, artistic, and so forth—should all be contrasted to apologetics and prophecy of every kind. Instead of continuously emphasizing the differences and divisions between disciplines (foolishly mis-interpreting the significances of those contrasts in a way that tends to make us narrow-minded champions of some cultural activities and ignorant opponents of others) we should more often recognize the profound family resemblances among all intellectual pursuits. We need to keep in mind the similarity of every kind of dogmatics to every other kind, of every sort of apologetics to every other sort, and of every variety of prophecy to every other variety.

In all areas of intellectual activity, it is the esoteric charac-ter of dogmatic (or amplificatory) analysis that makes apol-ogetic (or correlation) analysis a cultural necessity. When-ever a person is not operating in his field with prophetic originality, nor dogmatically addressing his fellow experts in that field, he will (in his professional capacity) very likely be doing apologetic or correlation analysis. Take the science of physics as an example. It has its continuous prophetic in-sights and its constantly unfolding dogmatic development of an esoteric terminology. But the overall activity of the science of physics also includes its attempts to translate the physicists' jargon and apperceptions into (i.e., to correlate them with) the common sense of ordinary language, or the less common sense of other esoteric disciplines. As with all other specialized forms of investigating reality or responding to human life, there is a side of physics, significantly similar to apologetic theology in method and intent, that is (like apologetic theology) simultaneously a specialized branch of philosophical analysis. Because this aspect of physics is not primarily concerned with the *prophetic accretion* of new physical insights, nor with the *dogmatic expansion* of physi-cal discourse—both of which activities might be denom-inated physics, strictly so called—but because it is primarily concerned to *correlate the language* of physics with other (sometimes radically different) symbolic responses to life, apologetic physics, like apologetic theology, is a specialized branch of analytical philosophy. As distinct from metaphysics and existential philosophy, analytical philosophy is that branch of philosophy which seeks to correlate various disparate areas of culture with each other and thus effect a kind of "translation" of the one into the other.

Being rational animals, men may be characterized as living languages. We both organize our facts and encounter them in our symbolic systems. The mountains and the subatomic particles we discover and discuss are very different kinds of objects, and, as such, they are integral aspects of the different kinds of languages that we use to describe them. But both kinds of objects are real, and they *appear* in our experience, although we experience them in very different ways as elements in different sorts of "facts."

Once again we see that we should not assume that some particular way (our way) of talking about "the world," or about "God," is the one right way. We should not presume that there is, at the heart of things, a privilege conferred on some one way of describing "reality" or on some particular way of addressing "God." Such presumption, in secular affairs, is narrow-mindedness, and it blocks the road of inquiry and social justice. In religion it is idolatry, and it dulls our sense of God's transcendence. Thus, as we so often do in ordinary parlance, we may distinguish between "secular" and "religious" speech and practice, but this should not make it impossible for us to see that every "secular" area of life may have its "religious" corollary and that the "secular theology" of some contemporary theologians—a theology that "waits for Godot" instead of "God"—has a proper voice in the total dialogue between man and Mystery. Nor should secular theologians insist, on their side, that the traditional distinction between "the secular" and "the religious" is necessarily inimical to the proper understanding of both.

213

The contemporary rush of Christian theologians to the Jewish Bible and its "this-worldly" theology is a valuable corrective of a centuries-long isolation of religion from common life in some quarters of Christianity, but we must not suppose for that reason (as some radical theologians seem to do) that all "other-worldly" and "churchy" stereotypes are therefore a threat to a renaissance of viable Christianity. There obviously are many ways of responding symbolically (intelligently) to reality in its relation to human existence. And each way is both a vision and a hindrance to vision. People who do not see trees are often those who organize their worlds in terms of forests, but they are not always simply mistaken. As some of my previous reflections in this book have suggested, both "religious" and "secular" folk who think that their particular vision is the one true or one most adequate perspective of reality should ponder the full implication of Yahweh's reluctance to give himself one proper name (Exodus 3:14-16). Yet, it is not surprising that the myriad "language games" that grow together and tangle in our general culture should often mislead us to believe that they are necessarily in conflict, even when they are not. Different modes of discourse sometimes embody vastly dissimilar signs, syntaxes, emotional attitudes, and contents. They are different orders of revealed being, different modes of consciousness, different "grammars" of experience: compare science to myth, experimental psychology to psychoanalysis, playwriting to dramatic criticism, and so forth.

Of course, some of our symbolic systems and the ways of life they determine may indeed conflict, especially on emotional and other practical levels. Some people, for instance, may be violently hostile to the way certain other people think and enact their lives. But the more radically different the logics and contents are that are involved in such psychological and practical conflicts, the less chance there will be of a formal conflict. What conflict there is, in such cases, will most likely be merely attitudinal—so many instances of man's repeated need to choose his way of life: to elect his values, his world and his very self; and to tolerate, even to love, his neighbor.

This is an important point! The more we are aware of the profound family resemblances that exist among the different types of intellectual life to which I have been pointing in my comparison of prophecy, theology, and philosophy, the more tolerant—even the more loving—we will probably become toward those people whose intuitions and traditions and choices are different from our own. Even when, in some extreme cases, the world may prove to be "too small" for some ways of life to coexist—even when this involves persons or states in bloody conflict—the inescapable tragedy of the situation, the mutual necessity for each party to sacrifice and be sacrificed for what each cares that much for, could hallow with charity the whole attitude with which each person engages himself in his struggle.

But understanding will often make tragic conflicts avoidable. If in secular matters we were all less narrowminded, and in religion less idolatrous, many ways of responding to life that are now assumed to stand unavoidably at cross-purposes with each other would become, instead, mutual supplements to the general enrichment of the human spirit.

Let me summarize the points I have made in this chapter before continuing:

1. In its biblical context, prophecy is the spontaneous appearance of the Word of *God* in the mouth of man. This Word is also conterminously the Word of the *people* who choose that Word—the Word of "the Chosen People"—the *choosing* people.

2. Traditional theology is the prophetic amplification of the Word of God (dogmatics) and the philosophic correla-

215

tion of the Word with other forms of language (apologetics). As, in the course of time, prophecy blends into dogmatic and apologetic theology, apologetic theology shades into analytical philosophy (linguistic analysis).

3. Analytical philosophy is, so to speak, the "theology" of *any* word. The philosophies of science, art, religion, law, and so forth are *all* forms of analytical philosophy. But, to the extent that they are *not* apologetic, to the extent that they are *not* concerned to "interpret" the languages of their respective specialites to people outside those specialties, to the extent that they are merely concerned to amplify those languages to the experts who are already at home in them, they are integral parts of those respective areas of specialized discourse and not of philosophy strictly so called. Thus "ordinary language" analysis (as practiced by Wittgenstein, for example), though it may seem at first to be an exception to this description of analytical philosophy, is instead a good example of it. For whoever experiences the "linguistic muddles" in ordinary language that Wittgenstein sought to eliminate, is not really, in his muddled capacity, a member of the area of discourse from which his muddle has isolated him. He must, through philosophic help, be reinstated.

In a broad but illuminating sense of the word "prophecy," prophecy is creation or inspiration in *any* area of discourse. It is the sudden appearance of a new meaning anywhere, of any kind.[18] Prophecy is the appearance of some brand new symbol, or symbolic system, and its peculiar realm of being. "In the beginning was the Word"—language of some appropriate sort is necessarily coeval with every revelation of being.

Prophets always give voice to orders of being that transcend the existing order of things. In this sense all prophets, secular or religious—innovators in any walk of life—witness

[18] See, e.g., Katherine Kuh, "Delacroix: Prophet in Paint," *Saturday Review* (June 22, 1963).

the existence of some one or other transcendent realm. They see what others do not see. But this does not mean that their apperception is necessarily closed to those who are willing to experience prophetic disruption in order to gain new vision. The transcendent world of every genuine prophecy only transcends our old linguistic ruts. And although such transcendent worlds are, indeed, "unknowable in principle" (as those who criticize metaphysics often point out),[19] nevertheless, when metaphysics is properly understood and properly practiced, the reason it troubles us may often be because it seeks to enlarge our philosophical perspective and deepen our ontological awareness. The general meaning or *weltanschauung* of certain metaphysical systems may be unknowable in principle, but that principle is sometimes our own, the measure of our own world view, which is not strictly relevant to the metaphysician's prophetically enlarged or different perspective. We must not try to understand what he says merely in terms of the syntax and semantics he has transcended. We must, instead, invite a dilation of our mode of apprehension. "Metaphysical descriptions are 'confessions' of the nature of things as seen from that perspective; hence there is a degree of circularity in metaphysical argumentation," says a commentator, Frank B. Dilley.

It seems reasonable, therefore, to borrow some of the language fashionable among modern theologians, to speak of metaphysics as confessional, to speak of it as being made up of *kerygma* (proclamation) and *apologia* (persuasion), in recognition of the fact that the presentation of metaphysical positions involves both proclamation that this is the way the world goes and apologetic justification of the conclusions that it works this way. Such views are set forth for others to hear, to bring them to the faith. Like-

---

[19] See Ayer, *Language, Truth and Logic*, chaps. i and vi; also Antony Flew, "Theology and Falsification," in *New Essays* . . . , pp. 96-99.

wise it seems reasonable to speak of metaphysical conversion for those cases in which radical shifts of view occur, since taking on a new philosophical perspective or faith requires a drastic restructuring of a world view—percepts, concepts, and fundamental assumptions.

Of course it is possible to exaggerate this resemblance between theology and philosophy; however, the real danger is not that of overstatement but of understatement. Theology and philosophy have converged to a remarkable degree in recent times, and can no longer be set at opposite ends of a continuum as though they involved methods radically different in nature, as is done both when theologians sometimes decry philosophy as devil-sent and when philosophers decry theology as sheer subjectivity. Each thinker is theologian in that he confesses the adequacy of a particular faith, and philosopher in that he builds this faith into a rational system.

Metaphysical systems are elaborated and criticized extensions of faith. . . . Such terminology as this serves to underscore the dependence of conclusions on starting points and provides a way of accounting for fundamental metaphysical disagreements which does not impugn either the logical ability or the perceptual abilities of philosophers. Philosophers disagree because they hold different faiths, because their views are formed by different languages and different assumptions, and perhaps because they commit themselves to different ultimates. No analysis which suggests that philosophical disputes are occasioned by simple factual or logical errors can do justice to man or his metaphysizing.[20]

Traditional philosophy includes both metaphysical and analytical activities, and we have now drifted into a consideration of metaphysics. The word "metaphysics" comes from the Greek, meaning, roughly, "beyond nature," or better yet, "beyond the things that are there." [21] It therefore connotes

[20] Frank B. Dilley, *Metaphysics and Religious Language* (New York: Columbia University Press, 1964), pp. 69, 72-73.

[21] Cf. Heidegger, *An Introduction to Metaphysics*, p. 14.

even more than Dilley describes in the quotation above. A new metaphysic not only prophetically bespeaks an interpretation of being-itself that has been as yet unspoken, it is often (and at best) an intimation of more than it can say—of something that is apparently unspeakable except by indirection. The enunciation of a truly prophetic metaphysical perspective—the announcement of an Aristotle, Democritus, Aquinas, Hegel, Nietzsche, or Marx—is (since the writers' words are inadequate) a partly strangled cry made by a philosopher in his inchoate, overburdened awareness of being-itself. Witness even Wittgenstein:

> It is not *how* things are in the world that is mystical, but *that* it exists.
> To view the world *sub specie aeterni* is to view it as a whole —a limited whole.
> Feeling the world as a limited whole—it is this that is mystical.
>
> . . . .
>
> There are, indeed, things that cannot be put into words. They *make themselves manifest*. They are what is mystical.
>
> . . . .
>
> What we cannot speak about we must consign to silence.[22]

These often debated words, and others, of Wittgenstein suggest that the innovating word of a creative metaphysician contains an overtone above and beyond the note that is relatively obvious; there is something enormously important to be discerned between the lines he writes. That which the metaphysician must pass over in silence is like the country-

[22] Wittgenstein, *Tractatus Logico—Philosophicus*, trans. D. F. Pears and B. F. McGuiness, with introduction by B. Russell (London: Routledge and Kegan Paul; New York: Humanities Press, 1961), pp. 149, 151. See Max Black's discussion of Wittgenstein's mysticism: Max Black, *A Companion to Wittgenstein's Tractatus* (London: Cambridge University Press, 1964), the last chapter.

side a driver sometimes glimpses beside the road at night while he is staring straight ahead at the illuminated area under the headlights. Metaphysical intuition is sometimes a shock of recognition—like that which occurs in our experience of wit in its profoundest reaches. What a person was ignoring is exactly what now begins to fascinate him. And the character of this revelation, qualified by his interpretation of it, becomes the "root-metaphor" [23] of the metaphysician's understanding of all reality. Nevertheless, his "metaphor" is always inadequate, limiting, truncated, and the reality that it partially illuminates stretches away into the darkness on every side. Every revelation is also a concealment, and perhaps no one knows this better than the great creative metaphysicians themselves. Kierkegaard's criticism of Hegel, for example, would better have been restricted to Hegel's disciples, or at least directed at Hegel more circumspectly when it was obvious that he had fallen into the trap of becoming a disciple of himself.

The task of all who try to follow the great innovators, the "world shakers" in philosophy, is not only to master a new principle of interpretation—in the faith that both its fresh syntax and its strange content will be revealed to those who try to follow that new hermeneutic—it is also a task of trying to see past it. The pity is not that prophets may have disciples—as, for instance, the prophets of modern science have made disciples of us all—but that those disciples are too often pharisaically committed to that one order, and thus they hinder the development of new insight and wider vision in themselves and others.

The great original metaphysicians of the history of philosophy are all philosophical *prophets*. The great innovators in art and science are also prophets in their spheres of influence.

[23] See Dilley, *Metaphysics and Religious Language*, p. 61.

Such men promulgate new symbolic responses to the otherwise meaningless, or less meaningful, shocks (the brute surds) of experience. And, in so doing, they "speak for another." As the prophets of the Bible created "the people of the Word" by addressing it to them—God being ingodded in the "Chosen People" as *they* chose to live in that Word—so the great creative metaphysicians of traditional philosophy and the great innovators in all other disciplines are prophets because, as witnesses of their respective sorts of intuitions, they each address an audience that they intend to inform by their mode of talk or thought—an audience in whom the appropriate kind of experience is impossible until that audience enters the appropriate manner of apprehension. The trouble is, however, that those who enter will often begin to act as though they had entered a tunnel.[24] "Seeing they do not see, and hearing they do not hear, nor do they understand" (Matthew 13:13; cf. Isaiah 6:9; Deuteronomy 29:2-4; 30:11-14).

6. Existentialism

The rebuke that biblical prophets once leveled at the People of the Word parallels the criticism that has more recently been directed at academic philosophy and inauthentic existence by the existentialists whom we have occasionally discussed on previous pages. The intention of nineteenth-century existentialists like Kierkegaard and Nietzsche, and of twentieth-century phenomenological ontologists and existentialists like Heidegger and Sartre, is to challenge men to accept their ethical responsibility for what they make of themselves and their worlds, and to recall them to an ontological awareness of being-itself, even when, as in the case of Kierke-

[24] Cf. the liberalizing spirit of Wittgenstein's *Tractatus*, par. 6.451 and the *Philosophical Investigations*.

221

gaard, it is indicated in terms of the familiar Judeo-Christian faith. That is why existentialists are so drawn to the prophetic element (Nietzsche's Dionysian spirit) in poetry, art, drama, and myth—to prophecy in every human activity in which being-itself, *Mysterium Tremendum,* is erupting into historical existence in the light of human consciousness and in the presence of language. According to Heidegger, for instance, the poets among us are the yet prophetic mouths from which being speaks its *glossolalia.*

The origin of language remains a mystery; not because men have not been clever enough, but because their sharpness and cleverness made a false move before even setting to work. The origin of language is in essence mysterious. And this means that language can only have arisen from the overpowering, the strange and terrible.[25]

Elsewhere Heidegger suggests that the typical mistake of lesser metaphysicians—the mistake of those who move in the wake of the great innovators—is to repeat and repeat the sin of intellectual pride, as though some philosophical system could actually stand proxy for the fullness, the presence, of being-itself; as though when one can recite the words of the original metaphysician one is automatically "standing in the truth" he stood in, as if what he expressed were nothing but a formal concept. " 'Disclosure of being' means the unlocking of what forgetfulness of being closes and hides," says Heidegger. "And it is through this questioning that a light first falls on the *essence* of metaphysics."

When we hear of disciples, "followers," as in a school of philosophy for example, it means that the nature of questioning is misunderstood. Such schools can exist only in the domain of scientific

[25] Heidegger, *An Introduction to Metaphysics,* pp. 143-44.

and technical work. . . . But the best technical ability can never replace the actual power of seeing and inquiring and speaking.[26]

The phenomenological analysis of human existence, which contemporary existentialists like Heidegger and Sartre have conducted, helps modern man recapture the old prophetic and primitive philosophical awareness that "everything is full of gods," as the pre-Socratics said. The existentialists' concern to make us aware of the mystery of being (as medieval and modern philosophers have not generally been aware of it in their conceptualistic refinement of primitive man's thunderstruck response to existence) returns us once again to the mood and attitude of prophecy and mythopoeic intuition. According to Heidegger, metaphysics is anything but a scholastic exercise that can be learned by rote, nor is it, when properly approached, a science that violates the phenomenological method. It is, as he practices it, a return to the great beginning of Western metaphysics before it became refracted into classroom chatter. Heidegger does not denigrate primitive man as one on whom we have improved in all branches of philosophy. Heidegger laments, instead, the passing of a certain receptive naïveté, a readiness to awe, from the sensibilities of most modern philosophers.[27]

Modern existentialism, including its phenomenological technique, is a prophetic call to attend once again to Mystery in the commonplace. Existential phenomenology is closer to prophecy than it is to dogmatics or apologetics: it asks us to stop "thinking" so much about the world in order to look at it afresh and to listen to it once again with the revolutionary attentiveness, the sort of naïveté, that is characteristic of prophecy in all walks of life. When it is approached in

[26] *Ibid.*, p. 16.
[27] *Ibid.*, p. 13.

this way, philosophy will be essentially untimely, prophetic, revolutionary, as Heidegger says:

> All essential philosophical questioning is necessarily untimely. This is so because philosophy is always projected far in advance of its time, or because it connects the present with its antecedent, with what *initially* was. Philosophy always remains a knowledge which not only cannot be adjusted to a given epoch but on the contrary imposes its measure upon its epoch.
>
> Philosophy is essentially untimely because it is one of those few things that can never find an immediate echo in the present. When such an echo seems to occur, when a philosophy becomes fashionable, either it is no real philosophy or it has been mis-interpreted and misused for ephemeral and extraneous purposes.[28]

By citing great metaphysicans and other innovators of the first magnitude, we come full circle back into prophecy—but now in an expanded sense of that word which includes non-biblical as well as biblical prophecy. To return to the metaphor of the colored line that we used at the beginning of this chapter, we have gone as far from biblical prophecy as we could—through theology to analytical philosophy, metaphysics, and existentialism—only to find that, although its shade may change, the *essential* elements of biblical prophecy still color every line of thought, even those which are radically nonbiblical and "nonreligious."

It might help to think of the colored line of my illustra-tion not as a straight line but as a circle or even as a point. Both ends of the line pass through each other to their op-posite extremes. Every form of prophecy is philosophical in the sense that it not only provides an immediate interpreta-tion of some event. but also entails a whole system, a dog-matic, of explanation. Every philosophy—clear or cloudy,

[28] *Ibid.*, p. 7.

224

examined or unexamined—is prophetic in the sense that it is always a miraculous appearance of meaning that cannot explain itself, except dogmatically (by some sort of circular argument) or apologetically (by a "leap" from one point of view to another).

Traditional theology is no more prophetic than any other interpretative response to life—nor is it necessarily more religious. It is not even more metaphysical. Of course, in a certain sense, traditional apologetic theology has often been more obviously "metaphysical" than many other intellectual pursuits—more so than chemistry or economics, for instance —but this only signifies that traditional religious apologists have used every viable philosophical system—Platonic, Aristotelian, Hegelian, and others—as mediums for correlating the Judeo-Christian revelation with other forms of experiencing. Often such secondhand metaphysical activity became, and still becomes, a degenerate form of almost empty talk, little more than high-flown chatter, far removed from the insight that it initially expressed. But this does not imply that any other intellectual discipline can avoid expressing a metaphysic of some sort, even when the practitioners of that discipline are unaware of its metaphysical foundations.[29]

A miraculous appearance of signs (prophecy) and a spontaneous interpretation (dogmatics and apologetics) are fused in every sort of intelligent experience, whether "sacred" or "profane." In the total spectrum of general culture, many ways of symbolizing reality may be properly distinguished. But even the most "profane" disciplines are only superficially distinct from the miraculous utterances of the Holy Spirit that we conventionally and properly call religious.

---

[29] Cf. Edwin Burtt, *The Metaphysical Foundations of Modern Science* (Garden City, N.Y.: Doubleday, 1932), Introduction, *et passim*.

We shall not cease from exploration
And the end of all our exploring
Will be to arrive where we started
And know the place for the first time.

T. S. ELIOT, *Little Gidding*

SUMMARY

THE MEANING OF "BELIEVING IN GOD"

Our study of sense and nonsense in religion began, in the Introduction to this book, with a brief description of the four most influential philosophical objections to traditional western religion at the present time. In Chapter I, I proceeded to amplify one of those criticisms by using the theological problem of evil as a frequently cited example of logical falsity (self-contradiction) in the Judeo-Christian religious tradition. Adapting the words of Stephen Toulmin to my inquiry, I concluded that the theological problem of evil posed a "limiting question" that tumbled us out of one area of inquiry into another—into a different sort of questioning, a different type of awareness. In this connection, I might have discussed an existentialist philosopher, Karl Jaspers, and his concept of "limit situations" (*grenzsituationen*),[1] but I did

---

[1] See Karl Jaspers, *Way to Wisdom*, p. 204; Jaspers, *Truth and Symbol*, trans. Jean T. Wilde, William Kluback, and William Kimmel (New Haven: College and University Press, 1959), translators' introduction and p. 33.

not. Instead, I moved on, in Chapter II, to consider the concepts of evil and absurdity as they appear in the phenomenological description of human existence that we find in contemporary "atheistic existentialism."

Once again, this time in the context of Sartre's thought, we were brought to a standstill by a tangle of ambiguous, vague, and paradoxical conclusions. Every human individual, we were told, is an "absurd project to be God," but "the idea of God is contradictory and we lose ourselves in vain." Even Sartre's definition of man as "a being which is not what it is and which is what it is not" was not free either of ambiguity leading to vagueness or of paradoxicality of one sort or another, a Scylla and Charybdis situation that either drowns us in a whirlpool of run-on equivocation (punning on the verb "to be," say some of Sartre's critics ruefully) or that dashes us to pieces on the rock of self-contradiction. Again we seemed to have arrived at a limit situation, this time marking the conceptual limitations of Sartre's thinking, but also, perhaps, of our own. What were the religious implications of these parallel occurrences, one in theology and the other in atheistic existentialism? Does Sartre's critique of religion violate the phenomenological method he professes? Could we combine the methods of linguistic analysis and phenomenological analysis and defend the essential elements of traditional religious belief and practice against both the linguistic and phenomenological critics of religion?

Using ordinary wit as a convenient model of the limit situations we had encountered in both theistic and atheistic contexts, I was able to show, in Chapter III, that certain features of religious life and language have a family resemblance to this most devastating form of humor. My purpose was not to suggest that religion is a joke (except in a very extended sense), nor did my comparison imply that existential philosophy and humor are the only "nonreligious" modes of expression that can be used to illuminate the essential nature of religious discourse. The variegated relatedness of all arts to religious consciousness and symbolism is, for example, fairly obvious, although much work still needs to be done to clarify and encourage our appreciation of the fact.

Because witticisms are closely related to puns (and since we had already observed the riotous ambiguity of theological and existential descriptions) we were led, in Chapter IV, to examine some family resemblances in the several areas of ambiguity in which we had become involved. The logical similarity between ordinary puns and biblical paronomasia was not difficult to see. But the punlike characteristics of miracle stories and (broadly speaking) of sacramental life, though less apparent, were seen to be equally real and maybe even more important. In this connection I attempted to bring out the way religious and theological language guides our understanding through vague and equivocal concepts in the direction of religious "wit"—in the direction of a "disclosure situation," as Ian Ramsey might say.[2] Had it not involved technical and historical considerations that lie a bit to one side of my primary purpose, I might then have shown how ordinary witticisms are related logically and phenomenologically to the sort of symbols that theologians call "sacraments" (the formal number of which varies from one Christian community to another) and how the logic of common puns resembles the function of those somewhat lesser blessings which are called "sacramentals" (in a sense that also varies somewhat from community to community). For the reasons stated, I did not do this, but it is perhaps apparent how one might proceed in those matters. My treatment, in Chapter IV, of the run-on "punning," which is implicit in

[2] Ian T. Ramsey, *Christian Discourse*, pp. 28 ff.

miracle stories and in the so-called analogical predication of traditional theology, supplemented the treatment of religious paradox that I developed in Chapter III. As a result, we saw how it is in principle possible to believe in the "witty" meaningfulness of the self-defeating utterances of religion even though we have not yet experienced the illumination that religious testimony promises to those who seek it. Religious faith is an *action*, like that of someone who listens expectantly to a complex series of puns and witticisms whose ultimately ineffable meaningfulness he has not yet been able to share with those who keep repeating the story in his presence.[3]

One result of my inquiry was the sort of insight expressed by John Calvin centuries ago: "True and substantial wisdom principally consists of two parts, the knowledge of God and the knowledge of ourselves. But, while these two branches of knowledge are so intimately connected, which of them precedes the other is not easy to discover."[4] The deepening mutual involvement of theology and existential anthropology, in my study, made the topics of Chapter V a necessity. Here I tried to distinguish between the concepts of knowledge and wisdom, and—using the examples of Job, Koheleth (Ecclesiastes), and Paul—to suggest how the idea of religious salvation relates to the existentialists' conception of "authentic existence." These considerations were in effect an amplification of my encounter with the theological problem of evil which first occurred in Chapter I, but they also led me ahead, in Chapter V, to contrast our workaday standards of morality to the moral wisdom that relates the Judeo-

[3] This is my explanation of how a person can believe a strict logical paradox which he does not understand. See Bernard Williams' presentation of the problem, "Tertullian's Paradox," *New Essays* . . . , pp. 187-211, esp., 208 ff.

[4] John Calvin, *Institutes of the Christian Religion*, trans. Henry Beveridge (Grand Rapids: Eerdmans, 1962), Bk. I, Chap. 1, Sect. 1.

Christian concepts of *Aggadah* to *Halacha*, of "Grace" to "works," of myth to the awakened conscience of the truly religious individual.

Still in Chapter V, I attempted to approach an understanding of the Judeo-Christian community's perennial mythopoeic enactment of the freeing of man from "Egyptian bondage" and the "sting of death." Involved with this attempt was an appreciation of the fact that biblical religion is essentially inimical to idolatry in every form, whether that idolatry is academic, moral, "religious," or egoistic. Far from being contradictory to liberal education, and instead of being a superstitious anachronism in a modern age, we saw that the religious spirit is roughly coterminous with the liberal mind. This in itself suggests a need for a renewed appreciation of mythic imagination and liturgical practice in our stultifyingly technological and industrial, computerized and success-oriented, mass-informed and misinformed society. Because each one of us is so tempted to ignore the "still small voice" that seeks to recall him to the painful idiosyncracies of his own personal existence and to deny his involvement in his farthest neighbor's life and death, some form of organized worship, some regular mythopoeic reminder and freely entered discipline is wanting in contemporary Western life. And yet, such forms of activity are present among us, if only we could effect a popular freshening and generally renewed appreciation of religious myth. That sort of renewal would repeatedly return us to the way of the free and prophetic spirit in every age.

Such thinking led me to my final chapter. Here I tried to illuminate the fact that, although it is convenient and often necessary to distinguish between "the religious" and "the secular," "the sacred" and "the profane," "God" and "man," nevertheless we must not forget that the form of human existence is ineradicably a blur and not a blueprint, that the variously defined and vaguely apprehended object of man's "ultimate concern" is sacred in "the secular" as well as in "the religious." Since modern culture has grown out of the primitive mind—since language, art, philosophy, and science have grown out of primitive man's broad religious stimulus and response[5]—we ought not to be surprised when we discover that some of the earliest characteristics of human consciousness are still present in contemporary forms of awareness, and that, conversely, the latest accomplishment of the human spirit was already nascent in the primitive.[6] All of man's interpretations of reality involve the essential and distinguishing characteristics of prophecy, theology, and philosophy—that is to say, of spontaneity, dogmatics, and apologetics. The *presentational* consciousness that is so characteristic of biblical prophecy (and of all forms of art, for example) is never utterly devoid of the *representational* mode of consciousness that is so characteristic of abstract reason (of traditional philosophy and modern science, for instance). Nor is representational consciousness ever wholly devoid of a presentational element. An object of some sort is *present* in every sort of intuition; and every kind of intuition understands what is present by *representing* it in some way.[7] This is as true of religious consciousness as it is of any other form of the human spirit.

God is not sheer transcendence and inscrutability. Every cult and every individual in a cult may encounter God as an imaginative construct, as a phenomenological presence in a religious myth, as a historical event enveloped in a mystery. Thus, *Mysterium Tremendum* has indeed entered the world in myths and has become incarnate in man in one or another

[5] Cassirer, *Language and Myth*, Chaps. 3 and 6.

[6] *Ibid.*; cf. Eliade, *The Sacred and the Profane*, pp. 201-13; *Myth and Reality* (New York: Harper, 1963), Chap. 1 *et passim*.

[7] See Justus Buchler (ed.), *The Philosophical Writings of Peirce*, pp. 74-98.

liturgical drama. This does not mean that all myths are equally adequate for the needs and the illumination of man —all forms of idolatry will ultimately prove unworthy, for example—but both Judaism and Christianity are anti-idolatrous, self-destructive, and equally true in the manner of religious "wit." Ideally, each leads its people through a punlike approximation process toward a witlike confrontation of the individual with *Mysterium Tremendum*.

Although I have stressed the difference between the language of religious witness and the sort of assertions that make up a large portion of ordinary language, I have *not* said that religious language is *totally* unlike all other kinds of linguistic activity. I have likened it to certain forms of humor, but also to painting, dancing, poetry, and drama—especially, in the context of our main approach, to the theater of the absurd.

It is helpful to think of religion as a form of drama, for if we wish to approximate a total understanding of a myth we must enter some myth and start to practice it the way we would enter a community theater production and begin rehearsals. To ask for the meaning of Israel or Christ is, in some important respects, like asking for the meaning of King Lear or Hamlet. In a very important sense, each actor must discover such meanings for himself—and *in* himself. In religious life, we must enact a myth the way method actors take on their roles—by becoming *possessed* by the character we play. We must respond to the Word of God as though it were a script that we want to act, and allow the phenomenological distance between ourselves and the characters we play to disappear; for we are each invited to move from role to role as the drama unfolds within us, as we fuse with the script. Those roles must become one's character, a unity of opposites and multiplicity: the total meaning of the myth becoming the erring, suffering, repentant, atoning, saving value of one's life—one's self. Then, since the principle role is both divine and human, tragic hero and a clown, our lamentations and our laughter will not be staged. And for some onlooker to ask for the meaning of another person's performance, as though it could be encompassed in a straightforward program note, shows that the questioner has hardly begun to appreciate what the script is all about. For the name of the play is "The Transfiguration of Man," and it was written expressly for the questioner by an "author" whom we must each discover for ourselves.

My replies to the four or five objections to traditional Judeo-Christian belief in God, with which I started this book, may now be summarized in a brief space:

In response to the philosophical criticism that religion is superstitious because it lacks good evidence to support belief in miracles, I have shown that this objection is fundamentally mistaken. Nor is it a deterrent to intelligent faith once we recognize the punlike character of miracle stories and religious legends. The proper function of such expressions is to act as syntactical and semantical switches over which members of the religious community can cross from one sense and syntax to another, from the language and life of a merely workaday world to the language and life of a world that is sacramental.

To the contention that the basic statements of religious testimony are either self-contradictory ("logically false") or so endlessly qualified as to be devoid of meaning ("cognitively empty") I, in a sense, agree. But I hasten to point out the similarities between the language of religious witness and the language of ordinary humor in this regard. The fact that analogical descriptions of God's character must be endlessly qualified when they are challenged—God loves us like a father, *but* not exactly like a father, *but* not exactly like a

233

teacher either, and so on—does not necessarily lead to a *mere* poverty of meaning. It can lead, rather, to a peculiar self-defeating surfeit of riches that is not *mere* nonsense. Thus, God loves us like a father *and* a teacher, *and* a judge, *and* so forth—which leads us, if we press on, toward an eventual explosion of religious "wit."

Punlike, certain forms of religious language dilate the significance of the commonplace in the direction of an ineffable insight that has the transcendental character of ordinary wit, but to an extraordinary and serious degree. Thus, the philosophical indictment of traditional religious belief as being patently or implicitly self-contradictory is both admitted and dismissed. It is not the case that every logical falsity is a mere mistake, like a mistake in a geometrical proof, and traditional religion is a case in point. Its basic testimony is paradoxical, but that is how it effects a presentation of its ultimate object, the ineffable, of which (as Stace points out) we cannot simply assert either that it is or that it is not itself a paradox.

The familiar criticism that religion is a neurotic crutch can now be seen as an exaggeration, which is often itself a neurotic refusal to admit that one is "lame," a refusal to accept the sort of healing of which traditional religions speak. Inasmuch as religion is not so much a system as a seeing through all systems—a *public* way of life and a *private* quality of awareness that is in itself the ostensive definition of "wisdom"—a nonidolatrous belief in God is not an illusion, but an escape from the illusions that enslave all of us who are not given the "wit" to see beyond the tyranny of the obvious and commonplace. As such, the ancient wisdom that our religious myths enact is certainly not irrelevant to contemporary life. Nor is it the case as some "modern" theologians seem to think, that the very idea of religion (of institution and cult) is necessarily in conflict with the notion of continuous prophetic revelation.[8] The concept of religion properly entails the idea of continuous reformation. A religious tradition is, ironically, a tradition that enshrines its own repeated surpassing, and such a heritage must be jealously preserved. The danger is that, if it is lost, it might be replaced by a thoroughly serious philosophy of life.

We have been told, by no less a theologian than Dietrich Bonhoeffer, that the world has "come of age," i.e., that it no longer needs the concept of God as a cosmological first principle to explain the universe; nor can man (nor need man) depend on Providence to act as a *deus ex machina* to solve the world's practical problems.[9] Not all philosophers and theologians would agree with Bonhoeffer—most Thomists, for example, would disagree to some extent—but even if Bonhoeffer is right, we cannot reasonably or safely jettison our religious heritage, although we might reasonably adapt our expression of it to the changing times. Bonhoeffer himself might have agreed with this. If, in an age of exploding population and technology, we do not safeguard our religions (both our institutions and our cult practices) and learn to *enact* our religious myths regularly—without superstition, but with a newly awakened faith in the Spirit of the Word—the temptation will be greater than ever to worship ourselves and our accomplishments, hating both, in an increasingly inhuman environment.

[8] A sensible explanation and discussion of contemporary theological rejections of "religion" is Daniel Jenkins, *Beyond Religion* (Philadelphia: Westminster Press, 1962). For his treatment of Bonhoeffer, see pp. 33 ff. Bonhoeffer, we must remember, was martyred before he could develop his theological ideas sufficiently.

[9] Bonhoeffer, *Letters and Papers From Prison*, p. 165 *et passim*. For an interesting corroboration of Bonhoeffer on this point, see John Wisdom's influential essay, "Gods." This article first appeared in the *Proceedings of the Aristotelian Society, 1944*, but is reprinted in Wisdom's book *Philosophy and Psycho-analysis* (New York: Philosophical Library, 1953), pp. 149-68. Note the problem with which the essay begins.

The Word of God is a warning. It is also a directional sign printed on the road in front of us: an arrow that points to where we are going—to meaningless life and meaningless death. But if we have the passion to follow that sign, it wittily brings us back to where we were. It repeatedly offers us another chance, if we take it. Now then, we are here for the first time again. The sign confronts us, pointing to itself, and we have moved into it. Still, if we think that we have reached the place it intends, we have missed it entirely. It does not mean what it means in that straightforward way. For the Word of God is circular, a spiral that repeatedly returns us to the same place, different. Paradoxically, it is, thus, the fundamental ontological proof of God's existence, but not in an academic sense. It addresses in the beginning what it addresses in the end: the presence of God in the center of human existence. And whoever enters the Word will encounter Him as the lyric relation that unites the Word and himself and his world. The meaning of the Word is, then, the Word itself. And the Truth of the Word is the Wayfarer on His Way.

BIBLIOGRAPHY

Books

Altizer, Thomas J. J. *The Gospel of Christian Atheism*. Philadelphia: Westminster Press, 1966.

_____, and Hamilton, William. *Radical Theology and the Death of God*. Indianapolis: Bobbs-Merrill, 1966.

_____. (ed.) *Toward a New Christianity*. New York: Harcourt, Brace & World, 1967.

Anderson, Bernhard W. *Understanding the Old Testament*. Englewood Cliffs, N. J.: Prentice-Hall, 1957.

Aquinas, Thomas. *Summa Theologica* in *Basic Writings of Saint Thomas Aquinas*. Edited and annotated with an introduction by Anton C. Pegis. New York: Random House, 1945.

_____. *Summa Contra Gentiles, ibid.*

Augustine. *Confessions*. Translated by F. J. Sheed. New York: Sheed and Ward, 1943.

Ayer, A. J. *Language, Truth and Logic*. 2d ed. revised. New York: Dover, 1950.

Barnes, Hazel E. *Humanistic Existentialism: The Literature of Possibility*. Lincoln: University of Nebraska Press, 1959.

Barth, Karl. *Anselm: Fides Quaerens Intellectum*. Translated by I. W. Robertson. Meridian Books; Cleveland: World, 1962.

Bergson, Henri. *The Two Sources of Morality and Religion*. Translated by R. Ashley Audra and Cloudesley Brereton. Anchor Books; New York: Doubleday, 1954.

Berkeley, George. *Sirius*. London and Dublin: C. Hitch; C. Davis, 1744.

Black, Max. *A Companion to Wittgenstein's Tractatus*. Ithaca: Cornell University Press; London: Cambridge University Press, 1964.

Blackstone, William T. *The Problem of Religious Knowledge*. Englewood Cliffs, N. J.: Prentice-Hall, 1963.

Bonhoeffer, Dietrich. *Letters and Papers from Prison*. Edited by Eberhard Bethge and translated by R. H. Fuller. New York: Macmillan [1953]; Paperback ed., 1962.

The Book of Common Prayer. Oxford: Oxford University Press. Queen Elizabeth II Edition.

Braithwaite, Richard B. "An Empiricist's View of Religious Belief." London: Cambridge University Press, 1955. This short monograph also appears in *The Existence of God*. Edited by John Hick. New York: Macmillan; London: Collier-Macmillan, 1964.

Brunner, H. E. *The Theology of Crisis*. New York: Scribner's, 1929.

Buber, Martin. *The Eclipse of God*. New York: Harper, 1952; Harper Torchbooks, 1957.

————. *Between Man and Man*. Translated by Ronald Gregor Smith. Boston: Beacon Press, 1955.

————. *I and Thou*. Translated by R. G. Smith. New York: Scribner's, 1958.

————. *The Prophetic Faith*. Translated by Carlyle Witton-Davies. New York: Macmillan, 1949; Harper Torchbooks, 1960.

Bultmann, Rudolph. *Essays: Philosophical and Theological*. Translated by James C. G. Greig. New York: Macmillan; London: S.C.M. Press, 1955.

————. *Jesus Christ and Mythology*. New York: Scribner's, 1958.

————, et al. *Kerygma and Myth*. Translated by Reginald H. Fuller and edited by Hans Werner Bartsch. Torchbooks; New York: Harper, 1961.

————, and Kundsin, Karl. *Form Criticism: Two Essays on New Testament Research*. Translated by Frederick C. Grant. Torchbooks; New York: Harper, 1962.

Burtt, Edwin. *The Metaphysical Foundations of Modern Science*. Garden City, N. Y.: Doubleday, 1932.

Calvin, John. *Institutes of the Christian Religion*. Translated by Henry Beveridge. 2 vols. Grand Rapids: Eerdmans, 1962.

Cassirer, Ernst. *Language and Myth*. Translated by S. K. Langer. New York: Harper, 1946.

_____. *The Philosophy of Symbolic Forms*. Translated by Ralph Manheim. 3 vols. New Haven: Yale University Press, 1953, 1955, 1957.

Copelston, F. C. *Aquinas*. London: Penguin Books, 1955.

Crombie, Ian. "Theology and Falsification" in *New Essays in Philosophical Theology*. Edited by A. Flew and A. MacIntyre. New York: Macmillan, 1955.

Desan, Wilfred. *The Tragic Finale: An Essay on the Philosophy of Jean-Paul Sartre*. Cambridge: Harvard University Press, 1954.

_____. *The Marxism of Jean-Paul Sartre*. Garden City, N. Y.: Doubleday, 1965.

Dillenberger, John, and Welch, Claude. *Protestant Christianity Interpreted Through Its Development*. New York: Scribner's, 1954.

Dilley, Frank B. *Metaphysics and Religious Language*. New York: Columbia University Press, 1964.

Edwards, David L. (ed.) *The Honest to God Debate*. Philadelphia: Westminster Press, 1963.

Einstein, Albert. *Science, Philosophy, and Religion*. New York: Conference on Science, Philosophy, and Religion in their Relation to the Democratic Way of Life, 1941.

Eliade, Mircea. *The Sacred and the Profane*. Translated by Willard R. Trask. Torchbooks; New York: Harper, 1961.

_____. *Cosmos and History: The Myth of the Eternal Return*. Translated by Willard R. Trask. Torchbooks; New York: Harper, 1959.

_____. *Myth and Reality*. Translated by Willard R. Trask. New York: Harper, 1963.

Eliot, Thomas Stearns. *The Dry Salvages*. London: Faber & Faber, 1941.

Ferré, Frederick. *Language, Logic and God*. New York: Harper, 1961.

Flew, Anthony (ed.). *Essays in Conceptual Analysis*. London and New York: Macmillan, 1956.

_____, and MacIntyre, Alasdair (eds.). *New Essays in Philosophical Theology*. New York: Macmillan, 1955.

Frankfort, Henri, *et al. Before Philosophy*. London: Penguin Books, 1951.

Freud, Sigmund. *The Future of an Illusion*. Translated by W. D. Robson-Scott. Anchor Books; Garden City, N. Y.: Doubleday, 1957.

Fromm, Erich. *Psychoanalysis and Religion.* New Haven: Yale University Press, 1950.

————. *The Art of Loving.* New York: Harper, 1963.

Gaster, Theodore H. *Passover: Its History and Traditions.* Boston: Beacon Press, 1962.

Ginsberg, H. Louis. *Studies in Koheleth.* New York: The Jewish Theological Seminary of America, 1950.

Glatzer, Nahum N. (ed.) *Franz Rosenzweig: His Life and Thought.* New York: Schocken Books, 1962.

Gordis, Robert. *Koheleth—The Man and His World.* New York: The Jewish Theological Seminary of America, 1951.

Greene, Norman N. *Jean-Paul Sartre: The Existentialist Ethic.* Ann Arbor: University of Michigan Press, 1963.

Hare, R. M. "Religion and Morals" in *Faith and Logic.* Edited by Basil Mitchell. London and Tonbridge: Whitefriars Press; Boston: Beacon Press, 1957.

Heidegger, Martin. *Being and Time.* Translated by John Macquarrie and Edward Robinson. New York: Harper, 1962.

————. *An Introduction to Metaphysics.* Translated by Ralph Manheim. Anchor Books; Garden City, N. Y.: Doubleday, 1961.

————. *Existence and Being.* Edited with introduction by Werner Brock. Chicago: Regnery, 1949.

Hepburn, Ronald W. "Demythologizing and the Problem of Validity," in *New Essays in Philosophical Theology.* Edited by A. Flew and A. MacIntyre. New York: Macmillan, 1955.

Hick, John (ed.). *The Existence of God.* New York: Macmillan; London: Collier-Macmillan, 1964.

Holmes, Oliver Wendell. *The Complete Writings of Oliver Wendell Holmes.* Boston: Houghton Mifflin, 1892.

Hume, David. *Inquiry Concerning Human Understanding.* First entitled *Philosophical Essays Concerning Human Understanding.* London: Millar, 1748.

Husserl, Edmund. *Ideas.* Translated by W. R. Boyce-Gibson. New York: Macmillan, 1952.

James, William. *The Varieties of Religious Experience.* Mentor Books; New York: New American Library, 1958.

————. *Essays in Radical Empiricism.* New York: Longmans, Green & Co., 1947.

240

Jaspers, Karl. "On My Philosophy," in *Existentialism from Dostoevsky to Sartre*. Edited by Walter Kaufmann. Meridian Books; Cleveland: World, 1956.

————. *Way to Wisdom*. Translated by Ralph Manheim. New Haven: Yale University Press, 1960.

————. *Truth and Symbol*. Translated by Jean T. Wilde, W. Kluback and W. Kimmel. New Haven: College and University Press, 1959.

Jenkins, Daniel. *Beyond Religion*. Philadelphia: Westminster Press, 1962.

Josephson, Eric and Mary (eds.). *Man Alone: Alienation in Modern Society*. New York: Dell Books, 1962.

Jung, C. G. *Modern Man in Search of a Soul*. Translated by W. S. Dell and Cary F. Baynes. New York: Harcourt, Brace & World, 1933.

————. *Psyche and Symbol*. Anchor Books; Garden City, N. Y.: Doubleday, 1958.

————. *Answer to Job*. Translated by R. F. C. Hull. Meridian Books, Cleveland. World, 1960.

————. *Psychology and Religion*. New Haven: Yale University Press, 1938.

Kaufmann, Walter (ed.). *Existentialism from Dostoevsky to Sartre*. Meridian Books; Cleveland: World, 1956.

Kierkegaard, Søren. *Fear and Trembling and the Sickness Unto Death*. Translated by Walter Lowrie. Anchor Books; Garden City, N. Y.: Doubleday, 1954.

————. *Concluding Unscientific Postscript*. Translated by David Swenson and Walter Lowrie. Princeton: Princeton University Press, 1941.

Lawrence, Nathaniel, and O'Conner, Daniel (eds.). *Readings in Existential Phenomenology*. Englewood Cliffs, N. J.: Prentice-Hall, 1967.

Mackintosh, H. R. *Types of Modern Theology*. London: Nisbet, 1952.

McPherson, Thomas. "Religion as the Inexpressible," in *New Essays in Philosophical Theology*. Edited by A. Flew and A. MacIntyre. New York: Macmillan, 1955.

Macquarrie, John. *An Existentialist Theology*. London: S.C.M. Press; New York: Macmillan, 1955.

Maimonides, Moses. *The Guide for the Perplexed*. Translated by M. Friedländer. 2d ed. rev. New York: Dover, 1957.

241

Maritain, Jacques. *Approaches to God.* Translated by Peter O'Reilly New York: Harper, 1954.

―――――. *Existence and the Existent.* Translated by L. Galantiere and G. B. Phelan. New York: Image Books; Garden City, N. Y.: Doubleday, 1957.

―――――. *A Preface to Metaphysics.* Mentor Books; New York: New American Library, 1962.

Martin, C. B. "The Perfect Good," in *New Essays in Philosophical Theology.* Edited by A. Flew and A. MacIntyre. New York: Macmillan, 1955.

Marty, Martin E., and Peerman, Dean G. (eds.) *New Theology No. 3.* New York: Macmillan, 1966.

May, Rollo (ed.). *Existential Psychology.* New York: Random House, 1961.

Menninger, Karl. *Man Against Himself.* New York: Harcourt, Brace & World, 1938.

Mitchell, Basil (ed.). *Faith and Logic.* London and Tonbridge: Whitefriars Press; Boston: Beacon Press, 1957.

Molina, Fernando. *Existentialism as Philosophy.* Englewood Cliffs, N. J.: Prentice-Hall, 1962.

Montefiore, C. G., and Loewe, H. (eds.) *A Rabbinic Anthology.* London and New York: Macmillan, 1938.

New Essays in Philosophical Theology. Edited by Antony Flew and Alasdair MacIntyre. New York: Macmillan, 1955.

Newman, John Henry. *An Essay in Aid of a Grammar of Assent.* London: Longmans, Green & Co., 1885.

Niebuhr, Reinhold. *The Nature and Destiny of Man.* New York: Scribner's, 1941.

―――――. *The Children of Light and the Children of Darkness.* New York: Scribner's, 1944.

―――――. *Discerning the Signs of the Times.* New York: Scribner's, 1946.

Nietzsche, Friedrich. *The Complete Works of Friedrich Nietzsche.* 18 vols. Edited by Oscar Levy. London: Allen & Unwin; New York: Macmillan, 1909 and later printings.

Nowell-Smith, Patrick. "Miracles," in *New Essays in Philosophical Theology.* Edited by A. Flew and A. MacIntyre. New York: Macmillan, 1955.

Otto, Rudolf. *The Idea of the Holy.* Translated by J. W. Harvey. Galaxy Books; New York: Oxford University Press, 1958.

Paissac, H. *Le Dieu De Sarte*. Vichy: B. Arthaud, 1950.

Peirce, Charles S. *The Philosophical Writings of Peirce*. Edited by Justus Buchler. New York: Dover, 1955.

Philipson, David. *Reform Movement in Judaism*. New York: Macmillan, 1907 and 1951; rev. ed. Ktav, 1967.

Pike, Nelson (ed.). *God and Evil*. Englewood Cliffs, N.J.: Prentice-Hall, 1964.

Ping, Charles J. *Meaningful Nonsense*. Philadelphia: Westminster Press, 1966.

Rahner, Karl. *The Christian of the Future*. New York: Herder and Herder, 1967.

Ramsey, Ian T. *Religious Language*. London: S.C.M. Press, 1957; New York: Macmillan paperback.

_____. *Christian Discourse: Some Logical Explorations*. London: Oxford University Press, 1965.

Richardson, Cyril C. *The Doctrine of the Trinity*. Nashville: Abingdon Press, 1958.

Roberts, David. *Psychotherapy and a Christian View of Man*. New York: Scribner's, 1950.

Robinson, John A. T. *Honest to God*. Philadelphia: Westminster Press, 1963.

Royce, Josiah. *The Problem of Christianity*. New York: Macmillan, 1913.

Russell, Bertrand. *The Scientific Outlook*. New York: W. W. Norton, 1951.

Ryle, G. *The Concept of Mind*. New York: Barnes & Noble, 1949.

_____, et al. *The Revolution in Philosophy*. London: Macmillan, 1956.

Sandmel, Samuel. *The Hebrew Scriptures*. New York: Knopf, 1963.

Sartre, Jean-Paul. *Search for a Method*. Translated by Hazel E. Barnes. New York: Knopf, 1963.

_____. *Being and Nothingness: An Essay on Phenomenological Ontology*. Translated by Hazel E. Barnes. New York: Philosophical Library, 1956.

_____. *Existentialism*. Translated by Bernard Fechtman. New York: Philosophical Library, 1947.

_____. *Existential Psychoanalysis*. Translated by Hazel E. Barnes. Gateway Edition; Chicago: Regnery, 1962.

_____. *La Critique de la Raison Dialectique (Précédé de Question de Méthode)*. Paris: Gallimard, 1960.

243

———. *The Transcendence of the Ego.* Translated by F. Williams and R. Kirkpatrick. New York: Noonday Press, 1957.

———. *No Exit and Three Other Plays.* Translated by S. D. Gilbert. Vintage; New York: Random House, 1955.

Schechter, Solomon. *Aspects of Rabbinic Theology.* New York: Schocken Books, 1961.

Scheler, Max. "Towards a Stratification of the Emotional Life," in *Readings in Existential Phenomenology.* Edited by N. Lawrence and D. O'Conner. Englewood Cliffs, N.J.: Prentice-Hall, 1967.

Schleiermacher, Friedrich. *Speeches on Religion.* London: K. Paul, Trench, Trubner & Co., 1893.

Sprague, E., and Taylor, P. W. (eds.) *Knowledge and Value.* New York: Harcourt, Brace & World, 1967.

Stace, W. T. *Time and Eternity.* Princeton: Princeton University Press, 1952.

Tillich, Paul. *The Courage to Be.* New Haven: Yale University Press, 1952.

———. *Systematic Theology.* Chicago: University of Chicago Press. 3 vols. 1951, 1957, 1963.

———. *The Protestant Era.* Chicago: University of Chicago Press, 1957.

Toulmin, Stephen. *The Place of Reason in Ethics.* London and New York: Cambridge University Press, 1953.

Trueblood, Elton. *The Humor of Christ.* New York and London: Harper, 1964.

Urmson, J. O. *Philosophical Analysis.* London and New York: Oxford University Press, 1956, 1967.

Vahanian, Gabriel. *Wait Without Idols.* New York: Braziller, 1964.

Van Buren, Paul M. *The Secular Meaning of the Gospel, Based on an Analysis of Its Language.* New York: Macmillan, 1963.

Van Doornik, N. G. M., Jelsma, S., and Van de Lisdonk, A. *A Handbook of the Catholic Faith.* Edited by John Greenwood. New York: Image Books; Garden City, N. Y.: Doubleday, 1956.

Von Hildebrand, Dietrich. *Liturgy and Personality.* Baltimore: Helicon Press, 1960.

Warnock, Mary. *The Philosophy of Sartre.* London: Hutchinson; New York: Hillary House, 1965.

Wheelwright, Philip. *Metaphor and Reality.* Bloomington: Indiana University Press, 1962.

244

_____. *The Burning Fountain*. Bloomington: Indiana University Press, 1954.

White, Victor, O. P. *God and the Unconscious*. Meridian Books; Cleveland: World, 1952.

Wild, John. *Existence and the World of Freedom*. Englewood Cliffs, N.J.: Prentice-Hall, 1963.

Williams, Bernard. "Tertullian's Paradox," in *New Essays in Philosophical Theology*. Edited by A. Flew and A. MacIntyre. New York: Macmillan, 1955.

Wisdom, John. "The Logic of 'God'," in *The Existence of God*. Edited by John Hick. New York: Macmillan, 1964.

_____. "Gods," in *Philosophy and Psycho-analysis*. New York: Philosophical Library, 1953.

Wittgenstein, Ludwig. *Philosophical Investigations*. Translated by G. E. M. Anscombe and edited by G. E. M. Anscombe and R. Rhees. New York: Macmillan, 1953.

_____. *Lectures and Conversations on Aesthetics, Psychology, and Religious Belief*. Edited by Cyril Barrett. Berkeley and Los Angeles: University of California Press, 1967.

_____. *Tractatus Logico-Philosophicus*. Translated by C. Ogden with introduction by Bertrand Russell. New York: Harcourt, Brace & Co.; London: K. Paul, Trench, Trubner & Co., 1922.

_____. *Tractatus Logico-Philosophicus*. Translated by D. F. Pears and B. F. McGuiness with introduction by B. Russell. London: Routledge and Kegan Paul; New York: Humanities Press, 1961.

Zilboorg, Gregory. *Psychoanalysis and Religion*. New York: Farrar, Strauss & Cudahy, 1962.

Articles and Periodicals

Aiken, Henry B. "God and Evil: A Study of Some Relations Between Faith and Morals," *Ethics*, LXVIII, (1957-58), 79-97.

Aron, Raymon. "Sartre's Marxism," *Encounter* (June, 1965), 34-39.

Farrell, P. M., O.P. "Evil and Omnipotence," *Mind*, LXIX (1958-59), 74-76.

Grave, S. A. "On Evil and Omnipotence," *Mind*, LXV (1954-55), 259-62.

Hamilton, William. "The Death of God Theology," *The Christian Scholar*, XLVIII (Spring, 1965), 27-49.

Kuh, Katherine. "Delacroix: Prophet in Paint," *Saturday Review* (June 22, 1963).

Laks, H. Joel. "The Enigma of Job: Maimonides and the Moderns," *Journal of Biblical Literature*, LXXXIII, Part IV (December, 1964), 345-64.

Mackie, J. L. "Evil and Omnipotence," *Mind*, LXIV (1955), 200-212.

Malcolm, Norman. "Anselm's Ontological Arguments," *The Philosophical Review*, LXIX (January, 1960), 41-62.

Pike, Nelson. "God and Evil: A Reconsideration," *Ethics*, LXVIII (1957-58), 116-24.

Ramsey, I. T. "The Paradox of Omnipotence," *Mind*, LXV (1954-55), 263-66.

Smart, Ninian. "Omnipotence, Evil, and Superman," *Philosophy*, XXXVI (1961), 188-96.

Spiegelberg, Herbert. "Husserl's Phenomenology and Existentialism," *The Journal of Philosophy*, LVII (January 21, 1960), 62-74.

Time. January 24, 1955, p. 44.

Tyson, Ruel. "Philosophical Analysis and Religious Language: A Selected Bibliography," *The Christian Scholar*, XLIII (Fall, 1960), 245-50.

White, Morton. "Religion, Politics, and the Higher Learning," *Confluence*, III (December, 1954), 402-12.

INDEXES

Index of Biblical References
(Boldface indicates scriptural passages.)

Index of Proper Names

Index of Subjects

God—*cont'd*
   78, 89, 92, 94, 107-8, 115,
   122, 127-28, 137-38, 186-
   87, 193, 201, 233-35
  death of, 14, 20, 102, 142,
   188
  existence of, 13-15, 54, 71,
   173, 236
  as immanent, 20, 106, 124,
   133, 201, 231
  knowledge of, 42, 103, 130,
   133, 201, 229
  names of, 121, 128
  as paradox, 29-30, 39, 95,
   121-23
  as personality, 123-24
  and Satan, 119
  silence of, 98, 102, 142
  as transcendent, 20, 39, 106,
   124, 133, 201, 231
  word of. *See* Word of God
God above God, 97, 111, 114
Grace, 92, 102, 132, 173, 189
Grenzsituationen or "limit situation," 44, 226
Guilt, 83-87, 171, 179, 185-86,
  190

Halacha, 182, 230
Hell, 83, 85
Hermeneutics, 15-16, 148, 151,
  220
Human existence (*passim*), 46-
  47, 54-66, 68-69, 76, 90-
  96, 98, 115-16, 121, 125-
  26, 160, 164, 173-75, 177-
  81, 185-88, 190, 213-15,
  236
  Kant's basic questions of, 56-
   58, 88-89, 164-65

Human existence—*cont'd*
  Sartre's description, 52-66,
   76-77, 79-80, 83-89, 227
Humor, 103-4, 111, 136, 227

I and Thou, 98, 141
Id, 62
Idealism, 53
I-It, 141
Immanence, 126, 133
Inauthentic existence, 80-86,
  114, 118, 169-71, 177, 181,
  190, 221. *See also* Authen-
  tic existence, and Human
  existence
Intuition, 40, 54, 67-68, 116-17,
  119-21, 178, 189, 220, 223,
  231
Ipsum esse subsistens, 54

Judaism (*passim*), 48, 181-85,
  190-91, 202

Kerygma, 217
Knowledge, 38, 73, 88, 117,
  121, 160, 229
  self-knowledge, 46, 66, 160,
   164, 169, 188, 229
  theory of, 52, 67-68, 72-73
Knowledge of God. *See* God
Komos, 134

Language, 34-36, 40, 101-2,
  117, 193, 198, 208-10, 212-
  14, 216, 222, 232-33. *See
  also* Religious language, and
  Linguistic analysis
Language games, 34, 214
Laughter, 116, 140
Libido, 62
Linguistic analysis, 15-16, 22,

Sin, 78, 80, 85-86, 90, 178. *See also* Original sin
Spontaneous upsurge, 54, 59, 61-62, 76-77, 87, 91, 93, 171, 181
Subject-object relation, 53, 72, 75-76, 98, 121-22
Subjectivity, 61, 69, 75-76, 90
Suffering, 83, 105, 109, 178-79
Suicide, 84
Symbols, 15, 37, 101, 106-7, 137, 145, 147, 151, 157, 194, 198, 204, 213-14, 216, 228

Teshuvah, 113, 181. *See also* Conversion
Theater of the absurd, 232
Theology, 193-97, 202-3, 210, 213-16, 218, 224-25
apologetic theology, 202-4, 207-12, 216, 225
crisis theology, 32, 115, 202
dogmatic theology, 202-7, 210-12, 215-16, 225
liberal theology, 202-3
negative theology, 106, 126-27, 162
pastoral theology, 202, 210
philosophical theology, 38, 40, 115, 210
positive theology, 106, 126-27, 162
rational theology, 33, 38, 155
theology of dialogue, 97
Theophanous events, 125-26
Theoria, 51
Thomism, 155
Thrownness, 85, 191
Transcendence, 126, 133, 217

Trinity, 131-32, 162
Truth, 19, 32, 35, 41, 116, 130, 142, 144-47, 155, 168, 178, 187, 190, 206, 236
Twice-born soul, 108, 119, 127, 149

Unhappy consciousness, 76, 88, 171
Upanishads, 47

Value and values, 33, 71, 78, 160, 166, 179-80
Via negationis, 123-24

Weltanschauung, 51, 217
Wholly other, 123-24
Will, 60, 62
Wisdom, 103, 105, 174-78, 180-81, 229, 234
Wit, 103-5, 109, 112-14, 116-19, 122-25, 128-29, 131, 134, 138, 156-57, 228
common wit, 122-23, 129-30
moment of wit, 122-23, 129-30
religious wit, 114, 129-30, 146-47, 201, 232, 234
Witticism, 104-6, 109-14, 123-25, 131, 134, 136, 138-39, 146, 149-50, 155-56
Word of God, 37, 102, 115, 118, 127, 134, 139-40, 189, 198-200, 203-7, 209-10, 215, 221, 232, 236
World, 51-53, 59-60, 68-69, 142, 167, 176
bondage to, 172-73
as man's creation, 52, 59, 82-85